PRAISE FOR
# Tending the Bones

"In this deep and heartfelt book, Pavini Moray offers a unique program to access your autonomy and your pleasure power. With this step-by-step guide, you can stay grounded as you engage with your ancestral trauma. [Dr. Moray's] writing is clear, accessible, and thorough as they travel with you on your journey. *Tending the Bones* helps you tap into all of your senses and sensibilities as you wend your way through ritual, poetry, journaling, and prayer toward your ongoing evolution. Dr. Moray shows us how our own healing is a tender practice we can weave throughout our life. What a beautiful gift!"

— CELESTE HIRSCHMAN, MA, cofounder of the Somatica Institute and author of *Coming Together*, *Making Love Real*, and *Cockfidence*

"From cover to cover, *Tending the Bones* blends and layers Pavini's intergenerational insights, compassion, sex research, and embodied experience. Their generous, uplifting guidance has the potential to heal us all—the walking wounded—with a fresh, visionary approach. This thirteen-month program rooted in ancestral ritual and somatic practice is eXXXXcellent psycho-magic, which gives me hope that we can create a more peaceful, pleasurable, loving society. *Tending the Bones* blew me away—in the best, sexy way."

— ANNIE SPRINKLE, ecosex educator, artist, and coauthor of *Assuming the Ecosexual Position*

"In this brilliant, essential book of healing, Pavini Moray offers a clear, practical, and pleasure-centric path back to your body after trauma. Using the simple, powerful tools I recommend to all my students—breath, movement, vocalization, imagination, and clarity of intention—*Tending the Bones* gives you gentle yet powerful guidance on how you can work with and through your past to arrive warmly and ecstatically back home to yourself in the present."

— BARBARA CARRELLAS, author of *Urban Tantra*

"In *Tending the Bones*, Pavini Moray, a wise witch and a somatic sex therapist, presents a guidebook for intergenerational trauma healing and imbues it with potent spells that can be used to nurture erotic embodiment. Moray's method for addressing trauma does not promise a simple cure but emphasizes a lifelong commitment to continuous practices, chosen because they foster sexual well-being in one's body and in one's lineage.

The book guides readers through a three-part journey: starting with preparatory practices that help reconnect with one's body, then moving through ways to deal with sexual trauma, and culminating in practices that savor the aliveness we carry in our bodies. This aliveness has been passed down from our ancestors. *Tending the Bones* reminds us to pass this on to our descendants."

—JOSEPH KRAMER, PhD, founder of Sexological Bodywork

# ALSO BY PAVINI MORAY

*How to Hold Power: A Somatic Approach to Becoming a Leader People Love and Respect*

# Tending the Bones

## Reclaiming Pleasure after Transgenerational Sexual Trauma

**PAVINI MORAY**, PHD

Foreword by Daniel Foor, PhD

North Atlantic Books
Huichin, unceded Ohlone land
Berkeley, California

Published by
North Atlantic Books
Huichin, unceded Ohlone land
Berkeley, California

Cover art © Baranovska via Adobe Stock and
Tanya Syrytsyna via Adobe Stock
Cover design by Jasmine Hromjak
Book design by Happenstance Type-O-Rama

Printed in the United States of America

*Tending the Bones: Reclaiming Pleasure after Transgenerational Sexual Trauma* is sponsored and published by North Atlantic Books, an educational nonprofit based in the unceded Ohlone land Huichin (Berkeley, CA), that collaborates with partners to develop cross-cultural perspectives; nurture holistic views of art, science, the humanities, and healing; and seed personal and global transformation by publishing work on the relationship of body, spirit, and nature.

North Atlantic Books's publications are distributed to the US trade and internationally by Penguin Random House Publisher Services. For further information, visit our website at www.northatlanticbooks.com.

**CONTENT DISCLAIMER:** This book contains material that may be triggering, including references to rape, sexual abuse, and trauma.

Library of Congress Cataloging-in-Publication Data

Names: Moray, Pavini, author. | Foor, Daniel, 1977- writer of foreword.
Title: Tending the bones : reclaiming pleasure after transgenerational
    sexual trauma / Pavini Moray, PhD ; foreword by Daniel Foor, PhD.
Description: Huichin, unceded Ohlone land, Berkeley, California : North
    Atlantic Books, [2024] | Includes bibliographical references. | Summary:
    "A holistic, multidisciplinary approach to healing from sexual trauma
    that includes body-based practices, ancestral connection rituals, and
    reflective empowerment exercises"—Provided by publisher.
Identifiers: LCCN 2024028515 (print) | LCCN 2024028516 (ebook) | ISBN
    9798889841203 (paperback) | ISBN 9798889841210 (ebook)
Subjects: LCSH: Generational trauma—Treatment. | Psychic
    trauma—Treatment. | Rape trauma syndrome—Treatment.
Classification: LCC RC552.T7 M67 2024  (print) | LCC RC552.T7  (ebook) |
    DDC 616.85/21--dc23/eng/20240715
LC record available at https://lccn.loc.gov/2024028515
LC ebook record available at https://lccn.loc.gov/2024028516


1 2 3 4 5 6 7 8 9 KPC 30 29 28 27 26 25

This book includes recycled material and material from well-managed forests. North Atlantic Books is committed to the protection of our environment. We print on recycled paper whenever possible and partner with printers who strive to use environmentally responsible practices.

*Dedicated to all past, present, and future generations.*

*May we practice and experience radiant,
consensual erotic wellness.*

# Contents

# Foreword

In reaching for what's useful by way of introduction, I'm brought back to a conversation Pavini and I had over a decade ago. After some years of shared ritual and work with the ancestors, Pavini and I were enjoying a hike through the cool, misted hills of San Bruno Mountain, just south of San Francisco. From this place of spaciousness, they asked, "How do you tell when something you're working with is more personal and when it's more cultural?" I responded, "I start from the assumption that it's all cultural and work back from there."

The generous and potent bundle of teachings and practices that is this book situates something deeply personal—our experience of sex, sexuality, and the erotic—in a much wider context of lineage, ancestry, and culture. The benefits of this approach are myriad, not inherently obvious, and worth appreciating from the outset.

For one, framing our challenges as intergenerational and systemic rather than solely personal is honest and kind. This especially applies to the erotic, as attitudes of sex negativity are already so prevalent, and often doubly so for queer folk. When combined with the view that we should be able to single-handedly resolve all forms of our individual suffering, the result can be devastating shame. We want to feel capable, but resolving collective-level transgenerational trauma with personal-level skills is an impossible task and a setup for failure. The framework in this book provides a tangible pathway out of this confusion and back into healing and pleasure.

Another implicit blessing in the experiential work of this guidebook is the subversion of extreme individualism. In recognizing that our pain is not only personal, *Tending the Bones* makes clear that our bliss, queerness, and erotic creativity are also ancestral gifts and ways of affirming our deep humanity and place here on Earth. In this way, reclaiming pleasure and erotic joy is also culturally subversive and one way of releasing colonialist fictions of a separate, isolated self.

A third usefully radical implication of this work arises from combining the subjects of sex and sexuality with a focus on blood and family ancestors. For essential reasons, family is often too simplistically understood as a space incompatible with sexual energy. And yet, to quote Pavini, "We're here through the sex of our ancestors." The erotic, in all its messy beauty and pain, is at the heart of family. An ancestral and generational focus that's broad enough to include both wounding and healing also functions to carefully recalibrate cultural taboos in ways that allow us to openly honor and embody erotic gifts from our lineages. In doing so, a kind of silence is lifted in ways that support safer, more conscious, sex-positive approaches to creating new families and life.

Unlike much of the increasingly popular material on ancestral reconnection and work with the spirits, the approach offered here is rooted in psychological and ritual safety. Because I know a bit of Pavini's personal journey, I know they've learned firsthand about how hazardous the troubled dead and related forces can be. This is reflected in a steady, systematic lack of naivete that balances healing with a regard for safety, regulation, and healthy boundaries.

Finally, I'm grateful that this work openly challenges reductionist materialist epistemology by encouraging and validating ancestral relationships. Colonialist frameworks, to this day, often invalidate and belittle our innate human capacity to relate with the dead, the Earth, and the unseen. These attitudes often unconsciously replicate white supremacy and cultural arrogance toward traditional peoples and ways of knowing, including those of our older ancestors. By presenting practices of ancestral reconnection as if they're no big deal or an innate human capacity, this work does a service to our greater humanity and to our ability to decolonize our relational and spiritual lives and families. This is culturally kind, generous, and healing.

For these reasons and others, I'm confident the good medicine of this offering can meet you and your people both in its explicit, stated intentions, and also in the implicit ways of deeply nourishing liberatory, sex-positive, queer-celebrating culture.

In this spirit, may you enjoy direct, healing, and inspired connections with your wise and kind lineage ancestors. May these relationships help you to be steady on your path of destiny and in a full expression of your particular brilliance. May you know the love and kindness of your people in your bones, and may the teachings and practices in this book support that prayer for your path, your family, and the world.

DANIEL FOOR, PhD

# Introduction

What if the transmission of transgenerational trauma is actually a brilliant response to healing trauma? You might think that unresolved pain passed down through the generations is an unwelcome inheritance and a burden someone (you!) has to clean up. It may sound counterintuitive to think such pain could possibly be an adaptive strategy that promotes eventual healing. However, some wounds take more than one lifetime to heal.

Trauma is held in the tissues of your body. It may or may not be yours, but it prevents you from accessing the fullness of your sexuality and the depth of your capacity for closeness and intimacy, even as you value those things. It's possible you could be physically close with a partner but with your heart remaining unavailable.

Perhaps it feels that you are holding old pain and blocks around sex and intimacy that come from your mother, your father, your grandparents, or even from older ancestors whose names you do not know. Perhaps your expression of your sexuality and your erotic self are blocked by something you can feel but cannot see.

As a child and teen, and later as an adult, I experienced sexual abuse and violation. It was many years before I was ready to even look at the impact I held in my body from those experiences, let alone start on a path of healing. I was lucky; after working with several talk therapists who were helpful in some ways but not in others, I found a somatic practitioner who works with sexual trauma. As we slowly worked through the layers, I found that I was dealing with impact not only from my own experiences but also from the sexual violations members of my family had experienced and perpetrated.

In my work as a therapist, as I started to guide clients in healing their sexuality, I found a similar pattern: many of the clients who were healing from sexual abuse and violence had ancestors who had also experienced these forms of abuse. Clients would say things like, "I was raped, my mom was raped, my grandma too . . . I think there is a connection." But what was that connection? And how to address it so it could heal?

My clients repeatedly said they felt the impact of sexual violence other relatives had experienced. Clients would come in and say things like, "I don't have any sexual trauma that I'm aware of, but my mom does, my sister does, my aunt does." They would talk about how their own sexuality felt inaccessible, broken, or stuck. In their own sexualities and bodies, they felt the impact of violations that had not happened to them directly. Sometimes they felt part of a long line of victims of sexual violence and felt that they, too, would inevitably experience what their ancestors had.

I also had clients who were aware that people in their families had committed sexual violence. These clients felt unable to effectively deal with the guilt and shame this created. They would say things like, "My grandmother was raped by her father." The terror they named around being so afraid of becoming like their great-grandfather was heartbreaking to hear.

I didn't know what to do about it. I figured there must be ways to work with it, but at the time, I didn't even have the language of "transgenerational trauma." I could see a problem, but how to address it?

As a white practitioner of European descent, I knew of no tools for the job. The dead had died, and that was it. You could place flowers on their tombstones if they had them, but there was no practice of communication of any type. What had happened had happened. There was no way to heal anything once someone was dead. In fact, speaking with the dead was considered taboo or a sign of mental illness.

The next logical step was to investigate ancestral healing technologies, of which there are many, deeply rooted in various ancient traditions. I learned that the recovery of transgenerational trauma requires transpersonal tools. The tools for resolving trauma in the individual, while helpful, couldn't address the trauma that individuals hold from their ancestral lines.

How can transgenerational sexual trauma be healed? How can a relationship with ancestors support the healing of sexual trauma in the living? These questions became the focus of my doctoral research.

The results I found were quite astonishing.

First, transgenerational sexual trauma exists. It can be treated as part of the process of an individual doing their own sexual healing. Second, for people who already have any type of connection with their ancestors, addressing sexual trauma of the past matters.

When I started looking for ways to work with ancestral healing, I was introduced to the work of Family Constellations, a modality based on the work of Bert Hellinger. At a Family Constellations event, a trained practitioner facilitates an experience for one client. There are multiple attendees who volunteer to represent various family members, living and dead. The volunteers move and respond as the person they represent. I took a few workshops, and the results seemed powerful but not quite my cup of tea.

The witchy communities I participate in often "call in the ancestors," especially around the holiday of Samhain, aka Halloween. However, there wasn't a lot of clear guidance in working with ancestors, especially around the topics I was curious about. It was more like, "Oh, that's a nice thing to do, call in the ancestors."

I found the work of Malidoma Patrice Somé, who taught about the importance and benefits of connecting with the ancestors, based on his beliefs from his native Dagara culture. He shared that his culture depends on their relationships with their ancestors for guidance, support, and clarity. Their ancestral reverence practices are widespread and common in that culture, and they include their ancestors in their everyday life.

I was next introduced to the work of Dr. Daniel Foor and the organization he founded, Ancestral Medicine. Daniel's approach to working with ancestors was linear and had boundaries, and most importantly, it was direct. You didn't have to hire a practitioner to intervene; you could learn to relate directly with your own ancestors. Over the next several years, I worked closely to understand the Ancestral Lineage healing approach, and I became trained as an Ancestral Medicine practitioner. I started to weave that approach into my somatic sex therapy work. Daniel's work has greatly influenced my own.

There is an impact from the sexuality of your ancestors. These impacts can be positive or negative, or sometimes both. To begin to unwind transgenerational sexual trauma, you must first have the framework that it exists.

## Do You Carry Transgenerational Sexual Trauma?

Ask yourself these assessment questions:

- ¤ Do you experience sexual shame?

- ¤ Have you experienced sexual abuse, including incest or rape?

- ¤ Is there any sexual trauma in your bloodlines because of war?

- ¤ Do you have or does your family have a history of interpersonal partner violence?

- ¤ Were you, any of your living relatives, or any of your ancestors kicked out of the family home because of early pregnancy?

- ¤ Do you experience an unexplained fear of sex or aversion to sex?

- ¤ Is there repression of sexuality in your family of origin that has led to shame, especially around marginalized sexual orientations?

- ¤ Are silence and secrecy ways that you know that your ancestors had problematic sexual experiences, even if you don't have access to the full information?

- ¤ Are you aware of having perpetrators of sexual violence as ancestors?

- ¤ Have you or your people experienced cultural or historical influences that repress the free expression of sexuality?

- ¤ Do you sense that you were the victim of sexual trauma, even if you have no conscious memories of victimization?

If you answered yes to many of these or feel a sense of connection to these experiences as you read them, then you do carry transgenerational trauma. With that, you also have the possibility of experiencing goodness in your sexuality that hails from your people. When there is wounding around sexuality, there is also a deep well of healing. To work through your transgenerational sexual trauma and allow yourself to feel all the sexual goodness possible, you must deepen your relationship with both your sexuality and your people.

You've likely tried different things to find a sexuality that fits who you are, such as therapy, bodywork, books, and courses. While all of it has likely helped you heal, you may still experience blocks around sexuality in your body and in your relationships. You may be starting to think that erotic freedom might just be for other people, not for you. And worse, you may feel a loyalty to that pain. How would the justice your ancestors call for happen if you didn't feel their pain?

We each carry sexual burdens that we have inherited from those who came before. Examples of ancestral sexual burdens you may be carrying include shame, repression, sexual violence (perpetrator or victim), or residual sexual trauma that has been passed down to you. If you personally have sexual trauma, these can all become entangled so that it's difficult to know what is yours and what was handed to you.

There are cultural sexual burdens as well, and I name some of these from the United States in Month 5. While I am not Black or Indigenous, and therefore can only reflect what I read and hear because these are not my lived experiences, it is essential to name the impacts of colonization and slavery on the sexuality of African Americans and Indigenous Native Americans as I understand them.

Transgenerational sexual messaging happened to us all in our families. In some cases, it was a complete lack of information or silence around sexuality education. In others, sex was explicitly deemed negative. For example, if you had a repressive religious upbringing, chances are that your sexual self-exploration has been affected without you ever having a chance to first figure out what your body does. You were not given the freedom to find what feels right to you personally.

But there's good news too! Just as sexual burdens are passed down, so are sexual blessings. Sexual blessings you may be heir to include lustiness, sexual freedom, strong libido, and erotic attunement. They may be things like feeling great about sex or your body. Perhaps you experience your ancestors as a source of support for sexual wellness, sexual freedom, and sexual self-esteem. Or you may have ancestral erotic role models who have given you an example of sexuality across the life span, who validate your current sexual self, and who provide examples of the capacity for committed relationships.

Perhaps you have or had a relative who nurtured your developing sexuality simply by giving you permission to be who you are. It's possible that you experience the power of your queer and gender nonconforming ancestors as a source of strength. Maybe your ancestors were good at pleasure, and you've inherited that skill.

In my research, people reported again and again that sexual healing happens. I'll be sharing their words and stories through this book. Healing is a process that occurs by degrees. Pleasure becomes very important in healing areas damaged by sexual trauma. One person I spoke with who has done a lot of work to heal their own sexuality offered this:

*Healing sexuality is a process. You have to first clear away some poison because you have to make room in the place—in the body, in the soul—where this damage has occurred. Then it's not over yet. You have to actively regain and reclaim pleasure in the place that was wounded.*

*I responded, "The pleasure is the medicine."*

*They said, "The pleasure can't fit if it's filled with poison."*

Transgenerational trauma is viewed negatively as a legacy of suffering. It's passed down through the generations, something to be rid of. While the impulse to pathologize trauma is culturally rampant, I invite you to consider another approach. If you hold a multigenerational perspective on developing sexual wellness, it becomes possible to reframe some of the ancestral burdens as blessings.

One way to think of the transmission of transgenerational sexual trauma is to see it as a savvy and beautiful evolutionary adaptation. As human organisms, we are always trying to meet our basic needs for safety and belonging. The passing of trauma to future generations ensures that there will be chances for healing that trauma and ultimately meeting these profound needs.

You've probably heard about the migration of monarch butterflies. It takes them up to five generations to travel from Mexico to North America. The butterflies that set out on the great migration are not the ones who arrive. There are many generations of butterflies in between.

Apparently, the butterflies were facing the dilemma that their bodies were too fragile, and they were too short-lived. They couldn't live long enough to complete the trek that is, for some mysterious reason, crucial to their survival as a species. So instead of giving up and saying never mind, they figured out a somatic transgenerational approach to survival. They realized they could send a wave of life, a wave of generations, out into the winds, which would solve the dilemma.

Here's the thing: wounds love to heal. When humans have been faced with unmanageable traumas, we figured out that we can pass our trauma downstream. While this might sound like a terrible idea, actually it's brilliant because we're smart enough to ultimately figure out how to heal. It may not be the person who experienced the trauma that gets healed, but the recovery does happen. The wounds of the ancestors can be healed through the living. There is a continuity between the living and the dead.

Consider that transgenerational trauma may be one of our best evolutionary adaptations to make sure the wounds of the past are acknowledged and tended to and that everyone, alive or dead, feels that they belong. If we reframe transgenerational trauma to show the somatic wisdom inherent within it, we give trauma ample time to heal throughout generations. We can then have hope, because wounds that seem unhealable can in fact, with time, heal. This is the new, healed story you are writing for yourself and your ancestors.

## How to Use This Book

The book is designed as a thirteen-month process to provide spaciousness for your healing, inquiry, practice, and integration. It is meant to be worked through front to back, in order, one chapter per month. The process is sequential and cumulative. It is a structure you can work with to heal personal and ancestral trauma, and it is designed to be followed in the sequence in which it is presented.

Each of the thirteen chapters (called "Months") includes guidance, a ritual, a poem, exercises, a suggested monthly practice, meditations, and worksheets that you will find in the appendix at the end of the book. You can also download all the worksheets at www.pavinimoray.com/ttb-bonus.html.

This information is intended for educational purposes only and is not meant to substitute for medical or psychological care or to prescribe treatment for any specific condition.

You may find working through this book with a sexual trauma–informed therapist or counselor deeply beneficial and supportive. We are not meant to heal alone, and this work increases in impact when done with kind, loving support. If you do not believe in ancestors or doubt their existence but still feel called to work with the material in this book, please know that no particular beliefs are necessary to get positive results.

**Each Month, you are invited to:**

1. Read the content.

2. Perform the ritual (which includes a prayer to read aloud, or you can make up your own).

3. Use the daily practice to help anchor you in your body and the work for that Month.

4. Enjoy the poem.

5. Complete the worksheets.

6. Complete other tasks, like building an altar, singing to your ancestors, and other delights!

## How to Work with the Rituals in This Book

This book contains thirteen sequential rituals that correspond with the topics of the chapters. The rituals are designed to stand alone but also to work as a cumulative process of healing transgenerational sexual trauma and reclaiming sexual sovereignty and pleasure. I suggest that you do each ritual in the order in which it is presented, and to notice the results that occur.

In the first ritual, you will begin by creating a connection with an elevated ancestral guide, and they will partner with you in this transformational journey of embodied healing. Each following ritual includes a check-in with this same ancestral guide.

The approach to ancestral connection and ritual I offer here is one of primacy. That is, you do not have an intermediary in the process, like a medium or a spiritual practitioner. You are directly connecting with your own ancestors. I prefer this way of direct contact because less is lost in translation. You have the birthright to connect with your own people, and you do not need to pay someone to do this for you. Connecting with your ancestors yourself also builds trust and a sense of belonging to the wellness inherent in your lines.

You may want to conduct your ritual on the same day of each month, perhaps in tune with the phase of the moon. Some may choose to do one ritual every new moon, for example. Other than the ritual for Month 1, you can do every ritual as many times as is helpful. You can always return and do any of them again.

If at any point you get stuck, have something unexpected happen, or are uncertain about the positive benefits of the rituals, stop. Slow down and seek professional guidance. Especially if you are new to ritual, know that it can have somatic, emotional, and psychological impacts. The most important thing you can do is to trust the speed of your intuitive process. If something feels wrong or off, trust that. This ritual outline is a framework you can use, and while it will work for many, it is not one size fits all. Your ancestors may need different types of relating or tending from what is offered here.

It's also important to note that many different cultures utilizing Indigenous or shamanic healing practices use ritual for healing. The evidence supports the efficacy of ritual to address trauma. From child soldiers in Mozambique and Angola, to victims of war rape in Sierra Leone, to Australian Aboriginal people seeking to heal from forced attendance at boarding school and loss of culture, to Native Americans seeking support for substance abuse issues, ritual is used to address personal and transgenerational trauma.

Many Westerners do not have much experience with ritual. Ritual results are often subtle and can unfold in ways you only recognize much later. A teacher of mine once told me that just because I don't like a particular ritual, that does not lessen its efficacy. For people who do not come from backgrounds that revere the ancestors or practice ritual, one question often comes up: Is it real? Is our connection with ancestors objectively real? I ask this question too. In response, I suggest that you try it out and see what kind of results you get. Does it matter whether these practices use mechanisms that are quantifiable by scientific standards? Lots of global cultures practice ancestral reverence, and if you had grown up in one of those cultures, you would probably not ask if it's real.

Instagram and other social media platforms offer the teaching that ritual is primarily aesthetic with crystals and antlers, but ritual is an ancient and powerful technology for creating healing and change. It takes years to become a skillful practitioner so that you can track all of the nuances and implications of ritual action. Personally I have found great benefit in working with practitioners so that I can be solely in the role of recipient and not have to hold the ritual container at the same time.

This is all to say, take ritual seriously, move slowly, trust your intuition, and ask your ancestors what will be most beneficial for them. Modify and personalize the rituals in small, carefully considered ways. Always attend to ritual safety, which means setting up a well-held ritual environment with good protection. Close things down when you finish. Do rituals when you feel grounded and present, and get support if things go wonky.

# What You Will Learn

## Part 1: Build Inner Resources

Months 1–4 provide a foundation of information and practices that help you move through the process laid out in the book.

**Month 1: Containment Moon** invites you to set an intention for your healing process. Then you'll learn spiritual protection and safety strategies, including setting boundaries with the unseen realms. This Month concludes with a discussion of altars and invites you to create an altar to anchor the work to come.

**Month 2: Grounding Moon** provides additional foundational resources as you embark on your healing process. This includes what it means to choose wellness, practices for grounding and connecting with the land, and feeling safe in your body. You'll learn a variety of ancestral reverence practices.

**Month 3: Belonging Moon** supports you in finding a feeling of belonging. Through addressing attachment wounds and patterns, you'll examine your attachment style. You will work with a bright, elevated ancestral guide to create secure attachment and belonging. This Month also offers you practices of spiritual hygiene and discernment.

**Month 4: Resilience Moon** helps you understand your resilience and supports you in increasing it. You'll explore the survival narratives of your ancestors and create a resilience plan. You'll also learn three somatic practices for resourcing yourself through embodiment.

## Part 2: Heal

Months 5–8 support you by providing a map for moving through sexual trauma. You'll move toward healing through delineated processes of acknowledgment, justice, freedom, and transformation.

**Month 5: Acknowledgment Moon** supports you in acknowledging the impact of the trauma you and your ancestors have experienced. The first step is to investigate the protective qualities of denial as a strategy. Then, you can gently move toward recognizing the personal and lineage impact of sexual harm. Acknowledgment is the first step in healing.

**Month 6: Justice Moon** invites you to contemplate what justice means to you. This Month begins by discussing different justice models and how justice is a personal experience. You'll explore and define justice for yourself within a nonretributive, embodied model.

**Month 7: Freedom Moon** provides a conceptual framework of body liberation. The Month begins by discussing the complex role of shame in the trauma healing process. This Month holds that your body is a source of wisdom rather than pathology. You'll get to explore the somatic strategy of disembodiment/dissociation as a wise tactic. Instead of enforcing mindful presence as an automatic stage of the healing process, you get a choice.

How can placing your attention in your body be a friend? When is it not helpful? This Month aims to give you more choice about how you live in your body.

**Month 8: Transformation Moon** provides you with somatic tools that support your embodiment and transformation. Beginning with a discussion of what embodiment means (based on choosing presence practiced in the previous Month), you'll receive practical guidance that builds toward erotic embodiment. This includes breath, sensation, movement, vocalization, and attention to the senses as tools you can use to connect more with your body.

In part 1, you built inner resources. In part 2, you practiced using tools to work through sexual trauma. Now your attention turns toward pleasure as meaningful.

## Part 3: Savor

Months 9–13 explore pleasure, the erotic, and the erotic/ancestor connection. Through building a sovereign sexual self and claiming pleasure, you'll move toward integration and erotic wholeness.

**Month 9: Sovereign Moon** empowers you to develop sovereign sexuality based on exploring who you are and who you want to be as a sexual being. You'll learn the concept of inner sexuality—the most sacred and intimate version of a person's sexual self. This Month also explores outer sexuality, where one's desires, fantasies, and boundaries meet the world, including the capacity to say "yes" and "no." The Month invites you to dream and expand who you can be as you inhabit your full erotic power.

**Month 10: Blessing Moon** helps you connect concretely with your sexuality. You'll begin this Month by considering the burdens and blessings you inherited from your ancestors around sexuality. Then you'll explore sexual freedom and sexual self-esteem and how you can embody blessings received from your ancestral lineages around sex and gender. This Month, you'll dive into your own sexuality, learning more about your body and your pleasure for your erotic embodiment.

**Month 11: Pleasure Moon** helps you vastly expand your concept of pleasure. By deconstructing capitalism and pleasure, you'll rewild your capacity for delight and feeling good. This Month, you're guided to practices of ecstasy and the healing power of pleasure, on your terms.

**Month 12: Ancestor Moon** helps you contextualize healthy sexuality within an intergenerational framework. This Month investigates healing as a community endeavor. Understanding the context of ancestral sexuality and giving it right-sized attention makes the transformation of sexuality within a blood lineage possible. You'll learn ritually safe ways to create healing at a potentially taboo intersection. Next, you'll get a vision of what radiantly healthy sexuality could look like.

**Month 13: Integration Moon** imparts the importance of integration and practical strategies for incorporating all the learning and exploring you have completed. Next, you'll pay the healing forward. By creating a pleasure bundle, you'll offer blessings and prayers for the sexual wholeness of all your descendants (blood, heart, and otherwise). This Month offers guidance for moving forward.

So what does all this mean for you? It means that the skills, experience, and protocols to help you heal are available. You can heal the impact of transgenerational sexual trauma on your own sexuality. This book is here to support you as you clear trauma in your body, both your own and that of your ancestors. Ready to begin? Let's get started!

# PART 1
# Build Inner Resources

The first part of this book is about building foundational resources for yourself so that when you move into active healing, you'll have the practices and awarenesses you need to stay steady.

# Month 1
## Clemency, to My Descendants

Dark blossoms from day.
I attend this ancestors' loch,
water smooth like glass.
It holds no justice (no truth nor lies)
about old bones nestling in ooze beneath.

My toes are wet.
Wind stirs the rowan tree.
Shattered, the water cracks.
I shake with old, familiar grief.

Rocking without knowing why,
I forget to breathe
and find the loss and ache not mine,
but someone's old undone,
my heartbreak legacy.

The ancient heart valve pumps corrupt,
centuries dissolved in water's wake and pull,
twined with mine, through blood
their unjust murder and what's bequeathed.

My voice skims the surface:
I am available only as I say
to heal these wounds not mine!
Not mine, but tangled history.

Tend the bones,
yes, that much I can do,
but there will be no assembling them again
into a twisted love,
but instead, something shining,
new.

Descendants, things I will not leave
you: heartbreaks, no inheritance from me.
You will not sit to mourn what I did not.
You. Are. Free.

## Moon of Containment Practice

**Each night as you lie in bed, call to you your magickal allies.**

Wait until you feel them arrive.

With their support, create a boundary of protection that encases you. Get clear on the sensory information for this boundary: color, substance, temperature, smell, taste.

You can experiment to see what works best. You may experience the boundary of protection as a tangle of blackberries, a coating of diamonds, a felt sense of armor at some distance from your body, or a thousand thousand other variations.

You may also wish to experiment with multiple layers.

Feel into the containment field you are creating. Stretch and build that energetic muscle. You can try using a felt NO. Once you are layered with protection, practice feeling protected. Breathe into your space. Fill it with you. Get into your body as much as you can and/or want to.

You get to discern what is in your best interest, and you get to practice until you are *exquisite* at it.

# MONTH 1

# Containment Moon

Welcome to Month 1 of *Tending the Bones*. This Month, you will set intention for your process and learn about grounding, boundaries, discernment, and containment of energies. You will also set up your own healing altar. Even if you have experience with these topics, I invite you to come to the material with a beginner's mind. Foundational practices can be returned to again and again for support and fortification.

How are you feeling? If you are nervous and a bit excited but also terrified, yep—you're in the right place. Remember, you get to go at the pace that is right for you and your ancestors. This process is designed to be slow, mindful, and incremental.

## Beginnings Matter, So Let's Set a Clear Intention

Deepak Chopra says, "Intentions compressed into words enfold magickal power." Intentions are born of our needs and desires. Intention is a way to be clear with yourself and the unseen realms about what you want in your life. An intention is your significant "why" for what you are doing. Intentions are our plans—what we're aiming for. You are laying the groundwork for what you desire to do. Power comes from deciding which direction to take your life in and then taking action.

Intentions are a systematic way for you to determine the course of your healing, your career, or really anything. Throughout this book, you are using intention as a tool of discernment. You are becoming crystal clear about what you want, what you don't want, and what you are up to. Intention becomes your boundary. It's a simple present-tense statement of your desire. You create clear intentions to get the results you want and leave room for beneficial surprise, creative outcomes, and magick. Intention helps you guide what your practices will be. It enables you to return to what's essential.

Intention setting is a practice that can guide many aspects of healing. For example, when working with ancestors, it's imperative to know who you intend to work with and what work you will attempt. The what and the who both matter a lot. One elder initiated in the Ifá tradition spoke about her intention for ancestral work and how important it is:

> *You just can't go into anything just because you can do anything, and you want to prove that you are powerful enough to do it. That ain't it. You got to be clear about the work that you're doing and who it's going to affect and how it's going to work.*

If you have participated in spiritual communities that involve ancestral work, you may realize there is a spectrum of how people work with ancestors. Some people just invoke "the ancestors" and hope for the best. Others invite only the well and bright ones, those who have demonstrated they are well in spirit.

I believe that the dead, like the living, are at various levels of spiritual wellness. Just because someone has died does not make them an *ancestor*. So if I invoke a dead relative and they are not in a state of wisdom and love, the results will be less optimal than if I invoke an ancestor rooted in love and compassion.

One person I interviewed who was on the more trusting end of the spectrum said:

*It seems like when I put the intention out that this is what I need or what I think I need. Then I ask for what I want or what interaction I want. I have to trust that it will happen and that the right entity will come forward.*

Another expressed the importance of intention setting a little bit differently:

*When working with ancestors of blood, be clear in your intention. Ask, and don't assume, that they're going to give you support. Just be really clear about the issue: can you help me with it? Also, be really clear about shielding yourself. I think it's always essential that you be really clear about what you're inviting in.*

As you begin this work, I suggest you commit to work only with elevated ancestors who can truly support your process. We'll discuss more about elevated ancestors in a later chapter, but for now, think of them as the dead who are trustworthy, supportive, and loving, and who will act only on your best behalf. But don't worry; the as-of-yet unwell dead don't get left behind. Instead, they receive healing from *their* ancestors. Everyone gets to belong.

Developing a clear intention for the next thirteen months will keep you on track. It's the thing you can return to in a challenging moment to help you reground and remember what you're doing and why you're doing it. Part of your initial work is to create a clear statement of intention using as few words as possible, but enough to define what this project is that you're starting. You will identify what you want and need for erotic wellness. Your choice of words is crucial: they need to be clear, spacious, unambiguous, and perhaps even poetic.

What are you doing? What great work are you setting out to accomplish for yourself, your ancestors, and your descendants in the next thirteen months?

Take a moment now and imagine who you might be after completing these next months. Imagine that you've completed this significant work; you're in an altogether different place in your life. Your relationship with your ancestors, your erotic self, your aliveness, and your embodiment have all undergone tremendous transformation. Stop reading, and form a snapshot in your mind's eye. Then go ahead and write this imagined outcome down on your worksheet page for this Month, which you can find in the appendix.

## Discernment, Boundaries, and Protection

Discernment and boundaries are really two sides of the same coin. Discernment is making conscious choices about how to proceed based on all of the information available to you. Knowing what is good for you and what is not is a capacity you can develop. Basically, you want the ability to make decisions that support your life. You want to choose things that uplift you and help you. This includes your environment, the people you surround yourself with, and the substances you imbibe, including food and medicine. You discern how to spend or save your money and what you do with your career.

Where do you choose to put your body on this Earth? What things do you do with your body? What kind of sex do you have? How do you invest your time, the time of your life? Whom do you trust? All of these are part of your discernment practice.

You are constantly discerning. All day long you discern. Discernment is a muscle. As you clear out your toxic loyalties to things that do not serve, your discernment becomes more skillful. Through experience, you learn to sort out what is good for you from what is bad for you. It's a full-body experience; your felt sense and your heart have as much input as your brain.

Discernment is the cornerstone of sovereignty. You come to trust your own input, your own learning, your own deciding. Getting to the place where you consciously practice discernment means you have already done some very significant healing. While you are constantly discerning day to day, trusting your own intuition is profound.

## How Do You Discern?

Discernment is a somatic and intellectual process. Part of learning how to discern is developing somatic awareness so you can feel what is good for you and what is not. You use your body to do that. You use your mind to consider the difference between short-term and long-term results. This sounds like: What do I want for myself right now? What do I want for myself as I move into later phases of life?

For example, right now you might engage in a practice that is not in service to your long-term well-being. Let's say you smoke cigarettes. While you intellectually know that smoking is not good for you in the long term, and maybe you even feel that in your body, you choose the relief it provides in the present moment, despite the long-term costs. Tobacco may be a necessary medicine for you right now, so it's worth risking the consequences. On the flip side, as you heal, it may become more important to you to care for yourself in different, more life-affirming ways. So you stop smoking and take up conscious breathing practices.

Discerning the right thing for the right moment is a skill you can practice. You practice by checking in with your body and your head, and asking: Is this good for me right now? Is this good for me in the long term?

To be clear, it is not necessary to always make the long-term self-care choice; but it is necessary to honestly acknowledge that you are making a choice. Discernment is the pause that provides you with rigorous self-honesty. When you take the time to discern, you are practicing self-worth. And luckily, practicing discernment also increases self-worth.

As you make choices based on what the wise part of you knows is in your best interest, you will notice that how you feel about yourself shifts. Perhaps you are more respectful of your own time, your own desires, your own boundaries. You may feel calmer, more loving toward yourself.

It really comes down to this: if you want to feel better about yourself, be nice to yourself. Make some choices that reflect love and kindness. There is no need to be perfect at discernment. If you always knew exactly what was right for you and chose that option, you would have few opportunities for growth and learning. When you choose what is good for you, especially in the long term, you value and protect the spark of life that is you.

## Using Discernment When Working with Ancestors

When working with ancestors, discernment is a necessary tool. Some of the dead are wonderful, loving, and elevated. Some of the dead are not yet well; and some of them want to be well. The dead, like the living, vary quite a bit in their degree of wellness. Some living people practice dignity, integrity, and wholeness. This is also true of the dead. Some living people engage in practices that create disintegration or harm; some of the dead do that too.

Death does not necessarily make someone into an elevated ancestor. Death is just death. What happens between being a dead guy and becoming an elevated ancestor is a mysterious process that I don't pretend to know about. My best guess is that there is a process where the individual dead person is ritualized and becomes an elevated ancestor through healing and transformation.

NOTE  *It's important to remember that the dead, like the living, can change. The premise of this book is that transgenerational healing is possible, which means that historic harm and suffering can be healed and atoned for, and justice can happen after the fact. Repair is possible.*

Every skilled ancestral healer I know believes that working with protection is a crucial safety protocol. In the way I've been trained, we do that by working with elevated ancestors. If you want to be well, work with well energies. You'll get better results!

How do you recognize well energies, especially since trauma can skew our judgment? You gather data and information. You ask your wisest self. You feel for the information your body provides.

Being able to protect yourself means:

- You recognize you are worth protecting.

- You discern appropriately what is good for you and what is not.

- Based on your discernment, you set boundaries.

- You enforce your boundaries.

Who will you work with? Who will you set boundaries with?

Discerning which ancestors are helpful for you to work with takes practice. You don't decide with your intellect, "Oh, I loved my grandma, so I will work with her."

You can only discern whom to work with after you know how to protect yourself spiritually. Think about it; you choose to protect what has value and what is precious. So in the beginning of the work, I invite you to make this decision: you are worth protecting. You deserve love and kindness. Work only with ancestors who are well and bright in spirit.

Not protecting oneself is a strategy born of trauma. In the aftermath of harm, our assessments can become skewed, and we can get confused. We may want to protect perpetrators, especially if that is how we survived. In another example, someone may protect aspects of themselves and their life that would be better off transformed and healed, while leaving gaping vulnerabilities undefended. As you heal and practice boundaries, protection, and discernment, and work only with well, elevated ancestors, this confusion will resolve.

We'll talk more about safety in a bit, but it's an unfortunate consequence of trauma—especially early trauma—that we confuse danger for safety. Because harm is familiar, we mistake it for what is not harmful. Relearning what true safety feels like is part of the work. If you are someone with trauma (which is my best guess, since you are reading this book), pay heed to what I say next. When you read about protection, if you think "Oh, I'm fine," or "I don't really need to protect myself from my ancestors," or "I'll just skip that step," I invite you to consider that doing this work without protection is dangerous.

While researching this book, I interviewed many people who had sexual trauma and had worked with ancestors to resolve it. Almost everyone I spoke with stressed the need for ritual safety. They made three types of safety suggestions:

- Work within an established tradition with well-practiced ritual protocols.

- Work with a trained spiritual elder who can guide your process and your progress.

- Develop the skills to personally shield and protect yourself when working with the dead.

In traditions that work with the dead, ritual safety is paramount. Some traditions highly value ritual form as a safety protocol. One person of Chinese ancestry said:

*My family wants me to go into ancestor work very carefully. There's a lot of safety built into the way Chinese people practice safety and superstition. My family said, "You can't just be making things up, because it's dangerous." When you go into a trance, you have a good person with you to make sure that the bad spirits don't come and get you, because you don't know what's out there. You have to stay in your body, where it's safer. The ritual forms can be protective.*

While some reverence practices are culturally specific, many are cross-cultural. Suppose you come from a distinct cultural background that practices ancestral reverence. In that case, it is best to learn those traditions. If you have an intact, living ancestral lineage, you should learn those traditions, because they are something your ancestors will respond to. Doing traditional reverence practices builds relationships with your healthy ancestors. Over time, you establish trust and consent. You can decide which paths of healing to go down with your ancestors.

Some spiritual traditions, like Ifá, highly recommend working with a spiritual elder to hone this skill of discernment. The elder you work with helps you discern which spirit you're working with and why that spirit wants to work with you. An elder practitioner of Ifá said:

*Well, you try to find out as much as you can, beginning with why they want to work with you. I have known folks who had to deal with ancestors who had crossed over, like someone who committed suicide, and they could only work with them under the guidance of an elder priest. They had to be clear about the work that they were doing and why they were doing it.*

I encourage you to find mentorship and be rigorous about quality. Finding a spiritual elder you can trust can help you get to where you can discern for yourself what's what. You have to follow your own knowing and intuition just to find a good teacher. You may have to try out several before finding someone who can help you build your discernment practice. There are many trained professionals who can support you in working with transgenerational trauma and ancestral healing. (Check the "Resources" section at the end of this book for some recommendations.)

To do this work safely, you also need to develop your personal skills of ritual protection. Discernment is one such tool. Others will be discussed a bit later. As noted above, you will be deepening your discernment for the rest of your life so you can discern who an appropriate spiritual mentor or spirit guide might be, among other things.

One person I interviewed said this about discernment:

*There's a process of discernment, and there's a process of actually learning to check our senses. People have been taught to mistrust themselves and to trust outside authorities in a way that's really pernicious, but in order to connect with the spirit realm, you have to be able to trust your own directed spirits. There are the eyes and the heart that have to be opened, and there is your felt sense in which you have to trust yourself directly, in the same way that animals do. Animals respond to the visceral input of their environment. They don't stop and ask questions like, "Wait, is this valid and real?" They're just responding directly to their perception.*

Ultimately, your personal safety during spirit work and ancestor work is your responsibility. You have to want to be in a well-enough state to make sure you work in a way that's safe for you. Make sure your mental health is good, and when you need support, get it quickly.

As part of your personal skill-building, you learn to trust your own knowing. For example, if a new spirit shows up and things seem mostly okay, but you still have a slight nagging feeling, trust it and don't work with that spirit. If a spirit you have built a trusting relationship with does something disturbing, seek further information or guidance from your teacher. Working with the dead becomes a litmus test of your own healing, and you are safest when you are going slow and checking facts. Trust is built over time. This is a safeguard in relationships with the living and the dead.

In spirit work, an essential skill you develop is personal protection. If you have an upsetting dream or feel the presence of something ominous, or if things start to happen on the material plane like your house getting broken into, you need to know how to shield and protect.

You start with a radical act of faith that there is that within you which deserves your protection. You become the guardian of your integrity and your dignity. You no longer settle for having your boundaries violated, and you're no longer content to violate your own boundaries.

You begin with the premise that your untouched inner treasure will eventually appear if you can learn to discern safety from harm and to protect and guard yourself in good ways. This new radical act of faith is where it begins—with saying no. You learn boundaries. Obviously, boundaries keep you protected, so you aren't all permeable and mushy with the living and the spirit realms.

One person I interviewed shared this with me:

*I think just in all situations, in any kind of work like this, you should be prepared to shield yourself, particularly when you think [spirit attention] is coming as a compliment and it turns out it's not. When you think they're being really helpful and it turns out they're not. You get to learn to discern ancestral spirits that are benevolent in nature. You get to learn to connect with the spirits of the dead that you wish to. You want to connect with ancestral allies who are sound, whole, and healthy, and who wish good things for you.*

To be clear, the gift of accessing information from the unseen realms is a profound gift. Having easy access to the spirit world is often a silver lining for survivors of sexual trauma. I think this happens because the liminal is a place we can retreat to when our boundaries are overwhelmed. If someone learns to dissociate from the tangible world, the spirit world is there to catch them. This is why it can be scary to set boundaries with spirits in the beginning. People worry: Will I lose access? Will I lose connection? Will the spirits abandon me?

When you develop a relationship with a well ancestral guide, it's essential to know that they represent the sound and thriving energy of the entire line. Chronologically speaking, if you go back far enough in your lineages, your ancestors were tended by the living up to a certain point in history. The forgetting had not yet happened (if the forgetting has indeed happened in your heritage; no assumptions).

And that means there is a lot of wellness for you to access. You want to tap into all of that. When you relate with a guide, you're not just relating to that particular spirit; you're connecting with thousands of souls who are all well behind them. You get to access *all* of the blessings and goodness of that line.

Helpful spirits will be respectful. They will never be intrusive. They might be bossy or opinionated, but you always get to negotiate with them around their suggestions. They will respect your agency. They are never mean, cruel, or punitive. They will not leave you just because you're taking care of yourself. They love you. They want what's best for you. To really reclaim your full power, you need to be able to say no to what you don't want. Having the capacity to say no allows you to truly discern what is best for you. That means shutting the door on spirit energies that aren't well. Saying no to something allows you to say yes to something else.

Suppose that spirits you believe to be your ancestors are sending you information that is not supportive. In that case, it's possible that whatever you are relating with is not radiant and loving ancestral energy. There is lots of cool sparkly stuff you can connect with in the unseen realms. And some of it is not-so-awesome stuff that doesn't have your best interest at heart.

We must know that we can lean into and trust the advice of the warm, wise, kind, loving elders who have our backs and want what's best for us. They're not going to be mean to us. Your guides are your intermediaries. They help you understand things and deepen your knowledge. They are wise elders.

Think about how you feel toward any descendants or future descendants of your body, heart, or family's line regardless of whether you have children or plan to. You have a desire to be intentional about what you embody in your own life and what you bequeath to your descendants. You long for them to be nourished, to live good lives; you desire their happiness, their fulfillment, yes?

I think about this a lot, and I pray about it a lot. When I use the word *pray*, I don't mean it in a particular religious paradigm. Anyone can pray without needing to be a devotee of a faith. Prayer is a heartfelt desire that you speak or send out into the world.

I pray for my descendants every day, both descendants I have and descendants yet to come. I send love forward in time. My ancestors did this. We want those who come after us to have good lives. I pray for those who come after me, of my blood, heart, and future generations of the Earth; I pray for their wellness. I pray for them to have a better world.

Praying for my descendants helps me remember that I can receive the benefits of prayer from those who, in their lifetimes, prayed for me. They didn't know me personally, but they did the same thing. It's a way I can lean into the love of my ancestors. As I do this, I can trust that they did this, and I can receive this love through time. Your ancestors did the same for you while they were alive. They do this now, just as you will support your descendants after you die.

If I choose to work with well ancestral guides, this becomes a blessing for my descendants. I am getting things current in the lineages, interrupting harm so that healing can move backward and forward in time. It becomes a blessing for you to choose to work with the good ancestors, and it's a gift to your descendants. Discernment is a practice that benefits all the Earth that you and your people embody.

Here are some questions to help you explore your discernment. You may wish to write about or meditate on these.

- ¤ What image represents discernment?
- ¤ What are the discernment practices you use?
- ¤ Do you move slowly enough to trust your own knowing, but quickly enough when a clean cut is necessary?
- ¤ How do you experience your discernment?
- ¤ How do you know what's good for you? How do you know who is good for you?

## What Are Boundaries?

I once watched a video of a new mother bear. She had cubs, and she was patiently lying down and allowing them to nurse. After a while, the cubs began to play with each other, still mainly on the mama bear's body. The play became more and more vigorous until the patient mama bear had had enough of it, and she swatted one of the cubs. It wasn't severe, but it was enough to get the message across: knock it off. She asserted her boundary: don't do that while you are on my body.

Boundaries are how you discern what is you and what is not you, what is yours and what is not yours. Some examples of physical boundaries are fences, walls, windows, gates, doors, your skin, physical distance, and time. Emotional boundaries include saying no, maintaining your truth, and standing up for your integrity. To feel safe, children need to be able to say:

"No, I disagree."

"I will not."

"I don't want to."

"Stop."

And they need to have those boundaries respected.

Boundaries keep what is good and desirable in and keep what is unwanted out. When boundaries are violated, this order can get reversed. It can mean that you can't accept or absorb goodness anymore. When boundaries are reversed, what is unsafe becomes "safe" and what is actually safe can be perceived as unsafe.

You set boundaries in many contexts, including your professional relationships, your living family, your friends, romantic relationships, the dead, children, and animals. You set boundaries with your money and your food, and you set boundaries with yourself. Because you set boundaries in so many different areas, it's very possible—and indeed likely—that you have powerful boundary skills in some areas and not in others.

As a child, did you feel safe saying no? How do you feel about it now? Most of us have to relearn boundaries as adults. You get to learn to say no and trust that things will be okay and that you will be safe. You may be able to say no just fine but struggle to say yes. Yes is also a boundary.

Whatever kept you safest as a child has informed how you set boundaries now. For that reason, your boundary strategies might be outdated. They may not match the person you are now, although they may have served you in the past. You probably have some work to do on updating your boundaries, and this is often fairly unpleasant. It can be uncomfortable. It can strain relationships. However, it is deeply worthwhile.

Reestablishing a working relationship with your own boundaries allows you to become more deeply connected with yourself. You are saying, "I've got me, I've got my own back, I'm taking care of myself, I am worthy of taking care of myself. I am worthy of learning to discern. I am worthy of learning to have boundaries."

As an adult, clear boundaries prevent resentment from building up in a relationship. You don't necessarily have to leave a relationship or a situation to take care of yourself anymore. You have more agency. Boundaries support you in staying in a relationship or meeting your need for autonomy. Hence, when skillfully used, boundaries increase the possibility of greater intimacy in adult relationships.

Your work in updating your boundaries to support the current version of yourself is about becoming more of an adult. You move beyond your childhood boundary strategies, and you determine what you want your adult boundary practices to be.

How do you know if it's an adult boundary? When you can say the following things to yourself about a boundary:

- I can choose it, and I know why.

- I can communicate it verbally; that's the most effective way.

- I stand up for it.

- I endure the consequences if needed.

¤ I'm solely responsible for upholding it.

¤ I don't depend on others to maintain my boundary.

¤ With this boundary in place, I feel more connected with myself.

When folks first start to learn how to set boundaries, especially after a boundary violation, sometimes the boundaries they set are impenetrable. They are like a fortress. Folks learning about boundaries can be hypervigilant, always looking for real or perceived violations. Sometimes people have really mushy, malleable boundaries that are only responsive to the needs of others. Everyone's boundaries change depending on who you're with, where you are, what moment you're in, and many other factors. Your boundaries are not set in stone.

The cool thing about boundaries work right now is that it applies to both your living human relationships *and* your relationships with the spirit realms!

Boundaries are not "set and forget." They need to be constantly and consistently maintained, just like a fence. When I set a limit, I expect both the living and the not-yet-well dead to test it. I expect that it will likely change the dynamic of the relationships it affects. I expect that I will get lots of chances to practice upholding it. I might test my own boundaries.

The process of setting and maintaining boundaries is complex. It's highly connected with your needs and desires. How do you develop this art? This is part of discernment: the art of holding firm boundaries without being brittle, supple without being mushy, responsive without being reactive, and loving without being aggressive.

You set a boundary in the following way: first, decide what you are saying yes to and what you are saying no to. Second, commit to enforcing the boundary. Instead of telling a friend, "Please don't call after 8 p.m.," say, "If you call after 8 p.m., I won't pick up the phone." And then don't pick up the phone!

While you don't ever need to explain a boundary, it can be relational to give people more context, which could sound like: "Hey, just want to let you know that I'm trying to get more sleep these days, and I've made a decision to not talk on the phone before bed, so I'm not taking any calls after 8 p.m. Thanks for understanding!"

## Containment of Energies

Boundaries are one way of containing energies. This principle will become especially important when we get to the part in the book where you're working with the dead. Containers keep things in and keep things out. Containers keep you safer.

Have you thought about what your container agreements are for yourself and your own magickal workings? What are you willing to allow into your space? What are you ready to exclude from your field for your own safety?

Setting your container informs what happens next. Give these questions some good thought: What is the container you're creating for your own magickal self for the next thirteen months? What are your container agreements? What gets to come in? What are you keeping out for the sake of your own safety?

Some suggestions for elements of your own personal container agreements:

- ¤ I will only work with elevated ancestors.
- ¤ If something feels off, I'll listen to that feeling, pause, and seek support.
- ¤ I'll get support if I find myself tangled up.
- ¤ I will set time for myself to do this work on my calendar.
- ¤ I will let my therapist know I'm doing this.
- ¤ I will work with my spiritual teacher to complete this process.
- ¤ I'll schedule monthly check-ins to assess how I'm doing and what I need.

There are many kinds of boundaries, including magickal limits. There are many technologies available to create magickal, energetic boundaries. For example, you can cast a circle. There are lots of different ways to cast circles: some call the four cardinal directions and the elements, whereas others draw a circle of salt on the floor.

One of my favorite ways to cast a circle is to call on allies I have a trusted working spirit relationship with. These are entities like specific plants, trees, animals, minerals, or deities—protectors I already know and trust. With their support, I create layers of protection that go all the way around my body, in every direction. I imagine a shield of love, protection, and blessing.

When I set up a container to do magick in, I imagine creating a force field that wraps around me in every direction. Once I feel that, then I take the time to fill it out. I imagine blowing myself into that container, filling it with all of me so nothing else can be there unless I invite it in. I hang out inside my force field, noticing what it feels like to feel protected.

What is it like to just hang out in a well-protected, well-boundaried, safe space? You can give your body this experience, and it will deepen with practice over time. It's an energetic way of telling yourself, "I've got me; I will honor and respect my own boundaries."

You can experiment with multiple layers of protection. One layer of security might be that you turn off your phone. Another might be that you go into a room and close the door. Another might be that you put on some magickal items of clothing or jewelry. Another might be this practice of calling your allies and then asking them to help you create a magickal containment field around you. You can say a prayer, inviting protection from your space, from the trees near where you live. Suiting up would be another way to think about it, such as putting on protective work gear.

Love is an exceptional magickal boundary. Ground and center in love.

It doesn't matter so much what specific technique you use, but rather that you take the time to call protection to mind and do it every time you are going to spend time with the unseen realms.

Once you have a sense of your container agreements and boundaries, write them on the worksheet for this month.

## What Does Safety Mean to You?

You are here reading this book for your own healing: healing of your sex, your ancestral wounds, and your trauma. Erotic freedom is best supported when your body feels safe to be vulnerable, so you have to figure out what safety feels like and how to feel it. So we need to ask: What does safety mean to you? This is an essential question because our culture conflates safety with comfort.

Many people equate feeling uncomfortable with feeling unsafe. Disentangling these concepts in your body is necessary because, in fact, many trauma survivors don't have an embodied understanding of what it feels like to feel safe. Knowing what safety feels like is often a piece of healing work. Learning to feel safe and notice when you feel safe is part of the process of becoming embodied and sexually free.

My favorite definition of safety comes from Master Somatic Coach Meredith Broome, who says:

*Safety is the capacity to act on your own behalf.*

Safety is the capacity to act on your own behalf.

Let's unpack that a bit. In your family of origin, was it okay to say no? Was it alright to be angry? Did you get to act according to your wishes and desires? Perhaps autonomy was woven into the fabric of your family. When you didn't want to eat something, your caregivers honored that. When you wanted to wear yellow tights, a plaid shirt, a striped skirt, and glitter to an important family event, your creative self-expression was celebrated.

Others among you may have been required to uphold the code of your family. You had to do what you were supposed to do, whether you liked it or not. For many of us, it's a mix of these two extremes. Your autonomy was sometimes recognized, and at other times, when you were required to adhere to someone else's rules, needs, or desires, it was not. When you are required to adhere to someone else's dictates or face the consequences, you may still have the agency to act on your own behalf—but the costs can rise if you do.

There have probably been moments in your life when you couldn't act on your own behalf. In these moments, you were powerless. When you feel helpless, you do not feel safe. Feeling truly powerless is (usually) the opposite of feeling safe. I say "usually" because there is work you can do to learn to deeply experience powerlessness and develop the capacity to be present with your emotions and sensations, but that's another book. I also say "usually" because in my head I can hear BDSM folks challenging the idea that feeling powerless is the opposite of feeling safe, and I mean no disrespect to consensual play.

Ignoring your own "no" or surviving having your no dismissed means your boundaries were violated. In these cases, it essentially becomes unsafe to even have boundaries. When personal boundaries are violated repeatedly or extremely, it becomes difficult to understand them.

Your own anger is a vital tool in boundary practice. If you grew up in a family in which you were not allowed to express your anger, delving into your rage might be part of your process of relearning boundaries. Feeling angry is often a sign that a limit needs to be reestablished.

When you feel angry, you can ask yourself, "What boundary needs to be established right now?" You can learn to feel safe with your anger, and with all of your emotions.

## Agency

Agency is your access to personal power. It relates to safety and to your felt experience of safety. A more effective way to name the felt sense of safety or the lack thereof is *agency* and *agencylessness*. Your sense of agency is intrinsically linked to your sense of self, your dignity. When you can act on your own behalf, you are powerful.

Once, I was driving down a crowded city street. In the middle of my lane was a crow, eating the remains of someone's tossed-out-the-window dinner. As I approached the crow, it stood defiantly in the path of oncoming traffic, pecking at its supper and keeping a sharp eye on my approaching car. At the last possible moment, the crow winged away. It took responsibility for its own life and safety. That crow embodied agency. It also knew its capacity and how much time it had to remove itself from harm's path. That sense of knowing our capacity, knowing our timing, and feeling our own agency is what really creates safety. Agency creates safety.

## How Do I Start to Feel Safe in My Body?

A lot of people don't feel safe in their bodies. As a result of overwhelming experiences, we often move our attention away from our body and from feeling. You may experience fear about feeling the sensations and emotions in your body. How do you start to feel safe in your body again?

Living outside of ourselves is so common, and we all do it. It's a beautiful gift of nature that we can dissociate in this way—well, it's beautiful until we want our attention back in our bodies and don't know how to get it there. (Much more on this topic later in the book.)

Assuming that you are physically safe and there is no ongoing harm in your life, somatic healing starts when you encourage this collaborative relationship between your mind and your body.

Your body begins to feel like a safe place when:

- You consistently make loving choices that support your needs for food, hydration, rest, companionship, movement, and work.

- You are kind to yourself inside your own head and stop thinking that you need to be mean to yourself for motivation.

- You give your body all the time it needs to reorient to a new way of being (as opposed to pushing your body to accept change on some predetermined timetable).

- You recognize that your body remembers and processes at a different (and usually slower) speed than your mind.

- You take a systematic and somatic approach (as opposed to a cognitive one) to address and renegotiate the trauma in your bodily tissues.

- You practice trusting the information that your body relates to your mind.

- You believe that your body is sage and wise.

- You give up your story of brokenness and trade it in for one of healing and integration.

- You recognize that muscular contraction in your body is valuable information and that the advice to "just relax," while well intended, misses the point.

- You allow your body to drive rather than your cognition; you listen deeply to your body.

These safety practices are available to you for free right now. You can start to develop this collaborative, trusting relationship with your body by believing that whatever it's doing, it's doing for a reason. Your body has not betrayed you. Your body is your first and final friend. Your body is where you are your entire life. The work is deepening this connection into the Earth that is your body and getting right with that. Inhabit your agency in a way that's not power-over, but power-with, by creating a consensual relationship with yourself.

## Altars

In general, altars are a place to externalize magickal processes and practices. They represent a threshold between this world and another.

There are many different types of altars. For example, altars can be more general, like a working altar, a place to gather spiritual items, light candles, and sit and say prayers. Alternatively, altars can be dedicated to a specific event or season, like a winter solstice altar. They can be devoted to a spell you are working on, like a liberation altar. They could be dedicated to a specific life event like wanting to graduate from college. And ancestral altars are specific physical spaces designed for communion with the dead.

Altars are where humans and deities, the living and the dead, engage. There are as many types of practices and protocols for altars as there are altars that exist.

The placement and orientation of an altar, and the items one includes on it, depend on the specific spiritual tradition one practices. Ancestral altars can be located indoors or outdoors, and they can face any direction, depending on the practitioner's spiritual purposes.

Some altars are permanent installations, and some are created for a particular celebration, such as altars created for Día de los Muertos (Day of the Dead). For this celebration, families place pictures of their ancestors, their favorite foods, and flowers on the family altar. They then venerate their ancestors by calling out their names.

Gravestones and grave markers are a particular type of shrine that commemorates the dead. Altars and shrines can be individual, like a small household altar, or they can commemorate the dead on a much grander scale, like the Vietnam Veterans Memorial in Washington, DC.

Altars created in honor of the dead communicate to them that you remember them and welcome them when you wish to be in communication. You can place offerings on ancestral altars. You can sit at your altars and sing and pray so that they know you are in contact with them.

The items found on your altar can be traditional or culture-specific. One subject I interviewed reported that many Chinese homes have a family altar where they pray to their ancestors. Such altars may also feature images of the Buddha, Kuan Yin, or other gods, as well as the ancestors' names or pictures.

Altar creation can also be combined with intention-setting practices for healing. When I asked what would be a good way to begin working with ancestors, one pagan practitioner I interviewed said:

*I build an altar with the intention that this is going to be my space of healing for that particular ancestor or ancestral line. Then the altar would include images of the people, things that they appreciated or liked, maybe a certain cigar, wine, flowers—something that connects me to them. Then I set the intention that this is what I want to do. I want to heal this aspect of my ancestral line and then get into a meditative space. I call forth and ask the energy to come forward that wants to be healed. I have, I guess for lack of a better word, a "conversation" as to what would help that person heal. Then I try to execute what they asked for. Intention and reverence go a long way with the ancestors. Having them know that we're willing to do acts of service for them makes everybody feel better. Build an altar, set the intention, create a meditative practice.*

## Building a Healing Altar

This is a good time to remind you that the process laid out in this book is meant to be followed in sequence. This month, I'm talking you through setting up an altar, but I'm not suggesting that you start to commune with your ancestors just yet. You are building the altar where you will eventually spend time with your healthy ancestors. In terms of altars you might wish to create, I suggest first setting up a simple space dedicated to your healing intention.

I suggest that you do not yet put images of your dead on your altar. As we're starting out, this is not an ancestor altar. You are not yet inviting ancestral connection, though it may already be happening.

To set up your altar, first choose a space you can visit comfortably that can be dedicated to only being used as your altar. You're not going to be setting your coffee cup or cell phone on there; it's your altar space. You might want to put a candle on it. You also might want to put some water, some Earth from where you live or from one of your sacred places, and perhaps some incense or a plant.

Maybe you have a particular object that represents healing. You might wish to add flowers. Some people like pretty altar cloths. It's okay to be as creative as you want. Altars are an expression of our magickal selves. You can be very ornate and elaborate, but know that simple is equally powerful. Let your altar be a place that nourishes you. We'll talk more about what to do at your altar in future chapters. For right now, it's time to set up a simple altar of healing.

## Last Thoughts for Month 1

You get to work with your ancestors in ways that feel safe and supportive to you. Your discernment and boundaries are tools to protect you from that which does not serve your highest good. While you will likely at times be uncomfortable as you do healing work, you will eventually develop an internal sense of safety with yourself.

**In conclusion, this month you will:**

- ¤ Complete the Month 1 worksheets in the appendix. You can also download this month's worksheets at www.pavinimoray.com/ttb-bonus.html.

- ¤ Set up your healing altar.

- ¤ Do a daily practice of boundaries: Call on your allies as you lie in bed, and create a layer of protection all the way around you. Feel safe inside it.

- ¤ Complete Ritual 1: Intention and Boundaries.

# Ritual 1: Intention and Boundaries

## Preparation

¤ The purpose of this ritual is to create a connection with an elevated ancestral guide on one of your four primary bloodlines. This guide will support you through the entire work of the book. The ancestral guide connection process comes from Dr. Daniel Foor's Ancestral Lineage Healing work, and is offered here with his blessing. You can find more in-depth explanation in his book *Ancestral Medicine*.

¤ This is a multipart ritual. It is likely the longest ritual in the book. You will need at least an hour. It is good if you also plan a buffer of time after the ritual when you can continue to process the experience and do not have to move directly back into task-oriented activity.

¤ You can do this at your healing altar or in another place where you will not be disturbed.

¤ You will need a notebook or voice recorder to take notes.

**Begin by setting a container of prayer as you read this aloud:**

*Beautiful, wise, elevated ancestors, respectfully, I honor your presence.*
*You from whom I descend.*
*I come as your beloved child, you who have wisdom, love, and guidance to share.*
*I come with good intention to offer you respect and reverence.*
*I come to tend your bones.*
*I seek your support, guidance, blessing, and protection.*
*As I traverse these healing paths, I want good things for myself and my blood and heart.*
*I want our lineages to be healed so that they may be a source of blessing, belonging, strength, and resilience.*
*Sweet ones, sweet ancestors, I ask for your attention.*
*Please, may a trusted ancestral guide make themselves known to me,*
*I ask to know you, to feel you, to be guided in all good ways by you.*
*Be with me.*

**Next, create a layer of protection with the help of your allies.**

Call out to the trusted spiritual sources of protection you already have. These may be deities, guardians, the elements, or relationships with animals, stones, holy places, herbs, or anything from the green world. Invite each to come toward you, and pause until you sense that they are present.

Then, with their support, imagine creating a layer of spiritual protection that goes all around you. You can visualize it if you like, or just feel it. Let it take form in your mind, a blanket of protection that allows only what is in your highest good to penetrate it, keeping anything negative at bay, and keeping you safe from unwanted impact.

This practice is a piece of ritual protection you will use in every ritual in this book.

Check in: Do you feel protected all the way around? Can you feel yourself?

**Choose a primary bloodline to work with.**

Now that you have set up ritual protection, you need to decide which of your four primary bloodlines you will focus on first. Choosing one bloodline to work with does not mean you are forsaking the others. Rather, you will work with one at a time. Spend some time in meditation to discern which line has the potential to be most helpful in your sexual healing process. Use your intuition more than your brain; no need to analyze what you already know. Instead, lean toward what feels best for you at this time. You are under no obligation to choose any particular lineage.

You'll know which lineage to work with because you will feel something inside that says "yes." Your decision should feel either pleasant or neutral. The recommendation is not to choose a bloodline that feels super troubled right away. If you get a sense of heavy energies, choose a different line.

Once you have determined which line you will work with, you will then open to a connection with an elevated ancestral guide on this line. In a lot of cases, guides come from many generations in the past, and many of them lived before a time of remembered or recorded names. To connect with a guide, first get present in your body. Your ancestors are part of you, your bones and blood, so you can connect with them by turning your attention inward.

NOTE   *The rhythmic sound of drumming may help your mind relax. You can find a web address for an online source of drum sounds in the "Resources" section at the back of the book.*

When opening to connection with a guide, you are not going anywhere. The safest place for you is in your body, in the room you are in. You are not traveling around the universe in search of your guide. They will come to you. The vibe you want to cultivate is curiosity, openness, friendliness, and welcome. Actually connecting with an ancestral guide can be very quick, or it can take some time. Remember that unless you have someone among your recent dead someone who practiced connecting with ancestors, it may have been a long while since a descendant has attempted to establish connection within that bloodline. Connecting directly with a blood ancestor may also be a new muscle you are learning how to use, and it can take time to learn to trust your experiences.

Many people describe meeting a guide as encountering a sense of presence. Ancestral attention from the elevated ones can feel like not being alone, or having a loving elder direct their gaze toward you. Some people visualize human forms, some hear their ancestors whisper in their ears, and others have a felt sense. Your ancestors will come to you as you are able to receive them. Often different ancestors show up differently, so what is true for one line may be different for another.

When you have a sense that there may be an ancestral guide present, ask the following questions to discern if this is a guide you should work with:

- ¤ "Are you an ancestral guide on this line of my ancestors?" Wait until you have a clear yes. If you do not get a clear yes, ask the spirit you are with to give a clear answer. If you don't get it, say thank you and move on. If you do receive an affirmative response, then ask:

  - ¤ "Are you willing and able to assist me?"

  - ¤ "Do you have the backing of all the well ancestors who came before you? If so, can you show me?" Wait until you receive confirmation that the ancestral guide presenting themselves is something akin to a spokesperson for all of the well energies and blessings of that line. This means that all who came before this one are well in spirit.

- ¤ If the answers to the previous questions are satisfactory, do a gut check. Do you intuitively feel safe with this spirit?

If at any point you get a no or it doesn't feel right to you, you have two choices: you can say thank you and move on to another connection; or you can ask this one if they can introduce you to a well ancestral guide on this line.

The guide connection is so important that I strongly advise you not to continue this work until you have established one. If you get stuck, I suggest you work with a practitioner trained in Ancestral Lineage Healing through Ancestral Medicine to support you. There are many highly trained and experienced practitioners who can help you make sure you've got the guide connection sorted.

Once you have encountered a guide and have worked through the discernment questions, next you will want to introduce yourself to your guide. Tell them your name, your parents' names, and where and when you are in the world.

At this point, you will ask them for a blessing for your life. You are asking the well energies of the line to give of their unique gifts and talents to you. You are asking them to recognize you as their beloved descendant, one in whom they are personally invested.

Receiving the blessing of your line is often a special and meaningful experience, especially if you have any type of challenge with your living family. You are entitled to the goodness your ancestors can offer.

When your ancestors give you the blessing for your life, it can take many forms. You may see it, hear it, or feel it. Take time with it; do your ancestors the honor of fully receiving the blessing they offer you. Take it in, and allow yourself to be changed by it.

Take all the time you need at this point in the ritual.

The last thing to do is to ask your guide about what offerings would be beneficial for them and for the line to receive. As you will learn later in the book, offerings are made to the elevated dead, not to the hungry ghosts. Offerings serve a dual purpose of feeding the lineage energy so healing can happen and helping you tend and develop the connection with your guide and the lineage.

Make a note of anything your guide asks for, and let them know if that's something you are willing and able to offer. If not, you can always negotiate. It's important to follow through, so say yes only to things you know you can offer.

Once you know your next steps in terms of offerings, close out the ritual with your guide. Offer gratitude and assurance that you will return to tend the relationship.

Then thank any allies you called in to help you hold the boundary of protection, offer your gratitude, and release them.

Dissolve the ritual circle, while keeping the protection in place.

It is complete.

# Month 2
## *Finding Ground*

I am homesick for this Earth.
Weight, gravitas of dirt,
will you let me in and bury me?

Funky downtempo dis-integrate
I'm coming home.
Let me in and bury me.

My dead built cairns
beneath the ground.
Passage to the spirit's realm.
Solstice winter light, cold standing stones.
Oh comfort, bury me.

Ground: I found you
through thumping raves in forgotten stations,
queer rings of mud and forest magick,
punk shows in opulent decay

that make this Earth
thrash and tremble
shake and sway.
Ground
please bury me.

Thrum of Earth, this humble dirt.
Weight, I'm yours to keep.
Ground my ground
please let me in
oh Earth, please bury me.

## *Moon of Grounding Practice*

One way to hold grounding is getting good at downregulating your nervous system. Allowing your energy and thinking to slow and drop down.

At least once each day, feel yourself as a creature made of Earth. Slow and feel the connection between your body and your Earthly home. Feel the action of gravity working on your body. Allow your skeleton to hold 5 percent more of the weight of your meat.

Surrender your breath, and just let yourself be breathed. Release all efforting.

Imagine dropping a cord of connection that is as wide as your body at its widest point . . . sinking that into the heart of the Earth.

*You are worthy of feeling calm, loved, grounded.*

# MONTH 2

# Grounding Moon

Welcome to Month 2! How has your work with your boundaries supported you thus far?

This Month you will be exploring wellness and healing with your ancestors. There is no imperative that says you must heal, you must heal your ancestors, or you must have an embodied, thriving sexuality. These are all choices you get to make. You have agency to curate the life you want for yourself.

## Choosing Wellness

Wellness and health are not the same, although they get conflated. Wellness isn't something you have to go to the spa or the acupuncturist for. I'm not talking about wellness culture, which can be another way to police people's bodies and choices.

Wellness is a choice, not an obligation. Often we don't see that we have that choice, because oppression obfuscates it. Wellness is not an outside metric that determines your worth. Instead, wellness is self-defined. You decide what your best life is. Define wellness on your terms.

There are many aspects of wellness, including physical, mental, emotional, spiritual, financial, community, erotic, and professional.

It is possible and indeed probable that you are well in some ways and need to heal in others. When you notice that a part of your life feels less vital or vibrant than you would like it to be, consider that an indication that it needs more healing.

What practices do you need to do to feel most mentally well? Most professionally well? The teacher and poet Krishnamurti said, "It is no measure of health to be well adjusted to a profoundly sick society." As we all know, Western culture loves to pathologize. Blame is a part of this system. If you are "unwell," you are told that your unwellness is undoubtedly your responsibility.

Humans are sensitive. We are animals, responsive to our environments. We internalize cultural unwellness, and then we blame each other and ourselves for doing so. We learn to pathologize ourselves. Pathologizing ourselves is born of a healthy impulse. It is an attempt to take responsibility for our lives—an intelligent strategy, albeit a misguided one.

If you convince yourself you are to blame for whatever happened, that prevents you from having to admit your powerlessness. If we are somehow to blame for what happened, then at least we are not powerless. All of this occurs on the subconscious level.

You can reframe healing as gifts you get to open. You get stuck so you can get yourself free. It is great spiritual work to find your way into your definition of wellness. If you are reading this, you have already decided to heal. You have already decided to seek out wellness for yourself. Some part of you has decided this healing of your heart is important.

In what ways do you want to be well? You may wish to think or journal about this question.

## Toxic Loyalties

You may find yourself loyal to things that are not good for you. These bonds are initially born out of love and your need to belong. The decision to stay connected with an unkind family member is one example. If you decide that person is no longer good for your life and set some boundaries with them, what would happen? Probably the relationship would shift dramatically, and in some cases it would end. In this case, choosing wellness for yourself means breaking ties with someone else.

We will be going into further detail with this concept later in the book when discussing shame. For now it's important to know that some relationships require you to be "unwell" in order for them to continue. For example, suppose your family historically has not had access to money. In that case, you may have a piece of your identity wrapped up in that lack of money. What happens to those relationships if you focus on financial wealth and well-being? Your loyalty may pull you toward staying out of prosperity so you can stay in the family system.

Another example is if your family of origin uses a lot of alcohol, and drinking is a big part of the family culture. If you choose to get sober or even abstain from alcohol, what happens to those relationships? Your loyalties can mean that choosing between drinking and sobriety also requires you to choose between belonging and separation. That is a painful choice. You would hope that those who love you would support you in doing your healing work, but the opposite can be true. If you choose to heal, loved ones can feel judged, implicated, or abandoned by you.

## Making the Choice

Choosing wellness is not without consequences. There can be an invisible cost to working for your wellness. It's important to understand why you are healing and what you choose to heal. The more you focus on your healing, the more the relationships in your life have to shift to support you or be completed. Choosing healing and wellness is a big deal.

It's also important to remember that the concepts of healing and curing are often conflated. Curing means fixing, restoring to a previous state of health, or getting rid of something detrimental. Examples are seeking a cure for the stomach flu or cancer. Curing is not the same as healing. Healing is a process, and it is not a destination where you finally arrive after a lot of work.

There is no "healed" state. Wounds continue to unfold and offer their necessary medicine upon the altar of your life. Healing is the practice of moving toward wellness. Healing is an iterative, responsive, life-affirming development without an expiration date. There is no magickal place you get to and say, "Yes! I am healed." That is not how healing works. So when we're talking about wellness and choosing wellness, we're talking about a spectrum, because no one exists in a fully healed state.

Some wounds can heal, that's true, and you will always be making your recovery. Choosing wellness is a paradigm, a mindset, and a placement of attention. It's a declaration of what's important to you, what matters. When you choose to heal, you decide to be in a commitment to permanent practice. You say to yourself, "I will always be on this journey; there is always more to learn, I am always a student of life, and I never stop." That's the paradigm you're stepping into. We all know people who have gotten to a particular place in their path and then say, "Okay, this far and no further." But not you.

Choosing to heal and committing to wellness are gifts you give yourself. You are saying, "I get to be here. I get to be well in all the ways." This mantra takes great courage to speak, because choosing to heal means embracing a process of exploring your own needs. You work to undo your cultural programming that says you don't get to have goodness and pleasure.

It's a profoundly personal decision, choosing to heal. It's also an act of revolution, because the empire thrives on our brokenness. Choosing to heal and committing to practice what is in your best interest is a radical act of loving yourself.

It's worth noting that choosing not to heal something—or not to heal something yet—is also an acceptable choice. We do not put the binary of "healed/unhealed" or "well/unwell" on ourselves. If something isn't ready for healing attention, make that a conscious choice. You can name that it is too much, or too much right now. Make a decision not to engage in that work. That way, you haven't just swept it under the rug. You are not in denial; you are not pretending it doesn't need attention. You acknowledge to yourself, "Oh yes, there's that thing, and I don't want to/can't deal with that. I'm going to put that on the shelf for now, and that's okay." Timing and readiness matter. You need time, space, and support to heal.

Prospective Immigrants Please Note
By Adrienne Rich

*Either you will*
*go through this door*
*or you will not go through.*
*If you go through*
*there is always the risk*
*of remembering your name.*
*Things look at you doubly*
*and you must look back*
*and let them happen.*
*If you do not go through*
*it is possible*
*to live worthily*
*to maintain your attitudes*
*to hold your position*
*to die bravely*
*but much will blind you,*
*much will evade you,*
*at what cost who knows?*
*The door itself makes no promises.*
*It is only a door.*

◇◇◇◇◇◇◇◇◇◇◇◇◇◇◇◇◇◇◇◇◇◇◇◇◇◇◇◇◇◇◇◇◇◇◇◇◇◇◇◇◇◇◇◇◇◇◇◇◇◇◇

It can be unbearable to turn your attention toward your deep wounds. Often, there is fear that if you pay attention to a thing that needs healing, a floodgate will open, and suffering will invade your life.

Your intuition here is spot-on, because you know your capacity. You know deep in your bones that you don't yet have enough capacity to deal with the torrent of feelings and sensations required by that particular piece of healing. You don't have the time to surrender to such a process. Perhaps you don't trust your capacity to return from the places of madness that healing sometimes insists that we visit.

The outstanding work of healing often involves building your capacity to be with what is. So much of the somatic contraction that many people experience—numbing, checking out, distractedness—is because you cannot bear to be with the sensations and emotions you experience. Here, healing means building enough capacity so you can endure this flood. You may have heard the expression "You've got to feel it to heal it." You do this for the sake of welcoming the entirety of your experience. Every piece of you gets to belong.

The reframe I offer is that wounds are the great gifts of your life. It certainly does not always feel like this. Still, a wound is an invitation into deeper layers of who you are. Indeed, you can calcify an identity around any wound and hold tightly to that identity. That is one choice. That is very often a part of the process of healing. You get very identified with your wounds.

Another choice is to move toward the wound, gently exploring its edges. First, you build the capacity to be with the edges. You tiptoe and go slowly. Then, as you build trust, you go deeper and deeper into knowing yourself, your embodied experience, stories, and beliefs. You allow the wounds to be a transformative experience here as an excellent guide and teacher on your path to becoming.

This is grace. When you have entered the wound on multiple occasions and come out the other side, you start to trust your capacity for resilience and return. You're beginning to believe in your power to feel the fullness of your humanity. You're not scared of your wound anymore. You start to believe in the goodness of these burdens because you believe in their transformational potential.

One last thought here about choosing to heal as a spiritual path: it is not for the meek-hearted. No one else gets to determine what healing means to you or to judge where you are in your process. Choosing to heal is a great act of faith in yourself—faith that you are worthy and deserving of love.

# Grounding

People who practice magick talk about energy a lot. Neuroscientists talk about the nervous system a lot. Somaticists talk about noticing sensations. These are all different ways of describing the same thing. If I ask you to notice your nervous system right now, how would you describe what you feel? Not what you're thinking, but what you're feeling?

Now, if I ask you to notice how your energy feels without giving it any words, are these feelings similar? Are they different?

Use whatever framework works best for you when practicing grounding. You feel what your energy is doing in your body, how it's moving and where. Your energy follows your intention. First, you intend, then you attend, and then your energy flows toward that placement of your attention.

Let's see this in action. Give this a try for a minute or two.

**Intention:** Intend to feel your left hand.
**Attention:** Place your attention in your left hand.
What happened? Did your awareness of your hand increase?

Before beginning any magickal practice, ritual, healing session, or difficult conversation, it helps to ground. Grounding means feeling your connection with your body and the Earth. The neuroscientific way to talk about this experience is to say you're regulating yourself—specifically, dorsal vagal regulation. Witches call it being grounded.

No matter what you call it, it's helpful to know how to do it for magick, ritual, and any other situation in your life. When you ground, you're focusing on connecting with the Earth. This allows you to slow down, deepen, and feel more. When you feel connected and part of the whole, you move with more skill and grace. You draw resources from that connection, not from your own nervous energy.

Grounding is an act of deep self-love. It's a profound practice of belonging to yourself while belonging to the Earth, because every molecule of your body is Earth. The Earth that currently forms your body previously belonged to your ancestors' bodies. You will return to Earth. You belong to the Earth. When you are grounded, your energy flows both downward and upward.

Grounding is a reciprocal relationship with Earth. You both give and receive. You love, and you are loved back. You are not collapsing down into the Earth. You are acknowledging and feeling into your sovereign connection so you can receive.

When you ground, you allow your awareness to first drop down, to connect with the Earth. People use various metaphors to conceptualize this principle: dropping down a tap-root, sending out currents, grounding cords, connecting with the layers of the Earth, or moving attention down to the core of the Earth.

One technique you can use is to first connect with your feet. Bring your attention to your breath, and on your exhale, imagine your energy flowing downward, spilling through the bottoms of your feet and flowing down into the Earth. You can imagine yourself growing a root or grounding cord.

You'll also hear yoga teachers describe grounding as sinking a little more into the floor with each exhale. What happens to the rest of your body? You can start to notice gravity more. You can notice the weight of your limbs settling. You can notice the places where your body is tight and where it is relaxed.

The Earth can receive all that you have to offer without judgment. Once you feel that your energy is flowing down into the Earth, you can imagine starting to receive energy from the Earth. Imagine that little doors in your feet open to receive love, kindness, holding, and care from the Earth, just as a plant does. Inhale, and imagine energy rising up into your body from the Earth.

Grounding is a vital ritual skill. It's also an excellent embodiment practice and a resource that you can return to whenever you feel a need for slowing, feeling, and receiving. You ground so you can notice and feel yourself more deeply.

In the "Resources" section of the book, you'll find a web address for an online grounding meditation you can do.

# Grounding, Earth, and Ancestors

Grounding is also a foundational practice for connecting with your ancestors. Grounding helps you feel associated with yourself and quiet enough to hear their whispers and subtle communications.

Meditation teacher Julia Rymut defines grounding this way: "Grounding is a metaphoric term for calming your mind and becoming aware of the present moment. It can be divided into two broad categories—connecting yourself to the Earth and connecting yourself with your body."

You probably have grounding practices. You probably have a good sense of what grounding is. Being grounded is the opposite of moving too quickly, feeling scattered, or writhing with anxiety. It is a quiet, deep feeling of presence at this moment, of connection and belonging. The mind is calmer when you are grounded, and your embodiment stronger. Being grounded is the felt sense of being part of the Earth.

In the words of someone I interviewed:

*My feet get me very grounded, and when we finish, even though it's snowing out, I'm going to go outside in the backyard and get my feet . . . squish around and get really connected to the Earth. Or go for a walk or something, but I need to be connected to the Earth right now. I'm feeling a need to get grounded.*

You can practice grounding from the inside out or from the outside in. Spending time putting your body on the actual Earth, the natural ground, is helpful. Be outside, away from screens, without agenda. You can ground in your garden, a park, the forest. You can ground by stepping outside and feeling the wind and the rain. You can ground in the bath, in the ocean, with a tree, or sitting in the sun.

# Connection to Land

A connection with the land is an essential piece of grounding and ancestral connection. It is both possible and necessary to develop a feeling of relationship between your sexuality and Earth, land, or the universe.

As a person choosing to be on a healing path, you get to feel connected to the cosmic roots of existence.

The roots of generations extend back to the beginnings of Earth and beyond, to the explosion of those first stars. Spilling out of the vastness of space to the womb of creation and connecting with the mother of all things.

Connecting with the creatures of the land can be a vital piece of practice. Sometimes embodiment comes from recognizing the embodiment of other species. If you connect deeply with animals, witnessing their embodiment can benefit you. Anytime we're connecting with our bodies, we're connecting with the Earth since we are made of Earth.

One person I spoke with said:

*I feel connection with nonhuman ancestors and their presence in my life regularly and easily. Animals, plants, fungus, etc. Through observing, being with, studying, and imagining the embodiment of other living beings, I feel my own body more deeply. Some of my childhood experience includes trusting animals more than humans, so certainly there is a connection.*

The land can give us a sense of belonging and connection, especially for folks who live on colonized lands. An explicit comparison can be made between decolonizing and healing your sexuality, and the necessary healing of occupied lands.

Another person I spoke with said:

*I was raised on the land of the Lakota and the Cheyenne. Images from the land, images of certain periods in history, will just evoke thoughts of my ancestors. I knew I needed to heal some larger story than just me and my immediate family, that there was a bigger story here and it included colonization, it included land, it included slavery. There are many ways to work with ancestors. There's the land. I go outside, get to know where I am. I need to find that sense of being connected, belonging. It is important I can get that from the Earth.*

Remember that you are Earth; you are made of Earth. Our bodies are not some other thing that dwells on the surface of the Earth. We actually are the Earth. When we are disconnected from our bodies, we are disconnected from the Earth. The Earth is made of the bodies of your ancestors. Everything you eat and drink has been the bodies of those who came before you.

## Ancestors

In terms of ancestors, think about the concepts of forgetting and remembering. Many of us (especially those descended from European settler colonizers) have forgotten how to connect. We have forgotten that we once lived in connection. In our present society, our capacity for being alive while simultaneously being profoundly disconnected extends from our bodies and our hearts and our sex to each other.

The disconnect extends to older ways of knowing that worked well for human survival for millions of years. We are also disconnected from remembering how to relate well with the other-than-human world: the trees, the rivers, the stars, the four-leggeds and more-leggeds. The watery ones and the winged ones and the crawling, squirmy ones. The green bloods and the gray bloods. All the other kinds of people who are not human. These are also our ancestors.

Forgetting our ancestors and the ways we once knew to relate across the veil cuts us off from the wisdom and blessings they have for us. Without knowing our ancestors, we can believe our painful narrative of disbelonging. Without knowing our loving ancestors, we lose our benevolent guides to the unseen realms.

Our ancestors are intermediaries with the gods. We are merely the ones who are alive right now, Earth shaped into flesh. The animating spark of life belongs to a lineage of sparkling heart stars that repeatedly pass from parent to child.

*Walking, I can almost hear the redwoods beating. And the oceans are above me here, rolling clouds, heavy and dark. It is winter and there is smoke from the fires. It is a world of elemental attention, of all things working together, listening to what speaks in the blood. Whichever road I follow, I walk in the land of many gods, and they love and eat one another. Suddenly all my ancestors are behind me. Be still, they say. Watch and listen. You are the result of the love of thousands.*

—Linda Hogan, *Dwellings: A Spiritual History of the Living World*

## Choosing to Heal with Ancestors

You get to decide if you want to include ancestors in your healing process. You don't have to if you don't want to.

Do you feel a sense of obligation to heal ancestral lineages of sexual trauma or ancestral burdens? Now that you are aware that transgenerational trauma is present, do you feel a duty to address it rather than passing it on?

Consent and choice are necessary when working ancestrally to heal sexual wounding. This is especially true if there have been violations of consent within the bloodlines. Valuing your own consent is a corrective. One participant with instances of interpersonal violence and sexual trauma in her ancestry said:

*I would be really careful about "You should work on this in your current life because you also gotta heal your ancestors." That seems like an unfair burden. That should be a choice.*

The choice to heal with ancestors really needs to be yours. You will have access to more of yourself and your sexuality when you consciously choose this work, rather than allowing it to choose you. You can make a space for your ancestors to be present in your life. You can choose to be open, giving you more access to all parts of yourself.

One interviewee said:

*I feel like my opening a space for my ancestors to be present in my current life, and to be open . . . this is what gives me more access to all of myself. The spiritual part of me cannot be whole if I'm not allowing space for my ancestors and healing my connections with my ancestors. If my spiritual self is not whole, I don't feel like I will have complete access to Eros.*

Whether or not you choose to have children, this choice of healing with ancestors (or not) exists for you. If you have children, you may feel the pressure to make sure you are the interruption of the harm and the beginning of the healing of the lineage. You may be determined to not pass along to your present or future children any of the harmful sexual legacy you inherited. If you do not have children, through choice or circumstance, you may feel the pressure of being at the end of the bloodline and wanting to leave things in a good and tidy state.

Suppose you have perpetrators of sexual violence in your lineage. In that case, you also have a choice regarding interrupting and not repeating patterns of sexual violence that are handed down.

One elder I interviewed said:

*Everything is a choice. Even though that blood is in you, too, that doesn't have to be your choice. You have consciousness, so that doesn't have to be your choice. It won't be your choice, and things will be different because of you and your family. Because there's a consciousness that is alive now that wasn't alive back then. That's what you need to always remember: your consciousness, your choices will make it different to whatever has come down the family line.*

To be clear, you will have this choice throughout your entire life. You can always choose to work with ancestors, or not. You may make either choice at different times of your life. Whether or not one decides to do the healing work with ancestors, the work is present. One person shared:

*That's the thing about doing ancestral work. You can try to skip it, but you're living with those stories in your body. They're in us. Either work with them or not, but they're there anyway.*

Working with ancestors to develop sexual wellness and heal sexual wounding and trauma is a specific choice. Creating an intention to work with ancestors to develop sexual wellness can help focus attention on particular practices. Having an intention means you know where you intend to go in your healing. Clear purpose produces more effective results and establishes a condition by which to assess outcomes. Why are you doing this? How will you know when you've done it? What is this great healing project you're embarking on?

Lastly, no matter your beliefs on ancestors, what is essential is that you get your desired results. There are many ways to work with the concept of ancestors. You don't have to buy into any particular dogma or worldview.

One person who works worldwide with transgenerational trauma on the cultural scale told me:

*So, you know, you go back in time, you reclaim parts of yourself. Imaginally, you can go back in the past and confront the perpetrators. I don't think of it in literal terms. I think that we've absorbed it. It's inside of us. These people are inside of us. And even if we don't know details, we have a felt sense. I see a lot of psychodramas as going back to rescue yourself. And sometimes it's important to engage with an ancestor. But really, that ancestor is not real; I don't think that we channel them. I think that they live within us. I don't think that we're actually engaging with a literal ancestor. But as a way of understanding and reprogramming ourselves, I think it's a useful idea. You take this ancestor from within you, and you externalize them, and then you reinternalize them in a different way. All of the energy fields that people tap into doing ancestral work can seem and feel very real. And really, it doesn't matter whether they're real or not. If it's healing for the person, then it's important.*

## Last Thoughts for Month 2

Part of healing is choosing wellness, and you get to determine what that means for you. Grounding practice is foundational; you will return to your connection with the Earth repeatedly. You can choose to heal with your ancestors if that feels right to you.

**In conclusion, this Month you will:**

- Ask your intuition about an offering your ancestors would appreciate. Leave it outside, and clearly say out loud that this is an offering for your well, bright ancestors.

- Build embodied safety by checking in with your body regularly and listening to what it suggests.

- Add something to your healing altar that represents grounding.

- Listen to a guided grounding meditation.

- Daily practice of grounding: At least once each day, feel yourself as a creature made of Earth. Slow down and feel the connection between your body and your Earthly home. Feel the action of gravity working on your body. Allow your skeleton to hold 5 percent more of the weight of your meat.

- Complete Ritual 2: Grounding.

NOTE *There are no worksheets in the appendix for Month 2.*

# Ritual 2: Grounding

## Preparation

- ¤ The purpose of this ritual is to ground and create a cocoon of prayer.

- ¤ You can do this at your healing altar or in another place where you will not be disturbed.

- ¤ You will need a dish of Earth or a stone from the place where you live.

- ¤ You will also need a notebook or voice recorder.

**Begin by setting a container of prayer as you read this aloud:**

*Ancient Earth, body of my body,*
*I pray for your wellness. I pray for your healing.*
*I pray for my wellness and my own healing.*
*I recognize that I am of you*
*that life flows through me*
*that I am a container made of Earth that life inhabits.*
*May I remember my connection.*
*May I feel my ground.*

**Next, cast a circle of protection with the help of your allies.**

Call out to the trusted spiritual sources of protection you already have. This may be deities, guardians, the elements, or relationships with animals, stones, holy places, herbs, or anything from the green world. Invite each to come toward you, and pause until you sense that they are present.

Then, with their support, imagine a layer of protection that goes all around you. You can visualize it if you like, or feel it.

Check in: Do you feel protected all the way around? Can you feel yourself?

## Ritual

Hold the dish that contains the Earth, or the stone, and quiet yourself. Just feel what there is to feel. Widen your perspective to a global one, and realize that this is the same Earth that your ancestors walked on, grew their food in, were made of.

Imagine you can feel the connection between the atoms of you and the atoms in what you hold. Then widen that field of connection. Imagine you can feel connected with the Earth beneath you, all around you. Everything your body is touching is made of Earth.

Try feeling part of, instead of separate from. Try having no distinction between you and Earth. Open to connection, however you can.

What do you know when you feel part of?

Make notes of the information you receive.

When you are ready, drop into connection with your ancestral guide.

Once you have reestablished connection, ask them if there is anything they would like you to know right now.

Have the offerings been received? Are there any other offerings that could be helpful?

In this ritual, your guide will create a cocoon of prayer around all the generations of dead in the lineage who are between your guide and your oldest living generation on that line.

A cocoon of prayer is a ritual containment field that your guide will create. The intention of the cocoon is to contain all of the generations of dead who may not yet be well. Your guide can place them into the container, and while they are in there they can heal enough to transition to the realm of the elevated ancestors.

This will help protect you from any harmful energies, and it will also give the dead a holding environment where they can gently heal.

To begin, ask your guide to create a cocoon of prayer starting with the generation just below them and containing all of the generations that fall between them and the oldest living descendant on the line. Living generations are not included in the cocoon of prayer.

Typically, this isn't a long process, but give it the time it takes until your guide indicates it is complete.

Close this ritual with a prayer for your own good life, and thank your guide and the allies who showed up.

Dissolve the circle while keeping the protection intact.

# Month 3
## *I Belong*

To my body, I belong.
To myself, I belong.
With you, I belong.
To my feet on this Earth, I belong.
To this Earth, I belong.

When I feel my own heart beat, I belong.
When I'm snuggled in your arms, I belong.
When I'm breathing my breath, I belong.
When I'm singing to my ancestors, I belong.

I belong on the Appalachian mountains.
I belong in the Pacific tides.
I belong at smoky backyard bonfires.
I belong beneath cold and silent winter stars.
I belong below the twisting moon, bright above.

When I love, I belong.
Letting myself be loved, I belong.
When I share my love, I belong.
Receiving tender love, I belong.

To the wind across the heath and through the pines, I belong.
To the redwoods, silent in crumbly sunlight, I belong.
To the ravens, cawing delight and trumpeting trouble, I belong.
To spring's emergent bloodroot and steady trillium, I belong.
To the bees, their warm honey in the hive, I belong.

When I pray to what I cannot see, I belong.
When I dance barefoot, I belong.
When I cook delicious food for my lover, I belong.
When I play in my garden, I belong.

I belong to my blood.
I belong to my ancestors.
I belong to my descendants.
I belong to this world.
And when this life is over, to the Earth my body belongs.

# Moon of Belonging Practice

At a quiet moment each day, call to mind a safe person, place, or other-than-human being, like a tree, river, or pet.

Imagine you feel the kinship as a physical sensation. The felt sense of invisible bonds of love and care, connecting you.

Lean in to the felt sense of your love for them. Imagine it pouring up from the Earth, through you, and out toward them.

Imagine them receiving your love, what it feels like landing.

Now explore the felt sense of reciprocity: safely receiving love. Your heart may warm. Know that this love is eternal. It will never end, even as the relationship shifts through time.

You are *loving*, you are *loved*.

# MONTH 3

# Belonging Moon

Take a moment to reflect on the work of the past two Months, particularly the positive resources you've been developing: boundaries, protection, discernment, and grounding. What can you notice about the differences you experience as you've been practicing these skills?

The purpose of the first part of this book is to help you develop supportive, positive resources and practices. Taking three months to build these skills may seem excessive. You may find yourself impatient to "get to it" already. I ask you to trust this process. It is tested by real humans. For most, learning to go slow and allow healing to be supported by spaciousness is a new (and deeply anticapitalist) skill.

This Month, we're heading more deeply into positive resources by talking about belonging, singing, and spiritual hygiene. You will also learn about many ancestral reverence practices.

## Attachment and Belonging

The perceivable connection between the Earth that our bodies are made out of and the greater Earth we are creatures of feels broken for many. That means our feeling of belonging to the Earth is muted. This primary attachment is hard to experience and really know.

Like you, your ancestors had bodies, and those have now returned to the Earth. Because your relationship with Earth is fragmented, your relationships with your ancestors are likely remote and distant.

In North America, so many feel like spiritual orphans without a land base. Most of us live on stolen lands without intact lifeways, without families of nurturance. We are the recipients of intergenerational trauma, with legacies of enslavement and genocide. Is it any wonder that many of us do not experience embodied belonging?

One way to think of this lack of belonging is as an attachment wound. The loss of embodied belonging permeates all of our relationships and societal structures. If we don't feel that we belong, it is difficult to feel connected. This is a tragedy. As mammals, we must form bonds to receive nurturance. Because we are pack animals, we need connection to thrive. We do much better when the connection sources are kind, supportive, and constant.

Secure attachment bonds are necessary. Psychologists John Bowlby and Mary Ainsworth were the first researchers to flesh out our understanding of attachment by developing attachment theory, which focuses on relationships and bonds between people, such as parents and children, romantic partners, and friends. Bowlby described attachment as a "lasting psychological connectedness between human beings."

Bowlby and Ainsworth believed that the earliest bonds children form have a vast impact upon them throughout the rest of the life course. Their work posits that humans are born helpless, so as a matter of survival, the first job of every infant is to develop attachment bonds with a caregiver who will keep them alive. Developmentally, finding belonging is the prime objective of our first days, months, and years.

Our earliest needs are body-based: food, warmth, soothing, safety, and contact. If things go well, caregivers desire to touch, rock, and snuggle their baby and tend to its needs. In response, the baby smiles, snuggles, and coos. If caregivers neglect or abuse a baby in their care, the natural instinct to seek connection for care and protection gets damaged. We start to feel others are not trustworthy or are frightening.

Out of these early experiences and attachments in childhood, we form persistent strategies and ways of being in relationships. Attachment researchers have defined three attachment styles:

- **Secure:** attunement and responsiveness provide the foundations for secure attachment.

- **Avoidant:** overly self-reliant.

- **Anxious:** overly other-focused.

There are also some combination styles, like anxious-avoidant, also known as disorganized.

Secure attachment takes hold when attunement is present between the child and the caregiver. People who grow up to have a secure attachment style can tolerate some distance in a relationship without taking it personally. They trust that the bond in a relationship will hold. In early childhood they had a caregiver who was responsive to their needs, and this experience built a foundation for a secure bond. People who are securely attached trust that their needs will be met most of the time.

Folks who are avoidantly attached have a hard time relying on others. Trust is often challenging. In their earliest relationships, needs were not consistently met, and there was a lack of caregiver responsiveness and attunement to their needs. These humans have learned to avoid contact and take care of themselves. They grow up to be people who are very independent and really can take care of their own needs. Sometimes they are hyperindividualists. They don't want to need anyone else and probably have a hard time receiving care and goodness from others.

People whose attachment style is anxious are overly focused on others. They worry about the relationship and fear abandonment. They ask questions like, "Are we okay?" and "Are you mad at me?" or "Are we still good?" The negative association with this attachment style is clinginess. They don't feel secure that the bond is stable and present.

You may find aspects of yourself in each of the attachment styles. Still, if you look at your relationship history, you will see patterns to help you identify your prevalent type.

Who you are in a relationship with also determines how secure you feel. If, for example, you are anxiously attached to a securely attached partner, over time, your attachment wounds can start to heal. Conversely, if you were in a relationship with someone who was avoidantly attached, you would likely be triggered often in the relationship.

Whereas children use familial relationships to establish a secure base, adults use romantic and platonic relationships. There are two essential factors in secure adult bonds: safe haven and room to grow.

A relationship that is a safe haven means that the relationship is just that: safe. It feels like a refuge where the person has your back. You trust that you're not alone in the world. They respect your boundaries and uplift your glittering destiny. Safe haven doesn't mean you never have conflict, but that when you do, you both show up to be accountable and make the repair.

Room to grow means that because you're safe and secure within the relationship, you can learn, grow, and fully expand into your potential. The other person is your cheerleader and wants you to have the best possible life.

In a secure adult attachment, you have a place to be when the shit hits the fan, and you know somebody has your back. It's a safe place to launch into the world and activate your potential. Secure adult attachment is also about interdependence. It's safe to rely on your partner to help meet some of your basic needs, and it's safe for your partner to rely on you, too.

A lot of folks fear being needy. However, people perform better when they have a secure base. When you feel safe and secure, you can take appropriate risks. There is a good and appropriate way to need your romantic partner or whoever you decide to do life with. I use the term "partner" loosely: it could be a romantic partner, a platonic life partner, or your best friend. We can form attachment bonds with people, places, animals, and energies.

## Strengthening Bonds of Attachment

Developing secure attachment in any relationship is possible, but overcoming early programming takes a conscious effort. To make this possible, reparative experiences need to happen. No matter what kind of attachment you experienced as a child, it is possible to heal and become someone who has a soft and trusting heart.

This becomes possible when you trust that your needs matter, both to you and to whomever you are close with. No one is 100 percent available, but secure attachment starts to be possible when you know your needs are considered and met consistently. The same holds true for the other person: they can securely attach to you if you consider and meet their needs with a degree of regularity.

We all come factory-equipped with the capacity to securely attach, but most of us must learn how to do it. We practice. If we are mistrustful because humans are freaky, we can practice with other-than-humans first: pets, places, trees, and rivers. Eventually, we can work up to practice being securely attached to people.

You can begin to trust your choices of friends and lovers, to trust that they love you and care for you, even if they are not always available. You trust that they attune with you and respond to you. You begin to trust your own capacity to do the same for them.

Years ago, I was on a dance floor, dancing to the music and thinking of all the people I loved in my life. I didn't have a romantic partner at the time. I was just really feeling the love for a given person, and then feeling the love for another given person. I felt so blessed that I loved all these beautiful humans. Huge epiphanies can happen when you're moving your body and breathing, and at that dance, I had one. I realized that all of those amazing people I loved and thought were so cool and amazing—well, they loved me too! And if they loved me, then I must have been okay. I must have been lovable!

Trust is built with practice over time. Conflict, rupture, and repair are necessary cycles for building trust. When working on attachment and trust, remember that intensity is not intimacy. You form secure attachment through discerning who truly has your back and whose back you truly have.

If you are partnered and not yet securely attached to your mate, this is a discussion the two of you can have. Do you both want to be securely attached? Are you both committed to working through previous relational trauma so you can be a person who gets to have a soft and trusting heart? If so, you can start to practice secure attachment with your partner.

You can practice secure attachment in various ways. One way is recognizing when you feel securely attached. Another is to pick the person (or animal, or place, or whatever you choose) to whom you're securely attaching and repeat this new narrative to yourself: "I have chosen a safe attachment partner." The second part of that practice is noticing that you are a safe partner—that you care and that someone else's needs matter to you, all the time. The currency of healthy, functional relationships is attention and attunement. You build secure attachment through attending to and through being attended to.

## What Is Belonging?

Belonging is an entirely subjective experience of feeling connected with others and feeling satisfied with those connections. Belonging doesn't necessarily mean being part of a group;

instead, it means finding meaning from connecting with others. Belonging can also relate to a place, a time, and the other-than-human world.

Most of us experience a compelling need to belong. We also are conditioned to provide belonging to others. This shapes our identity as a species.

Our need to belong can be traced back to our prehistoric ancestors, when group survival depended on cooperation. If a human didn't cooperate with others, they wouldn't last very long. Rejection by the group was a death sentence. The need to belong was that crucial. Hence, the fear of rejection is coded into our bodies and governs our actions. An absence of belonging has devastating effects on people, both physically and psychologically.

Belonging and our processes and experiences of it are woven throughout the trajectory of our life span. People who struggle with a poor sense of belonging have likely struggled with it for most of their lives. As kids in middle school struggle to adhere to imposed social norms, the attachment wounds of earlier years get reinflicted by peers, which can often build persistent and challenging narratives.

You can develop an identity around any wound. For example, suppose you create an identity around not belonging, being cast out, or being rejected. In that case, your identity limits your capacity to experience trusting, loving connections. You might grow up believing "I don't belong." From there, your brain mainly pays attention to information that confirms this core belief, regardless of whether you actually belong. You have developed a filter through which you experience the world.

Filters are tricky. It's so hard to notice them because all incoming information comes through the filter and gets warped by it. It's like looking at the world through the lenses in a set of goggles. A disbelonging or rejection filter is the lens through which you experience the world. But you can begin to notice the rejection filter.

For example, I have a friend I love very much who lives in Canada. In my head, he is more fabulous than I am. He is friends with another very good friend of mine who, in my head, is also cooler than me. They're both incredibly talented humans.

Once all three of us were going to a workshop. The night before the workshop began, my Canadian friend told me he would see me at the workshop, and he was going to drive there with our other friend. A story immediately started to spin in my head that he liked the other friend better. And I was sad about it; I felt really left out.

When I told my partner what I was feeling, he said, "Well, maybe he does like them better than you." This was a revelation. Possibly, my Canadian friend did like our other friend better. After all, there are some people I like better than others. That doesn't mean I am rejecting the people I like less; it just means I have preferences. My Canadian friend was not rejecting me. I was experiencing the world through my rejection filter.

To be fair, attachment wounds and disbelonging wounds come about as reactions to various stimuli. They didn't happen in a vacuum. You were affected by your caregivers. Perhaps you lacked a caregiver who was safe enough for you to securely attach to. Perhaps your caregivers were unable to securely connect themselves to you. When attachment wounds from the past get activated in present relationships, we tend to take it personally and think it's our fault.

Struggling to feel a sense of belonging and working to securely attach are distinct but related experiences. The remedy for both is practice. If you are not already a human with secure attachments, you can become one. You can become a human who belongs, who feels a sense of satisfaction in the quality of your relationships. This means you can trust others, let them close to your heart, share yourself vulnerably, and receive their love and care. It means you trust that they are not out to get you and are on your team, even when it doesn't feel like that. This is healing we can only do in a relationship, because attachment wounds come out of a relationship or lack thereof.

So ask yourself: Is an attachment or belonging wound at the core of what you are healing in this life?

Do you feel like you're an outsider, you don't belong, people reject you, or you're unworthy of love? This is what Buddhist teacher Tara Brach calls "the trance of unworthiness." If so, you can dance around it, go to therapy, and talk a lot about your issues—or you can go right to the core of it and practice belonging.

Ask: What makes me perceive things this way? What makes me act this way? How can I heal this core, central wound? Rather than putting Band-Aids in all these other places, how can I just go for it? How can I practice belonging?

## Healing Energies, Trauma Vortex

If you have issues around belonging, rejection, or abandonment, consider the role of relational trauma, aka attachment wounding.

In trauma healing, a crucial step is to tell the truth about what happened to you. However, telling that trauma story repeatedly is not the place to stay forever. We all know people who are really stuck in their trauma narratives, and they repeat them over and over, and nothing ever seems to shift for them. The trauma gurus on Instagram have huge followings because people need to heal. There is another, more insidious factor at work, though: trauma can be quite compelling to think about and talk about. It's highly marketable. Profitable. This should make you mad. It makes me furious.

In addition, trauma has a residue. As I said earlier, we can create an identity around any wounds. Those trauma wounds can be sticky. Trauma tells you that it's the one true thing, the most important story: "You're damaged goods." "There's something wrong with you." Ideally, however, you want to be informed by your trauma, not defined by it.

You want the ongoing harm to stop, whether it's interpersonal in nature or systemic and institutional, like sexism, racism, and transphobia. Once harm has stopped, then healing can begin. This does not mean you have to wait until oppression ends before you can heal; but in the face of ongoing hurt, wounds cannot fully heal. You can heal what is yours to heal, and society must do its healing as well. It's a choice. Healing trauma is a choice.

One of the necessary skills for healing is learning how to place your attention. Trauma narratives command our attention. They say, "Pay attention here, and *only* here." Freedom is being able to choose where and what you attend to.

For now, it's enough to consider that healing is about choice. Trauma narratives can be a vortex of thought and sensation that suck you in. There is an equally strong vortex of healing energies that you can turn toward. This is a choice everyone gets, all the time.

Questions to ask yourself:

¤   Where shall I turn?

¤   Which direction shall I move in?

¤   Where will I place my attention?

This is what we've been doing in the first chapters of this book. You have been building your healing vortex—constructing new narratives, practices, and tools—so that you have a choice and can choose healing if you want. This is not a bypass. I am definitely *not* saying, "Oh, just don't think about that silly old trauma."

Instead, consider how you feel and how you wish to feel. This is your *life*. It matters that you curate how you want to feel and be. You don't have control over what has happened to you. However, you have all the choice in the world about what happens next.

How do I wish to feel during my life? Speaking for myself, Pavini, I want to feel the total capacity of what it is to be human. I want to spend most of my time devoted to things that feel good. I want to feel regulated, connected, and joyful.

Not that that's all I want to feel. I don't want to suppress any emotion. Grief can feel deeply joyful. Sadness, anger, rage—all of those emotions can feel good. What I want, for you and for me, is the flexibility to move between them, to let them flow through.

So how do you wish to feel? Which feeling states that you wish to cultivate? Trauma is not a life sentence, and you do have agency.

Trauma is about the loss of connection—to ourselves, our bodies, our families, others, and the world around us. This profound disconnection is often hard to recognize because it happens slowly over time and becomes "normal."

Suppose belonging is a sense of connection and feeling satisfied with the quality of those connections. In that case, trauma is about disbelonging, or feeling disconnected.

## Practices of Belonging and Disbelonging

Belonging is a choice and a set of practices. Disbelonging is also a set of practices. When you are ready to belong, you choose to belong to a body. When choosing to belong to a body, you're choosing to belong to humanity.

One significant way to belong is to belong to your own body by choosing to be "all in," spirit in flesh. This initial choice opens a path to embodiment, and other practices become possible. Don't worry if you don't know how yet. Knowing how to feel more in your body will come with time and practice.

We sometimes think that we'll feel a certain way once we are healed, and we may not realize that we can practice feeling that way now, which will *help* our healing. For example, perhaps you want to feel like you belong and are at home in your skin. Would it surprise you to know that you can practice feeling like that instead of waiting for it to magickally happen? This is your agency in action.

When you practice belonging, you stop practicing disbelonging. Yes, you are practicing both. And you can become aware of how you practice belonging and how you practice disbelonging.

For your homework this Month, take an inventory of your disbelonging practices:

- ¤ What are all the ways in which you don't belong?
- ¤ What are all the things that you believe make you weird and an outsider?
- ¤ What are your practices of disbelonging? (What are you saying to yourself inside your head? How do you treat yourself internally?)

In addition, take a look at your practices of belonging:

- ¤ Where do you allow yourself to belong?
- ¤ Where do you feel satisfied with the emotional quality of your connections?
- ¤ Where do you trust that others are not the enemy and are indeed allies, even if they sometimes disappoint you?

Indeed, when we speak of belonging, the questions we're asking are:

- ¤ Where do you want to put your love?
- ¤ To whom or what do you want to belong?

You get to allow yourself to belong, especially if you have an outsider identity that precludes belonging. For example, sometimes I'll say, "I'm just not a joiner." I have an identity around these wounds that precludes my belonging. When I say I'm not a joiner, I'm practicing disbelonging, not belonging.

You will not belong to everyone, every place, every group. You must discern which groups to belong to. I don't want to belong to a fraternity of football players. You might. I don't belong with conservative right-wing separatists, and those could be your people. You get to choose who you want to belong with.

When you choose to belong, you are countering the narrative of disbelonging. No matter how long you have told yourself the story of disbelonging, it is fake news. Look: you are made of Earth. You don't live *on* the Earth; you *are* the Earth, living. You belong because you are the Earth. This may be a paradigm shift for you. Feeling connected with the land is a belonging practice. Feel yourself *of* the Earth and not *on* the Earth.

Another practice of belonging is the practice of belonging to your ancestors, especially if your family of origin was complex. You belong to a lineage of well, bright, and beloved elevated ancestors. Your awesomeness came from somewhere; you didn't spring up out of nowhere, right? You might sense a deep belonging with your family of origin; many people do, but many do not. If you're in the latter group and you feel like an outcast in your family of origin, you can connect with your ancestors as a deliberate practice of belonging.

Another practice of belonging is to actually feel belonging when you have it. If you're in a situation where you feel that satisfaction with the quality of your connection, or when you're feeling a part of rather than other, practice noticing and saying, "I belong here."

This Month, you are invited to make a timeline of your attachment and belonging history. This will help you connect some dots and string some of the stars together. It's vital to stop thinking that you have some internal flaw that makes you unlovable, and to get out of the part of you that thinks struggling to belong is somehow a personal failing. Everybody has wounds. What we're here to do is work with them. There's nothing wrong with you just because you're working on healing. You're not broken in a bad way.

## Ancestral Reverence Practices

There are many different types of ancestral reverence practices. Ultimately, you will practice what works best for you and your ancestors. You will find your way to what delights your lineages, and it will be different for each lineage.

What follows is a noncomprehensive list of ancestral reverence practices that emerged from my research. Many are cross-cultural practices. You can try any one you like and see how they work for you. Do note that if you are aware of practices specific to your lineages, those will likely be quite fruitful for you, since they were things your ancestors did.

### A Note on Cultural Appropriation

I live in the mountains of what is currently known as North Carolina, which is land stolen from the Tsalagi (Cherokee) people. I once attended a community singing event in my area, and while many of the songs were heartwarming and beautiful, there was a moment when a white-appearing song leader introduced a song she said was a Cherokee morning song. She gave no context for how she learned the song, if it had been given to her by someone of Cherokee heritage, or any other context except that she loved the song.

The group, which was mostly composed of white-appearing people, sang the song. I did not. At the end of the song, someone in the audience asked, "Can you share more context about that song?" The song leader repeated what she had said earlier, adding that she had read about the song in a book. Another song leader (a person with power in the room) jumped in and added that her understanding of the song was that it was a Cherokee song sung to greet the rising sun. At this point I left the event.

In my heart, a group of white people singing a Cherokee song without any framing or acknowledgment of the genocide committed against the Cherokee people on their ancestral land is unconscionable. I was, and am, heartbroken at the utter disregard for the crimes of the past and the lack of embodied compassion for the victims of those crimes. It is unbearable. I will not be willfully complicit in the erasure of history: killing off the people of a place, and then singing their songs as a celebration of them.

Ironically, in the ensuing discussions it came to light that the song wasn't even a Cherokee song.

Whatever your background, you are heir to a powerful inheritance of mystery, tradition, and spiritual technology. Stealing from other traditions is a less effective way to work because it weakens the bond between you, your offerings, and your people. To belong to your lineages, practice their traditions.

There is of course a more nuanced conversation that can be had here. Sometimes things are not clear-cut. In that case, check in with your ancestral guides and seek their help in discerning the right path to take.

## Making Offerings

Probably the most straightforward ancestral reverence practice is making offerings. When you offer, you relate with the unseen world, saying, "I believe in you."

Before discussing how to make offerings, let's talk about why you make offerings. As you are no doubt aware, living in a body allows you to access the material world and the powers it possesses. Being without a body enables one to access the spiritual world's gifts without limitations.

There are things ancestors can do that we cannot do. They have a far-seeing, clear view through time, and they understand the bigger picture. We have bodies; we can make things and do things that are nourishing for our ancestors. They have no way of getting energy, but we offer them power because we have an abundance of it. It's a reciprocal relationship.

When we talk about making offerings, that is why. It's a way of deepening relationships, and we want to hold up our end of the bargain. It's helpful for our ancestors as nourishment, and it's useful for us because it gives us a way to deepen a sense of connection. When we develop relationships with living people, we spend time together sharing meals, doing activities, and making memories. We can do the same thing with the dead, and a practice of offerings is a big part of that. Anything can be an offering if it has the right intention behind it. Making offerings to our ancestors and receiving their blessing is reciprocity.

Several people I spoke with said they made offerings as a way to nourish their ancestors, as well as to receive blessings from them. For example, one person explained:

*I have a formal weekly practice of making offerings to them, praying for the well-being of my ancestors, and asking for their blessings upon me.*

## How to Make Offerings

One way to make an offering is to name what you are doing out loud. As I light a candle, I might say, "I am lighting this candle as an offering for you, ancestors. May you enjoy this light."

If you are still learning to distinguish between well and unwell energies, make your offerings outside. Until you are completely clear, don't feed spirits inside your house. Feed them outside.

Different traditions have different protocols regarding what to do with offerings after they are made. Some traditions are clear that once you offer food items to ancestors, you should not eat it afterward. Other traditions are okay with food offerings being consumed after offering it. For example, one person stated:

*You'd bring all this food and you'd offer it and we actually eat the food afterwards because Chinese people are very practical and pragmatic, and maybe had starved. So, you offer them food, and then you eat it.*

When I make a food offering, personally I don't eat it once it's been offered to my ancestors. I don't have a cultural tradition that gives me rules for that, so I go with what feels right to me. If you offer food to your ancestors and they take their spirit bite, you're not going to leave it there too much longer before you remove it. It's my practice to leave it there until it feels complete. You can do what feels right with your offerings: compost them, bury them, burn them, put them in the garbage; it's okay because it all goes back to the same place. You don't have to be too precious about it.

People offer many different types of items. Offerings can be tangible or intangible. Many different types of offerings are listed here, so you can get a sense of the breadth of the practice. You do not need to take any or all of these practices on. With time, it will become clear what your ancestors like to receive and how they like to receive your offerings.

## Tangible Offerings

Tangible offerings include cups of water, candles, incense, pouring of libations on the Earth, flowers, creations of art and beauty, and special ritual objects like jewelry, goblets, cloth, tobacco, feather fans, and food. It is worth noting that food offerings play a unique role in the practice of making offerings.

*Interviewee: When we eat—especially at Shabbat or when we have community supper, but sometimes when it's just us in the house—we make a plate before we start eating it. It has a little bit of everything that's on the table, and we put it on the ancestor altar and ring the bell.*

*Pavini: What's the intention of that?*

*I: To feed them.*

*P: There's a belief that providing offerings feeds them.*

*I: Nourishes them, and then they help us.*

Several interviewees mentioned that preparing foods their ancestors liked is an integral part of the food-offering practice. For example, one participant discussed cooking for her ancestors:

*Yes, I make food offerings to them. I'll cook stuff just for them; I'll cook them stuff I don't eat and give it to them because they ate it. Luckily they don't ask me for pork often, they don't do that, I'm so happy; but if they tell me that's what they wanted, then I'll go buy some, cook it, and put it up here for them, because they asked for it.*

When you start developing relationships with your ancestors, you practice and see what result you get, and check in with your guides. Ask them if the way you did it was the right way or if they need something different. The muscle of deep listening gets built by trying things and checking in to see how they were received.

## Intangible Offerings

People often make all kinds of intangible offerings to ancestors. I am not suggesting that you do all of these practices; rather, I want you to know about various ways people make offerings to their ancestors. You will find which ones work for you and your people. Some of the following practices are often used as offerings, while others are practices of connection.

### Dance and Movement Practice

Dance and movement are practices people use to connect with ancestors. One person I spoke with makes an offering of her dance:

*I get to dance, and I'm dancing for them, not just for me.*

Other research subjects discussed the value of movement as part of the connection with ancestors, speaking gratitude for the "dancestors." If you want to offer a dance, perhaps find a piece of music that your people would find familiar, or learn a specific cultural dance from your heritage.

## Drumming as a Practice of Connection

Drumming is a musical practice of rhythmic sounding that occurs in cultures worldwide. Drumming can induce trance states. As one person said:

> *I try to look for connections to go back as far as I need to go to try to find a connection with a spirit that is not broken. I can do that when I drum.*

If you are interested in drumming as an offering, you could research the instruments and rhythms of the cultures of your lineage. Rhythm is a powerful way to entrain with the ancestors.

## Breath Practice

Making an offering of your breathwork practice consists of paying attention to the breath and then opening to connect with ancestors. One person I spoke with said that she breathes in front of her ancestor altar, and then she stills herself and listens for what her ancestors say. If you're interested in breathwork as a practice of offering, try out various techniques and see what happens. Which patterns help you feel more connected with your ancestors?

## Meditation Practice

Many people meditate to connect with their ancestors. People I spoke with said meditation caused a shift in consciousness, with results including trance journeys, nonordinary states of consciousness, deep listening, and ecstatic states. These different states of consciousness enable you to connect with ancestors and ancestral wisdom.

For example, here are some remarks from three different people I spoke with:

> *When I get into meditative space, I often imagine or feel a web of connection between myself and all beings, past, present, and future. I'm kind of in this cosmic web of how do I fit in and where do I connect, and how do I interact.*

> *When I meditate, they may come to me.*

> *There are ways of connecting with the ancestors . . . through dreams and through meditation, through journeying.*

# Prayer Practice

Prayer is a common ancestral connection practice. While prayer has a bad rap because fundamentalist religions have colonized the practice, prayer is your birthright, no matter your religious convictions. You do not need to participate in a formal religion to pray.

When you pray, you speak to the forces and powers of love and goodness in your life. Deity, your ancestors, the trees—whatever is holy to you. Consider prayer as a normal conversation that you have with your ancestors. You share what's important to you, and you hear from them.

Many people find it helpful to pray out loud, but you don't have to. When we start talking aloud to dead people, we break cultural conventions. It's validating to speak out loud for you to hear it, and it's validating to broadcast the vibrations moving through your body so the ancestors can receive them. You don't need to have any specific words, although if you do speak the language of your ancestors, praying in that language is powerful. Also, if you learn particular prayers from your ancestry, that is a wonderful way to connect.

In another interview, the person I spoke with made a case for praying aloud:

*Pavini: Do you mean you pray out loud? Or do you mean talk in your head, or both?*

*Interviewee: We can just talk to them if we can.... Yes, talk out loud. There's probably circumstances where we can reach out with our hearts and our minds. I think talking out loud is good.*

When you pray, you are engaging with the unseen realms. You are practicing believing in their realness and in their capacity to impact your life in positive ways. You are practicing belonging. Prayer can be speaking, writing, singing, chanting, or silent. Part of prayer is listening and receiving. Prayer is grounded in the principle of sacred reciprocity.

If you are interested in deepening your prayer practice, find a time when you have some privacy, and just start speaking aloud. Name who you are speaking to. Even if you feel awkward or nervous at first, you will find that it gets easier with time and practice. Some people pray only at their altar. Others pray whenever they need to. Trust your own intuition.

Many people I spoke with shared that they:

¤ Pray out loud.

¤ Pray for the wellness of the ancestors.

¤ Pray in memory of ancestors.

¤ Pray with ancestors who are well in spirit to support those not yet well in spirit.

¤ Pray to receive blessing and support from the ancestors.

You can also pray for the wellness of your ancestors. People pray by holding a person in their thoughts and sending them good wishes and love.

One person I spoke with, who had lost many beloved friends to AIDS, described his prayer practice that used prayer beads he had made:

*I have pagan prayer beads that I do every day. Prayer beads are a string of beads, and there's no specific way to organize them. The first part is about me, and the second part is about ancestors. I say a prayer about each of these people. I think about them when I do my prayer beads in the morning. In some cases, somebody gave me the bead. So, it really is about not even going through the process of picturing them or whatever; it's that this bead is a tool for them, and I pray for them. Each bead, in my psyche, is almost connected to them.*

You can also make requests of your ancestors during your prayer, like this person who said:

*I make requests by praying and by putting the notes on the board and ringing the bell.*

Cultures that practice ancestral reverence have traditional prayer protocols. For example, one person I spoke with said:

*In Chinese culture, you are supposed to be praying to your ancestors. And in fact, when you pray to your ancestors, you will be blessed with more luck and a better life.*

You can make prayer a part of your practice. If you have religious trauma, that probably needs tending first. If you are part of a spiritual tradition, you can pray in the manner you know. There is no wrong way to pray. At its heart, prayer is our plea to the universe to keep us from being alone. It is a way to acknowledge that more exists than what we see.

Without the counterpoint of prayer and gratitude, the world can seem bleak. Pray to uplift your spirit. Pray to feel supported. Offer prayer to your people, and pray for yourself as well. Center your own well-being in your prayer.

## Divination Practice

Divination is a way to access information that isn't derived from your senses or your own mind. When you divine, you seek to understand a situation or moment more deeply.

Divination can be used as a tool to communicate with ancestors. Divination techniques vary according to tradition, and they include divinatory tools like tarot cards, Norse runes, pendulums, casting the bones, dowsing, the I Ching, and scrying in water, fire, and smoke, among many other techniques. The basic premise is to find a method of relating so your ancestors can communicate important information to you.

In divination, your own discernment is active. You interpret the messages you receive from your ancestors through the lens of your own best judgment. As with prayer, if your ancestors used particular divinatory technologies, lean into them. Most cultures have methods of communication with the unseen realms, and the traditions of your own people will usually work best and are the least appropriative.

## Dreaming Practice

Dreams are often a powerful intersection with ancestors. Many people I interviewed indicated that dreaming was both a method of divination and a way to receive information from ancestors. Many participants took the information they received in their ancestral dreams to heart.

One way to practice ancestral connection through your dreams is to take a moment before you go to sleep to ask your ancestors to send you a dream. Keep a notebook by your bed so you can record any dreams that come.

## Photography Practice

Photography became available to the public in the late nineteenth century, so some people have photographs of relatives dating back generations. Looking at photographs of beloved dead can be a way to connect with those who have passed. Your discernment and ritual investigation with your ancestral guide can help you determine which relatives are a source of wellness and support.

You may wish to put pictures of your beloved dead on your ancestor altar. I do not recommend putting pictures of yourself or any living person on your ancestor altar.

You may also wish to explore having photographs of other-than-blood ancestors as a point of conneciton. One person I interviewed said:

*My bedroom altar has images of historic gay, lesbian, and trans ancestors.*

## Genealogy Practice

Tracing your ancestry through genealogy is a practice that can be complementary to ancestral reverence. Sometimes information comes to light that helps you understand what happened to your ancestors. For example, if you were tracing your ancestry and learned that your people came to the United States from the Scottish Highlands during the mid- to late eighteenth century, you could deduce that your ancestors were part of a forced exodus known as the Clearances.

Genealogy can be fun, validating, and rewarding. However, there are some issues of which you need to be aware. Genealogical records can be painful to receive. You may find out things that were hidden in your family, such as secret births or adoptions. If you choose to get a DNA test, you may find out things about your close blood family and parentage that have been unknown to you.

Because of slavery, information from popular genealogy sites can be difficult for African Americans to trace prior to the 1870 census. This is because that was the first census to include African Americans by name. If someone appears in a prior census, that means they were not enslaved at the time of the census. Records of enslaved Africans are often handwritten or poorly maintained, or they have been lost. That does not mean genealogy is not a worthwhile project, and there are resources like the Wisconsin Historical Society that can help (see the "Resources" section for more information).

Ancestors who were LGBTQ+ are also difficult to identify through genealogical records. Many of our queer ancestors were not out, and they may have lived their lives in heterosexual-appearing relationships. Many of our transcestors would be identified only by their deadname and gender identity, and their trans status wouldn't be reflected in the genealogical records.

All that said, tracing your roots through research can sometimes validate what you have divined during ritual. For example, I encountered an ancestral guide who spoke with an accent that sounded German or Dutch, I couldn't tell which. I believe she was an ancestor on a line that lived in Scotland before coming to the United States. When I would visit with her in meditation, we would often drink coffee at her kitchen table out of Delftware, a blue-and-white patterned china from Holland. As far as I was aware, I had no relatives from that part of Europe, and my ancestor presenting to me in this way was confusing. When I asked where she was from originally, she didn't answer. A bit later, I was doing genealogical research when I found an ancestor who had been born in Scotland but died in Holland. When I asked her in meditation if that person was her, she agreed. I don't know why she lived her life in Holland and died there, but the research confirmed what I had learned in ritual space.

In another example, when my first child was born, his dad and I legally changed our names to a shared last name. We chose Moray, because we liked the sound of it; no other reason. Years later, when I dug into the research, I found that my ancestors hailed from Morayshire, Scotland. Many generations back, I encountered Morays in my lineage.

## Forgiveness Practice

Some people who are curious about ancestral connection are also concerned about the harm their ancestors perpetrated. Many white people in North America hold guilt and shame about the actions of their colonizer ancestors.

When I was teaching ancestral lineage repair, we would have people come to our workshops who wanted to do the work but did not want to be associated with ancestors who had committed violence and atrocity. They often worried that they would be asked to forgive their ancestors.

Forgiveness is a process that you choose to do for yourself, not for anyone else. It is a deeply personal choice. There is no imperative to forgive. Forgiveness does not make you more holy or more elevated. I like to hold forgiveness practice as something I am doing for myself and my descendants. It's a self-love practice, not a magnanimous generosity of spirit. I forgive because what I'm holding on to is damaging me, so I'm going to let it go.

I am not suggesting you need to forgive anyone. But if your elevated ancestors are showing up relationally, ready to take responsibility for and repair the harm they did, it's an option. It doesn't mean we're letting anyone off the hook or sweeping anything under the rug. We must have accountability, and we must have justice. When there has been appropriate ritual and work, the forgiveness practice can be a ritual of intimacy.

Forgiveness is an ongoing practice, not a one-and-done event. It is often conducted ritually in stages. For example, although I did not know my grandfather well while he was alive, I have come to know him as a well ancestor. From family accounts, I knew he had committed profound harm while living; but as an ancestor, he continued to respectfully show up in my meditations for a couple of years. I set a boundary and said I wasn't interested in developing a relationship with him because of what he had done while alive.

Over time, as I saw him respecting my boundaries and still continuing to be present while not intruding, I got curious. Would it be possible to do ritual with other guides so that he and I could at least have an interaction?

With the help of other ancestral guides and a living human practitioner, I participated in a series of rituals designed to safely support an interaction. When I finally was willing to relate with him, I found him to be deeply apologetic, but without collapsing into a heap of abject sorrow. He was willing to face the harm of his actions with integrity. He was willing to make repair. And eventually, as I saw him acting in ways that were upstanding, I was able to offer forgiveness to his spirit self. This is an example of how the dead can change and how transgenerational harm can be addressed. The living can offer forgiveness to the dead, if the dead are willing to do the work.

What has been done cannot be undone, but receiving forgiveness from descendants can help restore the flow of love in a lineage.

## Music and Singing

Many ancestral reverence practices include singing. You can practice singing songs of reverence about ancestors and singing songs as offerings to ancestors. We're supposed to praise them and sing.

Singing is a powerful practice that you can use to belong. You can immerse yourself in your people's traditions, culture, and nourishing practices because your cells, your bones, hold the memory of these things, even if you do not have conscious access to them. Music, songs, stories—all of these things activate cellular memory and help you connect to your lineages. Memory can also be held in songs, stories, myths, and histories, and they can all be encoded into music.

Healing is not done in isolation but in community. Communal healing processes can involve dancing, prayer, ritual, movement, rhythm, music, and singing. When you sing, you join your breath with thousands of ancestors who also sang, whistled, and hummed. When you dance, you enter the echo of their footsteps and join the rhythms that pulsed through them.

As an embodiment practice, singing involves breath, sound, and vibration. Your vocal cords produce sounds that create movement in every cell of you. When the tissues of your body are being inwardly massaged through vibration, they are more awake and alive. You are more alive; you feel more. You are joining with life when you sing. You are allowing emotions and sensations to be fluid, to move through you.

There is something extraordinary about singing your prayers out loud and allowing praise, longing, and connection to be sent through your voice out into the ethers to connect with your ancestors. If you are blessed to know the songs of your people, or if you have melodies or lyrics from your parents or grandparents or even further back, sing them frequently.

Sound happens when a noise is made; then the sound travels in waves from the source out to the world and the universe. Think of waves in a pond after you toss a stone in, all the ripples forming concentric circles caused by something that happened previously. Sound is similar. Look at it this way: everything that has ever been said is still being said. The songs your ancestors sang are still being sung!

Even if you do not have access to the songs of your people, you can research the music of the part of the world where you came from. You can also just sing aloud by making any sounds you want. I often make up words, prayers, and conversations. I spontaneously sing them because the resonance in my own body is liberating.

One residue of trauma can be a freeze of the voice. There can be constriction in the throat. Many people have shame about their voice or singing publicly. This is a tragic loss of something you are entitled to by birth. The somatic value of singing is enormous: you work through any freeze or constriction of the throat and find your body as a refuge. This is home, and when you are home, you are unafraid to sing loudly, badly, and with great relish. Make a joyful noise!

Lastly, song and music can be ways your ancestors connect with you. Perhaps scraps of songs come in dreams, or you have magickal and synchronistic experiences with certain music. Songs have a spirit of their own, and many are widely traveled. Maybe you had an experience of a song coming back to you years later in a different context, spanning time and space to help you integrate something. Or have you ever listened to a song for years, only to come to a new and deeper understanding of some meaning?

One person I interviewed shared an experience she had while on pilgrimage in her ancestral homeland:

*How could I feel their presence? I could hear them singing at some point. There is a hill that I climbed up, and I could hear them calling the cattle. There are moments where I can really sense and feel that they were with me.*

This Month, sing every day. Sing a little bit to your people, for your people, and for your own embodiment. You can make up songs, sing songs you already know, or even research the ancestral songs of your people and learn those—maybe in another language! The point is, start using your voice to connect.

We've reached the end of Month 3. You have some enjoyable practices ahead of you this month.

# Last Thoughts for Month 3

One reason to work with ancestors is to find belonging. You can practice secure attachment, which is one part being a safe person inside of yourself and one part extending trust to another being. One way to deepen attachment is through the practice of making offerings. The offerings that fill you with the joy of giving are the right ones.

**In conclusion, this Month you will:**

¤ Complete the Month 3 worksheets in the appendix. You can also download this month's worksheets at www.pavinimoray.com/ttb-bonus.html.

¤ Sing aloud to your ancestors, and feel your body.

¤ Daily practice of secure attachment and belonging: At a quiet moment each day, call to mind a safe person, place, or other-than-human being, like a tree, river, or pet. Imagine you feel the kinship as a physical sensation. The felt sense of invisible bonds of love and care, connecting you. Lean in to the felt sense of your love for them.

¤ Add something to your healing altar that reminds you to whom and what you belong.

¤ Complete Ritual 3: Belonging.

# Ritual 3: Belonging

## Preparation

¤ The purpose of this ritual is to cultivate a felt sense of belonging.

¤ You can do this at your healing altar or in another place where you will not be disturbed.

¤ You will need at least one picture of a trusted loved one—e.g., a human, a pet, or a place—and you can use as many of these as you want.

**Begin by setting a container of prayer as you read this aloud:**

*Ancestors, sweet and well ones,*
*I pray to feel a sense of belonging. I pray to remember how to feel like I belong.*
*I long to form loving connections with my well ancestors of blood and heart, full of mutual respect and care.*
*I pray to fully belong to myself, and with my loved ones. I pray to be in right relationship with the land, and the land of my body.*
*May I be in integrity in all of my connections.*

**Next, cast a circle of protection with the help of your allies.**

Call out to the trusted spiritual sources of protection you already have. This may be deities, guardians, the elements, or relationships with animals, stones, holy places, herbs, or anything from the green world. Invite each to come toward you, and pause until you sense that they are present.

Then, with their support, imagine a layer of protection that goes all around you. You can visualize it if you like, or feel it.

Next, drop into connection with your ancestral guide.

Ask them if there is anything they want you to know: How are the offerings being received? Are there any other offerings that could be helpful? How is the cocoon of prayer?

Hold the picture you have chosen; or if you've chosen more than one, arrange them around you.

Say the following out loud, and notice how your body responds:

*I belong to myself and my well ancestors.*
*I belong with you and your people.*
*I belong to the Earth.*

Go slow and keep saying it, noting your internal reactions. Continue until you have a moment of feeling that you're speaking the truth.

Notice how it is to feel that you belong, even if just for a moment.

Is there anything your guide wishes to offer in terms of belonging?

Close this ritual with a prayer for your own good life, and thank your guide and the allies who showed up.

Dissolve the circle while keeping the protection intact.

Make notes.

# Month 4
## *Resiliate*

**We**

While we humans
    could probably
stand to care more,
What a miracle that
each day finds us loving; I don't know
anyone who doesn't love someone.
Wow.

**You**

Often,
your breath
catches in your throat
taking in some brutal beauty,
then returns and again
your chest rises.
Now.

**Me**

Each day waking, I return
from the dark's dreaming.
It's a
terrible joy
wake, stretch, pee, drink water, pray.
Here.

**Yes**

We scoff at you growing between the
cracks.
Spray you with poison, and DIE we
mumble
to the Green
but
still
the Green persists and
rises.
Phew.

It is possible, still
to be this newness,
this dawn
of rightening.

## *Moon of Resilience Practice*

*Breathing in, rejuvenate.*

*Breathing out, shed.*

Breath is the core resilience practice.
Breath is the determining factor of aliveness.

If you want to be more alive, breathe.
If you want to feel more, breathe.

No matter what has happened to you, they
cannot steal your aliveness if you refuse to
give up.

Make revenge of your joy, justice of your love.
You are here to do what you are here to do.

*Be resilient and you have
succeeded.*

Feel all, feel deep, and then let it go and breathe
again.

# MONTH 4

# Resilience Moon

Welcome to Month 4 of *Tending the Bones*. Over the past three Months, you have worked to build foundational practices of grounding, discernment, ancestral reverence, and wellness. With this foundational work in place, you may now build your healing on top of it.

## So What Is Resilience?

No matter what kind of life you've had, everyone experiences twists and turns: Loss. Hardship. Pain. Confusion. Unexpected circumstances and situations. Sudden change. Change you did not ask for and do not want.

Resilience is adapting in the face of adversity, trauma, tragedy, threats, or significant sources of stress. It is being able to cope with family and relationship problems, serious health problems, or workplace and financial difficulties. Resilience is about coming back to your center, coming back to yourself. It is about bouncing back.

Resilience does not mean you don't feel feelings. It doesn't mean you are not profoundly affected by loss, tragedy, or change. It is an internal process of belonging deeply to yourself and your good life. Resilience means you have the inner resources to deal with whatever comes your way.

Resilient people are those who:

- ¤   Have social support
- ¤   Hold positive views of themselves and their abilities
- ¤   Possess the capacity to make realistic plans and stick to them
- ¤   Have an internal locus of control
- ¤   Are good communicators
- ¤   View themselves as fighters rather than victims
- ¤   Have emotional intelligence and manage emotions effectively

The good news is that resilience is a muscle that can be trained. Resilience involves behaviors, thoughts, and actions that anyone can learn and develop. The ability to learn resilience is one reason research has shown that resilience is ordinary, not extraordinary. Resilience is a deep part of being human.

There are four aspects of resilience:

¤ Connection

¤ Mindset

¤ Wellness

¤ Purpose

## Connection: Isolation Is Not the Way

When you're focusing on resilience, you work to feel connected. You realize that isolation is not the way to heal. You don't go away and lick your wounds, even if you want to. You stay in connection with loved ones and with your supportive community.

## Mindset: Your Thinking Influences Everything about Your Life

You have agency in choosing which narratives you believe. How you think about a situation influences that situation. A resilient mindset involves attending to how you're thinking, which stories you're telling, which narratives you're embodying, which ones you're choosing, and which ones you're not choosing.

## Wellness: Take Care of Your Body

Wellness is another facet of resilience. This means taking care of your body and focusing on the things that make your body feel strong. These include nourishing yourself, getting enough sleep, resting when you need to, drinking water, moving your body in ways that feel good, and getting sunlight and fresh air. All of the things that you can do to support your embodied wellness will support resilience.

## Purpose: Find Meaning and Choose Service

The last area of resilience is your purpose. Your purpose is how you find meaning and what you choose to be in service to. Your purpose is taking action that is meaningful to you. Being on your purpose also means you're taking action, moving forward, and acting in your agency and sovereignty.

Those are the four ingredients of resilience. These are skills that you can develop: You can choose to focus more on connection. You can work with your mindset. You can practice self-care. You can act in ways that are meaningful to you. This is how you build the muscle of resilience.

## Why Focus on Resilience?

Much in this world tries to convince you that you are not resilient, that you can be broken by grief, that it is not safe to feel your feelings, and that your feelings are too much. There is much that benefits from you not believing in your own strength.

Who or what benefits when you do not actively strengthen your muscle of resilience?

Resilience is a choice you can make. You can train that muscle well before you need it. Resilience can keep you out of overwhelm and burnout when faced with challenging situations, or it can help you recover when you are crushed and burned out.

Remember, just because you practice being resilient doesn't mean you don't feel your feelings. You still feel, and you bounce back. Whatever the hard thing is, it doesn't destroy you. It doesn't end you.

One way to think about resilience is to consider what happens if you *don't* practice your resilience. What happens when you isolate yourself for long periods? What happens when you think negative thoughts without reprieve? What happens when your self-care practices fall off, or you don't do the things that make your life meaningful? We have all been there, which is why practicing coming back when you get knocked down matters so much.

Part of justice is you getting to live a good life. Your resilience is also your resistance. It is also your sovereignty. Becoming more resilient is a way to deeply honor your ancestors.

Sometimes people feel tired of being resilient. This is valid. We must pick ourselves back up so frequently that it can be tempting to just lie there next time we fall down. If this is you right now, I'm sending you love and compassion. It's okay to wallow in despair for awhile. It's okay to not do all the things. But when you get bored with that, come back to your resilience practices.

## How Were Your Ancestors Resilient?

When thinking about resilience, it is helpful to lean into your people. You come from people who survived; otherwise, you would not be here.

Granted, some of those survival strategies are maladaptive and are not things that you necessarily want to do. However, they worked, and those folks survived; and more importantly, the lineage survived, and it got to this point here where you get to choose to be resilient or not.

Resilience is not about denial or minimizing impact. In fact, part of resilience is developing the capacity to feel all that you feel. Your people experienced what they experienced. Whatever happened to them happened to them. Chances are, not only did they survive physically, but their hearts and minds were also resilient. This does not mean they were not scarred. It merely means they were able to continue life, hopefully living whole lives and having hope for their descendants.

This is not to equate being alive with being resilient and really *feeling* alive. These are different states of being. Some are not resilient in this way.

In 2012 a trio of psychiatrists studied transgenerational trauma by conducting in-depth individual interviews with fifteen people whose parents had survived the Holocaust. In the article "Transgenerational Transmission of Trauma and Resilience: A Qualitative Study with Brazilian Offspring of Holocaust Survivors," the researchers reported that "not only traumatic experiences but also resilience patterns can be transmitted to and developed by the second generation."

This is really interesting, because not only can you inherit transgenerational trauma; you can also inherit transgenerational resilience. Here is where you can lean in. Trust your transgenerational strength.

Many of my research participants shared how they gained an awareness of their own resilience through healing sexuality with their ancestors. Reported one participant:

*My direct-line ancestors offer patterns of resilience as much as they do trauma. That weaves into developing my sexual wellness deeply.*

One person I interviewed talked about resilience as a principle of their life:

*The tide of life is working to bring about wholeness and reconciliation.*

Life is passed transgenerationally. It brings trauma, but it also offers healing, resilience, and wholeness.

## Survival Narratives

One thing that helps us learn resilience is having role models and stories of others who have been resilient in the face of adversity. Do you know of people from your lineage who endured hardship and stayed committed to feeling?

You might not know the stories of resilience in your lineages, but undertand that they are there whether or not you are aware of them. The amazing thing is that your people, no matter what hardships they experienced, did survive. This is a source of immense strength in your lineage, and you have access to it by birthright.

Reading or remembering the survival narratives of those you admire can be a resource. When you lean into transgenerational resilience, it helps if you have stories as anchors. They do not need to be from your direct lineage to be effective.

Finding those role models of people who have faced adversity without losing their humanity—folks who have faced challenges and remained committed to their own wellness and to justice—is essential.

Can you think of anyone you admire who embodies resilience?

If you have living elders you communicate with, this is a good moment to approach and ask them to share stories with you. For example, "How did you survive hard things?" is a good starting point. If possible, you can go deeper: "How did our family survive hard things? Do you know any stories you want to share about survival in our family?"

Because one of the transmissions of transgenerational trauma is silence—the absence of stories and information—be aware that this may be tender for your elders. You may need to go slow, take breaks, and bring them snacks. It may be just a story to you, but it's something they or someone they loved actually lived through. It may be the first time they have ever spoken of this. This is a time for gentleness and attunement.

## Practicing Resilience

If you're going to increase your resilience, you must deliberately practice.

You are always practicing something. Freedom is choosing what you practice. You can practice having more of what you want in your life. You can deliberately spend time doing things that bring you more joy, more aliveness. You can do things that restore and nourish you.

This means that you're consciously focusing on developing resilience skills. Resilience happens on its own; it's a force of nature. Healing is a force of nature. Your body will heal from wounds. And you can obtain additional benefits by creating a plan for your resilience practice. You can create a resilience plan for both the short term and the long term. When you think about your good life, you're thinking about the long term. When you think about what you need today, that's the short term.

## What Resources You?

There are no rules you must follow as you build a resilience plan. There is no single correct model for resilience. What is nourishing and restorative is unique to each person.

In creating a resilience plan, you need to first consider what things bring you the most tremendous sense of aliveness. What are the activities, places, people, and ways of spending your time that help you feel most like your best self? Where is the place where you feel good, where you feel centered, where you feel resourced?

The next part of a resilience plan is deciding your practice frequency. You may have daily resilience practices, monthly practices, and even annual resilience practices that bring you goodness.

## Resilience Days

When I first started practicing resilience, I chose one day a month as my resilience day. Each month, I decided how to spend that day ahead of time.

Resilience days are days you schedule on your calendar during which you tend to your own well-being. You can schedule these at whatever frequency works best for you, and it may take some experimenting to find the right rhythm. *Important note:* once you put a resilience day on your calendar, it becomes nonnegotiable. I speak from experience of placing a resilience day on the calendar and then saying to myself, "Oh, but there's no time to meet with so-and-so, so I'll just put it on my resilience day."

Holding your boundary around your resilience day must be nonnegotiable. You realize that your well-being is crucial for staying present and engaged in your life, so you hold a *very* firm boundary with yourself about scheduling. During your resilience day, you choose to do things that bring you a sense of aliveness. You can make that plan ahead of time, or you can be responsive in the moment by continually asking yourself, "What do I want to do right now?"

Know that resilience practice is a long-term self-care practice. You tend your muscle of resilience over the long term because you want justice for your lineages, and your good life is one way to get it; and resilience will help you live your good life.

## Resilience Minutes

Resilience is something you can practice many times a day. Perhaps you take one deep breath for the sake of your own wellness. Maybe you meditate for one to three minutes in the middle of your day. Perhaps you dance to one song on your lunch break. Whatever the things are that bring you delight and pleasure, you can do those multiple times a day to enhance your resilience.

To be clear, this is not a to-do list. For instance, you may say to yourself, "I should brush my teeth twice a day." Okay, but does brushing your teeth make you feel more alive? Brushing your teeth is taking care of your physical wellness. Resilience is taking care of your emotional and spiritual health.

You can weave resilience into your day. Every time you notice that you're hunched over your computer, just take a deep breath, and use that action to bring your energy up and above and out. That's a resilience practice.

## Spiritual Hygiene Practices

Spiritual or energetic hygiene means paying attention to *how* it feels inside and around you—paying attention to your energy body. This practice is found in many religions, including Buddhism, Christianity, witchcraft, Hinduism, Ifá, and Santería.

It means you acknowledge that unseen layers of reality need tending just as much as the physical layers of reality do. Just as you clean your physical body, you clean your energetic body. You clean your physical house, and you clean your spiritual house. I know this can all start sounding very woo and ungrounded pretty quick. So let's talk about the importance of your physical living space and its impact on your well-being.

Your space affects how you feel in your life. I'm guessing you already know that when your area is tended—e.g., the plants are watered, the laundry is folded—you feel better. Here I'm speaking not about the physical aspects of your space but the unseen ones.

For example, things flow better when you are *on* in your practices. You feel more connected to yourself, your magick, and your purpose. And when your practices fall off, you probably feel worse in your confidence, self-esteem, and mental wellness.

We are all affected by the people and situations all around us. If those aspects of our lives are grounded and calm, that's awesome. We also get the opportunity to interact with situations, people, and energies that are not always in our best interest. You've been doing a lot of discernment practice around this. Take a moment to notice: How does the space where you're reading this feel right now?

Sometimes you must remain in less-than-optimal circumstances. You might be experiencing energies that don't feel great to you. And sometimes they're sneaky, and you don't notice them for a while.

## How Do You Know If You Need Spiritual Hygiene?

Just as you take care of and cleanse your physical body with personal hygiene practices, you can do the same on a spiritual level.

Imagine if all the bad vibes, negative thoughts, and nasty troll comments were little bits of dirt and grime that get stuck to you. If you were a car, you'd give yourself a wash.

If you notice any of the following conditions in yourself or your life, and there are no physical causes, it's time to do some energetic hygiene:

- Your brain is chattery and won't quiet, even during quiet times.

- You're exhausted, even though you may not have been doing much.

- You feel stagnant.

- You're irritable.

- You can't connect with your ancestral guide.

- Your space feels funky or heavy.

There are lots of techniques for cleaning up your spiritual energies. You may already know some. Ask yourself—or do some research to find out—"How did my people do this?" Lean into what they did.

Maybe you even have access to some of this knowledge now. Do you have traditions from your grandparents or parents about how they cleansed? There are traditional practices that many people do, such as burning white sage or using "Florida water" perfume. However, these are spiritual hygiene techniques from specific spiritual lineages that may or may not belong to you.

Let's sidestep the conversation about cultural appropriation, because here's the truth: you will get better results from the hygiene practices of your own ancestors. If your ancestors burned sage, use sage. If your ancestors used Florida water, have at it. But if not, do some research.

If you grew up Catholic, you could reclaim the burning of frankincense, which has been used for the past six thousand years. If your ancestors are from the British Isles, they may have burned meadowsweet and cedar. Basically, people did what they could, using whatever was available in the environment around them:

- Doing rituals in the fresh air and sunshine
- Exposing oneself to the ocean and ozonated air
- Burning incense or plant material
- Taking salt baths
- Spritzing oneself with vinegar water or other botanical sprays
- Using essential oils like rosemary, lavender, or eucalyptus
- Opening windows
- Putting one's body directly on the Earth
- Holding minerals such as obsidian, rose quartz, or amethyst
- Doing visualization practices, like imagining oneself being swept clean
- Wiping eggs over the body
- Using brooms or feathers to sweep off the energy

Your energetic well-being is crucial. I can't emphasize this enough. It took me a long time to figure out this piece of it. I thought I could just minimize the various impacts I underwent, but now I notice when I'm off my practices and I feel yucky. Spiritual hygiene is important for both your body and your dwelling.

Spiritual hygiene is a nonnegotiable daily resilience practice. The longer you do it, the easier it becomes to notice when things feel off.

## Somatic Resourcing

Resilience resources exist both inside and outside of you. External resources include:

- Attending a community event
- Sharing a meal with friends
- Having a therapy session
- Taking a hot bath
- Getting an acupuncture session

You also have many internal somatic resources—psychological, emotional, and spiritual. All the healing you've already done. The love you have for yourself. The inside voice that speaks kindly to you.

As you heal from traumatic impact, you engage your preexisting external and internal resources, and you build new ones.

I want to share three somatic practices that will help you move trauma through and out of your system. They can be beneficial when you're in a trauma flare-up or dealing with triggers. If you practice them when you're resourced, grounded, and centered, they become tools accessible to you when things are hard because you'll already have them as known practices and tools to reach for in your tool belt.

## Shaking

Shaking is a practice that is exactly what it sounds like: shake your body.

Because trauma is a physical wound in your tissues that restricts spontaneous movement, one antidote for it is to provide opportunities for liberated movement. Free-form dance is a wonderful trauma-release practice, but people can feel anxious about "dance." In contrast, I've found most people can shake fairly easily. Even if the movement is slight, shaking provides a way for your system to release stuck energy.

I learned about shaking from my body. I was processing a lot of trauma and would wake up in the middle of the night having an intense feeling inside of something trying to come out. I couldn't be still. I couldn't lie there. The only thing that helped was to stand up and start bouncing, shaking, and jiggling. Sometimes my movement was vigorous, and sometimes it was more gentle. I had to move my body, so I vibrated and bounced. It worked, and eventually, I would be able to sleep again. This went on for months.

Years later, I discovered that author and therapist Dr. David Berceli has developed a whole technique called Tension and Trauma Releasing Exercises that uses the body's natural shaking mechanisms to process trauma. The practice of this technique is so simple. I usually do it standing, so if you want to try it with me, why don't you stand up right now?

Stand with your knees slightly bent. Now, just start bouncing up and down by slightly bending and straightening your legs at the knees, over and over. Sometimes I put music on to do this. I find that very helpful, as it becomes a rhythmic practice. As you shake, you can imagine that one of those very hard rubber bouncy balls you used to get in gumball machines is bouncing around in your pelvis.

Move your center, and let that ball bounce all around inside your body. Allow your body to shake, including your hands and feet, one at a time. Let your head go; shake it! (Also keep in mind that you don't want to keep your head stiff while you're shaking or bouncing.)

There's no wrong way to do this. Just move your body. I typically find that the movement gradually becomes more vigorous as I continue to shake and bounce. You might start out feeling a little frozen, having a hard time getting into it, but then it builds and builds, especially if you have music on. You can put on any kind of music, although music with a faster beats-per-minute tempo is preferable, like electronic dance music.

Let the big muscles of your body move any which way. Shake it out and shake it off. There's a reason why animals shake once they have encountered a stressful situation, and our bodies do the same thing.

This shaking practice is a vast resource. You can shake for one minute, ten minutes, or an hour. You can do it for as long as you want. When you do this practice, you're discharging any adrenalized energy that's stored in your tissues. Shake it off. You don't need to set a rhythm; you just shake, vibrate, twitch, and let it come out. You will know when you're done. As you complete the practice, pay particular attention to how your body feels afterward. Can you feel your aliveness?

Shaking is a huge practice, and it's a vigorous practice. Maybe the shaking is too activating for your nervous system. Sometimes you may want or need a somatic resource that is a little bit more sedate. Discerning the proper practice for the moment is essential.

## Orienting

Another somatic resource is orienting. I learned this practice from the Somatic Experiencing modality, and I use it all the time. This is a less vigorous practice than shaking. When you orient, you bring your attention to the present moment and notice where you are.

For this practice, you can be seated or standing. To begin, open your eyes, and allow them to take in the environment.

Start looking around slowly.

Let your gaze move, noticing colors, shapes, lines, and curves.

In your head, you can name what you see—brown wooden corner, round white lampshade, hardwood floor—but you don't have to. You could just let your eyes see what they want to see.

Look in every direction. Look up, look around behind you, and turn your body. Really notice: "Oh, I'm in a space, and this is what else is in this space."

If you find that your eyes want to gravitate to a thing, let them rest on it, let them deeply take it in. Become curious with your eyes. Remember to breathe as you notice the edges, the contours, the shapes. See how the light plays on the thing you're observing. Notice what that thing is like in relation to other things.

Notice the empty space around that thing. Now notice: right now, how are you?

This is the orienting practice. You orient yourself to the space you are in. This is profoundly settling to your nervous system. You can use this practice wherever and whenever you need to bring yourself into the present moment, where you are safe.

## Anchoring

I want to introduce you to a third somatic practice called anchoring. The first two somatic practices were more externally focused, but anchoring is an internal practice.

In the practice of anchoring, you turn your attention inward. You can close your eyes if you want. Allow your attention to scan your body until you find somewhere that feels neutral or pleasant. Somewhere that doesn't feel tight, doesn't feel like it's in pain, doesn't feel like it's dancing in your chair. A neutral place. It could be your left elbow, right cheek, or belly. Wherever you feel neutral and calm right now.

As you find that place, allow all of your attention to pool toward it. Just let it sink and pool and pour toward that one place in your body that feels neutral or pleasant.

Notice the size of that place; is it small? Is it big? Notice if there's any pressure on that place. Is it pressing up against anything, or is there anything pressing against it? Notice temperature; does it feel warmer or cooler? Allow yourself to hang out in this somatic anchor.

Good. This is your anchor point.

Now, bring your attention up and out into the room again. Look around, and maybe look back at the thing you were looking at before. Put your attention there, and then let it return to your anchor. Move your attention back and forth from your external orientation to your internal anchor point. You are creating a safe hangout spot inside your body.

## Last Thoughts for Month 4

Resilience is the practice of developing self-trust. In leaning into your own resilience, you're proving you are flexible, responsive, and adaptive to change. You watch yourself be affected by something, and then you watch yourself come back to life. Feeling confident—like "I've got me!"—is really powerful. You know and trust yourself to return from whatever impact you have experienced: "I know I'm gonna come back, I know I'm gonna bounce back at some point, I know I have the capacity to feel this feeling."

Knowing that you can trust yourself to return, to bounce back: this is resilience gold! It's a gift to your ancestors, it's a gift to you, and it's a gift to any descendants. You know you can come back.

**In conclusion, this Month you will:**

¤ Complete the Month 4 worksheets in the appendix. You can also download this month's worksheets at www.pavinimoray.com/ttb-bonus.html.

¤ Perform a daily practice of spiritual hygiene.

¤ Perform a daily practice of resilience: "Breathing in, I rejuvenate. Breathing out, I shed." When you lay in your bed this Month, do a few rounds of this.

¤ Try out the practices of shaking, orienting, and anchoring.

¤ Add something to your healing altar that represents your resilience.

¤ Complete Ritual 4: Resilience.

# Ritual 4: Resilience

## Preparation

- ¤ The purpose of this ritual is to increase your resilience by trusting your boundaries and reclaiming your self-power.

- ¤ You can do this at your healing altar or in another place you will not be disturbed.

- ¤ You will also need a notebook or voice recorder.

**Begin by setting a container of prayer as you read this aloud:**

*Bright ancestors of my blood*
*who survived countless terrors with hearts intact,*
*who braved change and growth, wanted and unwanted*
*and lived bravely and thriving,*
*bless me with your embodied wisdom*
*so that I may manifest*
*the courage and humanity of my blood*
*in gorgeous tenacity.*

**Next, cast a circle of protection with the help of your allies.**

Call out to the trusted spiritual sources of protection you already have. This may be deities, guardians, the elements, or relationships with animals, stones, holy places, herbs, or anything from the green world. Invite each to come toward you, and pause until you sense that they are present.

Then, with their support, imagine a layer of protection that goes all around you. You can visualize it if you like, or feel it.

Check in: Do you feel protected all the way around? Can you feel yourself?

**Drop into connection with your ancestral guide.**

Check in and ask if there is anything they want you to know right now.

How are the offerings going? Are there any other offerings that could be helpful?

Check in on the cocoon of prayer. Are there any in there who are ready to transition to the realm of the well ancestors?

If so, allow the guide to undertake that work before continuing.

Once that part is complete, ask your guide about the gifts of resilience of this line.

How has this line practiced resilience? What guidance can your guide offer?

Ask your guide to receive the blessings of resilience carried by this line. This can show up in a variety of ways. Your guide may want you to know tales of courage and survival. They may whisper words of learned wisdom in your ear. They may gift you an object, a felt sense, a song that represents the resilience of your line, or a thousand other blessings. Be available to the blessing as it arrives.

Allow yourself to receive the blessings in your body, like a system update.

Make notes of the information you receive.

Close this ritual with a prayer for your own good life, and thank your guide and the allies who showed up.

Dissolve the circle while keeping the protection intact.

# PART 2
# Heal

This part of the book is designed as a path to follow as you actively seek to heal from transgenerational sexual trauma. Through the processes of acknowledgment, creating justice for yourself, freeing yourself from shame, and returning to your body, you work through layers of healing in a linear fashion. Healing is cyclical, so feel free to return to these tools and concepts as needed.

# Month 5
## *Everything That Happened, Happened*

No one says to the bee:
Summer wasn't.
You never flew out in the hot sun.
No rose welcomed you.

No one murmurs to the river's edge:
There is no river.
You are not eroding, washing away,
even now.

The praying mantis isn't told:
Don't bite his head off,
he's good at heart,
consider letting it go,
we wish
you would.

At what point did their nos
become your didn't happeneds?

When your moment of reckoning comes along
(What a gift! Finally!)
conceding what was demands a price of you.

Grief,
the most patient lover.

When *No, that never happened* becomes
*Yes, my sweet sweet heart,*
it's grief's hour.

Graveyard dirt scrabbled beneath
your nails.
A bad case of the howls.

That happened. That happened. Scream.
That happened. Sob.
That happened.

At first, terror
but then, pleasure.
How can it feel so good to feel so bad?

Feeling at last!

Growing the indelible strength
of scar tissue.

# Acknowledgment Moon

Here you are in Month 5 of *Tending The Bones:* the acknowledgment moon. We begin with a prayer. You can read this aloud if you like, or you can make one up:

> *Ancestors,*
> *I call out to you for your support,*
> *I call out to you for your witness, your presence, and your guidance*
> *as I enter into the work of this Month.*
> *I ask you to be a resource for me.*
> *A resource of healing as I turn my attention*
> *toward what needs healing and justice.*
> *Sweet ancestors,*
> *be close with me, be near me.*
> *Bless me.*

We have entered part 2 of this book, which focuses on healing.

You may wish to dial up the volume on your support for these next two months. Put on your hazmat suit; we're going in. Make sure that your therapy/professional support is in place and that you have ample support in your network. Let people you love know that you might be extra tender. You might need more spaciousness and help over the next two Months.

This Month we work with inherited sexual burdens, trauma, denial, and acknowledgment. We work with the lineages of harm and the lineages of healing. We work with having clarity and right-sizedness in your responsibility to ancestral healing.

## Inherited Sexual Burdens

In terms of your erotic self, ancestral burdens that you may have received from your personal lineages can include sex negativity, shame, repression, homophobia, transphobia, body shame, silence about topics of sexuality, and pleasure prohibition from your family, your culture, or your religion. You may have received negative gender messages or messages about which kinds of desires and sex are appropriate and which kinds are not.

You have no choice about the burdens that are handed to you. Your choice lies in whether you accept and embody them or not. It's important to note that the choice can itself be unconscious. You can practice or embody things that operate beyond your current awareness. Sometimes you will then become aware of them. When you become aware of a negative burden you have inherited, you can say, "The buck stops here; this [fill in the blank] will not be passed on. I will be the person to end this particular practice, belief, or behavior."

Another way some humans handle receiving a sexual burden is white-knuckling. For example, if you notice that your parents' beliefs around sexuality were based on shame, you could feel that same shame without speaking or acting in ways that perpetuate it. You haven't precisely healed it, but you still might act in sex-positive ways around your kids, for example.

That's one way to get through it, to say it's going to stop here; you're not going to embody that sexual shame. But unless you transform that burden at its root, the burden does indeed often get passed down.

The best thing to do is to work to transform the burdens you've been handed so that the patterns change. This means breaking cycles of shame, sexual violence, silence, homophobia, and other oppressions through active and intentional healing. You can change those patterns in you and your life so that they do not pass to those who come after you, whether or not you have biological offspring.

Your own work of acceptance, welcoming a diversity of desires, deconstructing gender roles and norms, and inviting in the fullness of your sexual potential is a healing force for you, for your descendants of blood and heart, and for the wider community and the world.

Although everyone probably inherits sexual burdens, it's good to remember that there are also sexual blessings—all the wonderful stuff coming toward you from those who came before.

We all carry a mixed inheritance of blessings and burdens in our sexuality, which is deeply rooted in our lineages and historical contexts. For those raised in the United States, acknowledging the weight we bear involves confronting the painful legacy of sexual violence used as a tool of control during the genocide of Indigenous people and the enslavement of Africans. These are not distant echoes; these systems of harm and oppression live within us, in our bodies, and they shape our sexualities.

Delving into the sexually inherited burdens specific to the United States is a painful and rage-inducing journey. If you come from an Indigenous background or are a descendant of enslaved Africans, these truths are likely not new to you. I extend to you my utmost compassion and my unwavering allyship for justice.

The contemporary battle over women's reproductive rights finds its roots in the birth of capitalism. In simple terms, women's sexuality was demonized when patriarchy sought control over an inherently uncontrollable force: the erotic. The haunting legacy of the witch trials, where thousands of women were murdered, remains an unhealed wound and a horrific example of how white men exploited women's bodies and knowledge to forge the foundations of capitalism.

To put it bluntly, capitalist economies thrive on workers' labor, and people with uteruses produce the workforce. The regulation of women's sexuality and reproductive choices laid the groundwork for the enduring patriarchal control we witness today in the fight over access to safe abortion and birth control. Capitalism requires access to cheap raw materials, land, and labor. The disturbing reality is that children became commodities, serving as a resource to fuel profit. The practices of patriarchy and capitalism converged, sparking colonization and slavery.

When Europeans colonized the land that is now known as the United States, sexual violence became a weapon deliberately used to dehumanize and subjugate Indigenous peoples. I'm going to say it again: the sexual abuse and murder of Native women were strategic tools of conquest and genocide during European colonization.

Before colonization, violence against and sexual abuse of Indigenous women were alien concepts in traditional societies, where these women were revered and were viewed as integral to maintaining tribal cultures.

Yet Indigenous women in the United States today face disproportionately high rates of sexual violence. The Department of Justice reports that sexual violence rates for Indigenous women are approximately 2.5 times higher than those for white, African American, or Asian American women.

Most shockingly, an estimated 86–96 percent of the sexual abuse against Native women is committed by non-Indigenous perpetrators. Since 1978, tribal courts have lacked jurisdiction to prosecute tribal nonmembers for many crimes—including sexual assault and rape—committed on tribal land, enabling most perpetrators to escape justice. This isn't just history; it's a present-day perpetuation of historical oppression.

Sexual violence wasn't accidental; it was a deliberate strategy wielded by male colonizers. If we recognize that sexual violence serves both conquest and profit, the repetition of these tactics on enslaved African people by white men is tragically unsurprising.

Enslaved African women endured systemic sexual exploitation and violence. White slaveholders wielded arbitrary authority, frequently raping enslaved women with impunity. These women bore children to their rapists, and these children were considered property and a potential source of profit by the white men who fathered them. Imagine having a child and viewing them as your property and a source of profit.

There's no eloquent way to capture the enormity of this injustice. My intention is to name these truths with compassion and emotion. The echoes of hearts breaking resonate across the years, reverberating in this room where I write and you read. How do we bring these "facts" close, allowing the truth to hurt, whether this information is new to us or we're already numb to it? For those who have been feeling this impact for some time, what is needed for our hearts to heal when violence is still directed against Black and Indigenous women?

White women were also complicit in the abuse. Instead of being allies in shared gender struggles, the stories that I read tell of how they furthered the abuse. They were jealous of their husbands' rape of enslaved African women, so they took their jealousy out upon the women whom their husbands had raped. Victim blaming has deep and unconscionable roots. While we can acknowledge that capitalism was built on slavery, which created power dynamics along race lines, I find myself as rageful at the white women who supported sexualized violence as I am at the white men who instigated it.

Slavery has had a lasting, multifaceted impact on the sexuality of Black people. For example, racialized sexual stereotypes that portray enslaved African women as hypersexual and promiscuous and black men as the "Mandingo" or the Black "buck" persist. Black survivors of sexual violence typically have worse outcomes than white survivors. The structural racism within health systems impedes access to adequate, appropriate care for Black survivors. As writer Lecia Michell states:

> Nearly 150 years later, the Black community still suffers the aftereffects of slavery. Colorism and sexual violence—both rampant during slavery—are commonplace even now.

> As a Black woman, I've encountered many white men who believe Black women are "easy." They make comments like, "I've heard that Black women are wild in bed." Or "You just seem so sensual." He made this comment when we were having lunch. I was dressed casually. Or this one: "I've never been with a Black woman. I want to know what it's like." Every Black woman has these stories.

But what about the impact on people's erotic bodies? I want to acknowledge the tremendous impact of systemic violence, abuse, and dehumanization on the nervous systems and bodies of the descendants of enslaved Africans. While each person's experience is uniquely their own, atrocities leave scars. Each of us inhabits our sexual burdens in our own way, but the impact is the impact. I may not be able to name what you personally experience as a recipient of this burden, but I hold space for it in my heart.

Until we acknowledge these harms on personal and cultural levels, they persist in our inheritance of sexual burdens. Time has passed, and it's likely no one alive today personally knows a woman who was raped while enslaved. Yet the impact endures. These harms cannot be inflicted or experienced without causing profound damage to our capacity for trust, intimacy, and pleasure.

What would an uncolonized sexuality feel like?

What access to intimacy and pleasure might be possible if these burdens were resolved?

## What Is Denial?

Denial is a strategy. It's what we live inside of until we're ready to be in acknowledgment. We are either in denial, or we are in acknowledgment. Some families have a strong history of denial, meaning they turn their attention away from what is painful to confront. They may use strategies of silence, numbing, gaslighting, or pretending as part of denying the truth.

The poet David Whyte writes:

*Denial is a beautiful transitional state every human being inhabits before they are emancipated into the next larger context and orphaned often against their will from an old and a very familiar home. Denial is ever-present and unavoidable in a human life....*

*Denial can be a prison if inhabited in a too concrete and unmoving way. Denial is also a necessary stepping stone and a compassionate foundation for viewing those unable to take the next courageous step....*

*Much better to pay attention to what beckons than to try to look at what, by definition, we are not ready to look at.... Denial is the crossroads between perception and readiness. To defy denial is to invite powers into our lives we have not yet readied ourselves to meet.*

Denial is a strategy you use to protect yourself until you grow the capacity to be with what is and what happened.

There's a lot of compassion and forgiveness available from within and without. You don't have to be mad at yourself because you weren't yet ready to see or acknowledge something. You can choose to be sweet with the places where you currently experience denial in your life, or where you have in the past.

The absence of acknowledgment is the absence of attention to something. It can be challenging to observe how you're not paying attention. You don't know what you don't know. But you can recognize that there are things you do not know. You can recognize that your healing will unfold as the time is right and you are ripe and ready.

## What Is Acknowledgment?

Acknowledgment looks like the following statements:

- ¤ That happened.
- ¤ That happened to you.
- ¤ That happened in your lineage.
- ¤ That affected you.
- ¤ This is the impact you experienced.
- ¤ This is the impact in your life caused by the impact you experienced.
- ¤ This is the way your life has been shaped because of that impact.
- ¤ Your life will never be as it was before the impact.

Acknowledgment work is grief work. It means you are willing to allow the past to be what it actually is. Another name for acknowledgment is *acceptance*. It means you give up your fantasy, your desire, your wish that it will ever be different.

My somatic coach once told me, "Pavini, the ship of having good parents has sailed." It was time for me to stop wishing that it was different. It was time for me to acknowledge and accept what is.

The pain of acknowledging an event can be more painful than the actual event because, in essence, you admit powerlessness over the event. It happened, and you cannot go back in time and rewrite history. There will be no different outcome, no different past. There's no other story than the story that happened. Everything that happened, happened. Acknowledgment means looking squarely at what you wish were different and giving up the dream of a possible narrative. Acknowledging is hard, and it's honest. It can be brutal, and it's also necessary for you to move forward.

Acknowledgment is what you move into when you move out of denial. It means you're ready to move from absence to presence. You move from ignoring and pretending to accepting.

Acknowledging what happened means:

¤ You've done a lot of healing.

¤ You mostly trust that you can bear your own grief.

¤ You trust your resilience; you trust your ability to come back.

There are multiple layers of acknowledgment:

¤ There is acknowledging what happened to you personally.

¤ There is acknowledging what happened to your ancestors.

¤ There is acknowledging what was done by your ancestors.

Acknowledgment is a turning toward knowing. To acknowledge means to confess knowledge. You admit that you know something. I believe that acknowledgment is a synonym for love. When you acknowledge, you are deeply present with what is. You bear witness to the truth. You are not in hope. You do not wish it were different. You're living inside of what is, and that is love.

In healing, you move from denial to acknowledgment and then to acceptance. You may then possibly move on to forgiveness. I'm not referring to hokey "I forgive you" BS. More on forgiveness later, but for now, drop a bookmark onto that concept and know that if you choose to forgive, you do it for *you*. It is not owed or required for healing to happen.

During the acknowledgment process, first you acknowledge what happened. Then you acknowledge the impact of what happened.

Impact is not inherently negative or positive. When something happens, you experience impact on psychological, emotional, somatic, and relational levels. Impact is what shapes you as well as all the ways it shapes you.

It's not enough to acknowledge impact intellectually. The impact you experience from a traumatic event creates emotions, sensations, oppressions, wounds, and ruptures. It also creates resilience, joy, and sustenance. It creates narratives and practices that can be passed between generations. What happened creates burdens, and it makes blessings.

## Acknowledging Impact at the Personal, Lineage, and Community Levels

When you acknowledge the full impact of what happened, you look at attachment wounds and relational implications. The impact creates outward ripples. This is why it must be recognized at the personal level and on the levels of family, community, and culture. The impact is never limited to the person who experienced the traumatic event.

Let me give you an example here. My grandmother lived through the Great Depression. As a kid, she lived in a rural area, and she often didn't have enough to eat. After she grew up, she raised her children, my mom and her siblings, during World War II; food was scarce. By the time I came around, the impact of food scarcity was an embedded narrative in my family. Our food practices were based on that narrative, which led to my mom not feeding me enough when I was a baby. That affected me by causing me to have an eating disorder.

Although I acknowledge the impact and how I was shaped by it, it still affects my kids. They have witnessed my healing and my struggle with food. Three generations down from my grandma, her trauma has affected them, and it will probably affect their kids if they have them. This is an example of impact moving down the line.

It's also an example of how you can acknowledge the impact and the truth of something. This is what happened, and there are many other layers that it needs to be worked at. It's not just an intellectual process of saying "that happened." Healing is changing the practices, the narratives, the choices, and the beliefs.

## The Layers of You

Acknowledging what is includes acknowledging who you are.

You are a complex and multilayered being. You contain multitudes: your parts, your personality, your conscious and unconscious. All of your selves, past and present. Your values and beliefs. Your brain, including the way you think, your mindset, and the knowledge you have. The stories and narratives you carry. All of the history and experiences you've had. Your survival strategies. How you react to stress, conflict, joy, boredom. Your intimacy and relationship patterns. Your chosen and habitual practices. Your sense of humor. And, of course, your body, where you experience your sensations and emotions.

One mind map you can use is that of concentric circles.

Before you existed, your ancestors lived with all the same parts you have. These affected your parents and, in turn, you. As a babe in the womb, you received impact—positive, negative, and neutral. This was your initial shaping.

You received impact and learning from either biological family or caregivers. You received shaping from all of the practices that happened in your home. These practices were, in turn, informed by outside influences of culture, religion, place in the world, access to resources, and tradition. Each of these factors is a concentric circle that shapes who you are.

Beyond these influences are other spheres of impact: the community or communities you dwelled in as you grew up. The institutions like schools or religion that you participated in, and the values and practices of those organizations.

Then there is the broader culture that you grew up in—the governments that assert legal authority over you. Also the physical environment you live in and are part of, including the food, water, and air you take in. In these larger layers, you can start to notice how systemic oppressions touch you.

For example, I once had a client who had experienced childhood sexual abuse. This issue felt deeply personal to her, because it was. However, once she noticed the systemic power imbalances at work, she saw that her abuse had occurred within a wider framework of misogyny and patriarchy. It was then that she could be appropriately angry at both her perpetrator and at a system that ignores harm to children. My somatic coach always says it takes a village to harm a child.

You receive positive and negative impact from all of these spheres. You develop in response to the impact that you receive. You may be very grateful for some of that impact. You might feel pissed off about some of that impact. Some parts of that impact are invisible to you because it's the water you swim in. (Hence, feeling the privilege you have access to can be really challenging.)

When acknowledging impact, it's helpful to consider where it lands in your concentric circles.

Where and when did you receive that shaping? Which ring of your circles visited that impact upon you? Did it happen at home? At school? On the playground? Within a wider system, like racism and white supremacy? It's good to place impact into a context.

For example, let's say you want to consider the impact of a sexual violation you experienced in college. While working with your therapist, you realize that there was an earlier impact from middle school, where you learned that in order to fit in, you needed to be considered sexually adventurous, which had led to you pushing through your own boundaries about what you were ready for. That pattern has continued throughout your life as a young adult. Leading up to the sexual violation, you had ignored your intuition. Acknowledging the earlier impact provides more context as you work to unpack what happened in college.

Generational trauma is a secondary form of trauma resulting from the transfer of traumatic experiences from parents (or caregivers) to their children. It's also referred to as intergenerational, transgenerational, or secondary trauma.

Unhealed issues in previous generations can continue to be expressed in subsequent generations. This expression shows up as repeated patterns and stories, and it's transmitted through psychological, physical, and spiritual mechanisms. Physically, trauma can be passed through the process of epigenetics. Psychologically, there are four primary mechanisms of multigenerational trauma transmission:

- Silence or lack of communication of relevant information
- Overdisclosure by adults to children of their past traumas
- Identification of children with their caregivers' traumas
- Cycles of traumatic reenactment

Transgenerational sexual trauma can mean sexual violation experienced by each subsequent generation. But children who have parents with sexual trauma can also experience transgenerational sexual trauma—reexperiencing the parent's trauma and exhibiting the parent's trauma symptoms—even if the children have not experienced sexual trauma of their own.

Unprocessed sexual trauma leaves residue. Devroede and Schutzenberger (2005) write: "The body remembers sexual abuse and keeping family secrets causes illness. Unwittingly and unwillingly, our parents, grandparents, and ancestors often leave us the legacy of their unfinished mourning, their 'undigested' traumas, and the hidden shame of their secret family history. Sexual abuse and other traumas experienced in the family's past create insurmountable or unresolved emotional wounds that leave their mark on future generations."

Symptoms that a child experiences from child sexual abuse (CSA) often present alongside the untreated CSA symptoms of a caregiver. Additionally, the research shows that many perpetrators of sexual abuse have themselves been victims of sexual abuse. However, the cycle of transgenerational sexual trauma can be interrupted by learning appropriate boundaries.

## Lineages of Harm, Lineages of Healing

Obviously, you inherit your looks and features from your ancestors. You may have also noticed that you've inherited many beliefs and behaviors related to sexuality, intimacy, and relationships from those who came before.

Some of these beliefs and behaviors may be beneficial blessings. For example, you might have inherited a commitment to sexual freedom or erotic giftedness. However, you have probably inherited burdens as well—unwanted things like sexual shame or repression.

Becoming aware of what you're working with in terms of burdens and blessings enables you to make choices about how you will be in your sexuality, and more widely in your life.

This Month you will make a map of the messages you've received about sexuality, intimacy, and relationships. Expressing these will help you become aware of the sex-related burdens and blessings you carry.

Some ancestral sexual burdens you may need to acknowledge include shame, repression, sexual violence (either as a victim or as a perpetrator—and sometimes it's both), or residual sexual trauma you inherited. If you have personal sexual trauma, your personal trauma and your lineage trauma can become entangled. It isn't easy to know what's yours from your own life and what you inherited as an unpleasant legacy.

For example, suppose you had a highly repressive religious upbringing. In that case, your sexual self-exploration through masturbating may have been affected before you had a chance to figure out what your body does. Or, if you received and accepted someone else's beliefs about sexuality, it will be a challenge for you to sexually self-determine. You never got to embody what felt right to you without the overlay of religion.

In these examples, someone could feel bad about themselves for not being sex-positive or not having lots of hot, slutty sex. It's imperative to acknowledge that this isn't a personal shortcoming; the person in question received impact from an institution that shaped their being.

I have worked with many queer clients who grew up Mormon or as members of other cultish fundamentalist religious groups. The similarity they share is that they were deeply shamed around sex, queerness, and gender fluidity. Often they were punished or slut-shamed, or they received violent repercussions for their beingness. Many were also the direct recipient of sexual abuse. Religious shaping tries to stifle the sexual and creative impulse and ensure conformity with a patriarchal, violent system. If this is you, coming home to your body and your healthy, loving sexuality on your terms is a great life work. You are the most courageous people I know—you who insist that you get to experience embodiment and pleasure after that kind of rigorous spiritual genocide.

It takes time to acknowledge that kind of impact. Often, people have grown accustomed to minimizing the actual impact they've received. When clients talk about sexual trauma, I frequently hear them say things like, "Oh well, it wasn't great, but I know it wasn't as bad as what many people have gone through." Minimization, like denial, is a strategy we use to protect ourselves. When you're ready, you can slowly start to acknowledge everything that happened, and its impact. There will be grief; there will be rage.

Once you can acknowledge the full impact you have experienced, you can start to make choices about narratives and practices that align with your deep self. You get to find out who you are as a sexual being. There is a morass of sexuality within and between the ancestral and the personal. It's yours to untangle if you wish. The reason for doing this work is to enable you to heal and develop sexual wellness.

On the flip side of the inherited burdens are ancestral sexual blessings. You may be heir to lustiness, sexual freedom, strong libido, erotic attunement, or being a great lover. It might be that you feel great about sex or your body.

You also may have ancestors who worked hard at their own healing or who were completely sex-loving. So even while we dig through the swamp of trauma, hold an awareness that there are glimmers of pleasure and beauty in even the most wounded of lineages. Remember, as Linda Hogan writes, that you are the result of the love of thousands. Somewhere in there were some awesome fuckers (pun intended).

Acknowledgment means thoroughly reviewing your sexual past, your choices, your sexual woundings, and your sexual wonderfuls.

I often work with folks who have survived sexual assault. In digging more deeply, they frequently find that they are the descendants of ancestors who suffered similarly. Knowing what is yours and what is ancestral can be quite helpful for your healing.

Families are complicated. You have to make room for paradox and complication because you can receive mixed messages about sexuality from different people—or even from the same person.

For example, I lived with my father when I was a teenager. He supported me in obtaining birth control at the age of fifteen. He would allow my boyfriend to sleep over. But then he also called me a slut one time when he found me in bed with someone. To process this on a body level, I have to get wide in my body to make space for both the sexual permission and the sexual shaming my dad gave me.

Families get even more complicated when sexual boundaries are not respected or violated. The incest taboo is there for both biological and social reasons.

## Acknowledging What Is and What Happened, Then Processing What Happened

Until the sexual wounding that you or your ancestors experienced or caused is acknowledged, it negatively affects your sexuality and unconscious mind. Truth is held in your body as trauma stored in tissues.

If you don't acknowledge or process that trauma and you choose to procreate, then you can just pass that bag of gross right along to your kids. One person I spoke to it said like this:

*When my daughter was born, I suddenly realized, "Oh my God, I have to get my act together, or this kid is toast!"*

You will likely have to hold complicated or conflicting truths when you acknowledge what is. Working with sexuality through an ancestral lens is often a practice of holding contradiction. Your ancestors may have committed sexual harm, or they may have been the recipients of sexual wounding in the same bloodline. Sometimes a single ancestor can simultaneously be a victim of harm, a survivor embodying wellness, and a perpetrator of harm, just as a living person can.

This contradiction—healing and harm, blessing and burden—is also found in our capacity for resilience. Capacity for resilience emerges from the practice of being resilient in the face of harm. That's trippy.

The paradox of blessing/burden and healing/harm shows up in many places in ancestor work. For example, people often want to identify with the well, bright ones of their lineage or those who were the recipients of harm. Very few people are super stoked to find out they have an ancestor who caused harm, even though we all do, if we go by the numbers (and the systems of oppression!)

A part of us wants to distance ourselves from any ancestors who caused harm. Unfortunately, that doesn't work very well. You don't get to pick and choose who your ancestors are, because they were who they were.

Choosing to heal is another paradox, another contradiction you must hold. To choose to heal, you must acknowledge injury.

New healing spaces open up when we're willing to hold up all these contradictions without judgment of ourselves or our ancestors. As we discussed earlier, consider that transgenerational transmission of trauma may be a powerful evolutionary adaptation. This mechanism makes sure that the wounds of the past get acknowledged, tended, and cleaned up.

I find it helpful to remember that yes, there are burdens, and yes, there are blessings. There is harm. There is healing. There are many contradictions. There is paradox. There is clarity. There is discernment, and all of it, all of it, is true.

## Being Clear about Your Responsibility: No More, No Less

Part of tending ancestral wounds is getting clear about your responsibility. You want to be right-sized about it. Many people with ancestors who committed harm struggle with this equation. They ask, "If I acknowledge the harm, then what?" Of course, North American white domination culture does not have good tools for helping descendants of perpetrators acknowledge and repair harm. In this way, the question they ask is fair. Are you responsible for things your ancestors did? If so, to what extent?

Many people have both perpetrators and victims of sexual violence in their bloodlines. This is also true for other injustices, like slavery, colonization, and genocide. You can be descended from those who created impact as well as from those who experienced it. You can be descended from a colonizer and from a person whose land was colonized; a person who owned slaves and a person who was enslaved. It is complicated to be with this.

Again, this is a place where people tend to distance themselves from particular ancestors and focus on those who align more closely with their own values and beliefs. I once worked with a mixed-race woman of African and European descent who claimed only her African ancestry because it was too complicated and painful to hold the entire picture. No judgment from me, and I hope, in time, she can embrace all of her origins. This work clearly calls for an increase in one's ability to hold nuance and complexity.

Another example of this conundrum is my friend Sonja, who is of French and Vietnamese descent. The French colonized Vietnam, and Sonja describes her embodied experience as feeling paradoxical. She also talks about trying to hold honor for each lineage, and the pain of that truth.

I believe it's on us to figure out how to take those internal paradoxes and make enough space for them, make it okay enough inside ourselves to hold it all. It's not very helpful to sit in judgment of ancestors, especially if we remember they can change and become accountable. Often they want to do so and are very willing to do it. We have to be willing to let them change. We have to be willing to update our beliefs about them, while also not excusing the harm of their actions and working continuously for justice and repair.

Here's the truth: you are not responsible for your people's wrongdoings. It's just not a helpful lens. You are not responsible. That said, you can still be in right relationship with them by attending to what happened. What are you right-sized responsible for, no matter what's in your blood?

You're obviously responsible for any harm that you do. You're responsible for how you continue to benefit from the damage your people perpetrated. For example, if you're white and haven't done your work around whiteness and how you continue to benefit from white supremacy, you need to. You have to be responsible for that. It would be best if you actively worked to acknowledge what is and what was so you can be right-sized.

However, doing this work does not mean that you committed those original harms.

Narratives around privilege can be a way to collapse. You've heard about white women's tears. This kind of collapse happens when you make the situation of historic harm all about your own feelings. In response to historic harm, some choose to take too little responsibility. Others become overly responsible, more or less saying "I owe my entire life as reparations," and being stuck in guilt because they've taken on more than their share of responsibility.

It does no good for you to become mired in shame or guilt. Part of healing means turning toward what happened while still having a spine. This means turning toward it with your dignity. This sounds like, "This is what happened. I will look at it without turning away. I will not crumble in shame. I will not take on more than I can take on. I will acknowledge the impact on myself and on everybody who is involved."

In my own life, some of my ancestors were antislavery abolitionists, but they also participated in the genocide of the Native peoples of northeastern Ohio: the Wyandot, Seneca, and Shawnee tribes. While I did not personally commit harm against these people, I undeniably have benefited from the egregious injury my ancestors caused. My family did and does own stolen land. If I were to crumble under the weight of shame, I would not be able to work toward reparations. Acknowledgment is the first step of repair. I hold my ancestors' complicated choices and politics with compassion. I do my work to dismantle systems of violence and oppression, and I take action to make repair. I continue to find my way to a right-sized responsibility, which will take the rest of my life.

Being right-sized in your responsibility means you are acknowledging harm and working toward repair. You deal with your shame in the right contexts, such as therapy and conversations with others of your background. You don't make the labor of your shame the work of those who experience oppression and marginalization.

Getting right-sized in your responsibility allows you to cultivate appropriate, right-sized ancestral pride. For example, I am proud of my Quaker ancestors who organized against slavery. You get to be in your dignity. I believe this is what our ancestors are asking of us. They want us to embody the blessings, work through the burdens, acknowledge the harm, and then embody the healing and do the hard work of repair.

The flip side to overresponsibility is being underly responsible, being in denial, and being unwilling to examine or acknowledge things that have happened and your relationship to them. If you cannot accept the choices and lives of your ancestors, you cannot move toward healing.

It's essential to discern what is yours, what repair you wish to do, and how you can support collective liberation. I believe the greatest gift you can give toward cultural healing is your willingness to acknowledge all impact. You can learn to turn toward acknowledgment. You can learn to not minimize at any level: personal, family, cultural, or systemic. My wish is that we came to this work with more playfulness, excitement, curiosity, and joy. It doesn't have to be so heavy and laden with shame. We get to do the work of acknowledgment. As a descendant of settler-colonizers, I get to do the work of repair. It is a blessing and an honor, not a hardship.

You can build capacity to be with what is. It's a vast work. And it doesn't end with acknowledgment. This is life work we remain engaged in.

## What If I Committed Harm?

While the focus of this book is on helping survivors of sexual violence find their way home to their bodies and their pleasure, it's important to note that we all have the potential to cause harm.

If your boundaries were violated, especially at a young age, it may be that you have also violated someone else's boundaries. You can also violate someone without being violated. If so, part of your healing will include acknowledging the harm you perpetrated. While you likely have huge amounts of shame about your actions, it is important to get compassionate support that can help you bear the weight of your actions.

Just as your ancestors may have both created and received harm, the same may be true of you. How do you start to acknowledge the impact you have created? How do you begin to forgive yourself, or at least have compassion? Because until you practice some self-love, you are stuck in shame's shadowy grasp. Trust that painful as it may be, the process of acknowledgment will do you good and help you step into accountability. This is the path back to dignity. Again, get loving support. Be completely transparent with a practitioner whom you trust about what happened. Allow them to help you come back home to yourself so you can repair and move forward with your life without this big, terrible thing hanging over your head. Your integrity demands it.

## Last Thoughts for Month 5

Acknowledgment is an initial stage of a healing journey, as well as a practice you return to again and again throughout your process. There are ever-deeper layers of impact that can be noticed and acknowledged. Acknowledgment is also the beginning of acceptance. It is a naming of what is and what happened. It is the foundation that justice is built on.

While it can be scary to turn toward what is and name it, it is also profoundly powerful. When you are finally ready to move out of denial and face truth, you embody courage. Acknowledging is scary work, so move slowly, sweetly, and gently with your psyche and nervous system, and get immense loving support.

**In conclusion, this Month you will:**

- ¤ Complete the Month 5 worksheets in the appendix. You can also download this month's worksheets at www.pavinimoray.com/ttb-bonus.html.

- ¤ Practice for the Month: acknowledge the not-ready-yet of denial with compassion.

- ¤ Return to your resilience practices from Month 4 as needed. Go slow and gentle in your acknowledgment work.

- ¤ Add something to your altar that represents your work of acknowledgment.

- ¤ Complete Ritual 5: Acknowledgment.

## Ritual 5: Acknowledgment

### Preparation

- ¤ The purpose of this ritual is to acknowledge what has happened in the past and to understand the unacknowledged trouble in your ancestry.

- ¤ You can do this at your healing altar or in another place where you will not be disturbed.

- ¤ You will need a notebook or voice recorder.

**Begin by setting a container of prayer as you read this aloud:**

*Sweet and bright ancestors,*
*I pray to you*
*for all that is unacknowledged in our lines*
*to be acknowledged.*
*I pray for what has been hidden or obfuscated*
*to be known and seen*

*so justice can follow.*
*Please help me know what is necessary to know.*
*Please help protect me from overwhelm*
*so I can support healing in moving through time,*
*so I can support healing to happen in me.*

**Next, cast a circle of protection with the help of your allies.**

Call out to the trusted spiritual sources of protection you already have. This may be deities, guardians, the elements, or relationships with animals, stones, holy places, herbs, or anything from the green world. Invite each to come toward you, and pause until you sense they are present.

Then, with their support, imagine a layer of protection that goes all around you. You can visualize it if you like, or feel it.

For this ritual in particular, extra layers of protection will not be overkill, so take your time.

Invite connection with your ancestral guide.

Check in and ask if there is anything they want you to know: offerings received or offerings requested, cocoon of prayer, any dead ready to transition to the realm of the ancestors, and so on.

When this is complete, ask your guide to help you understand the trouble in this line, but in a way that is accessible and not too much for your system to bear.

When you invite in acknowledgment, you counteract any strategies of denial or minimization in the line. To be clear, you are not asking to understand the specific details of every trauma, but rather the overarching shape or themes of the trouble.

This could be a viewing of the trouble from thirty thousand feet above it, or seeing it on a movie screen. Basically, you're giving your bloodline the opportunity to have any harm witnessed, so that afterward healing can occur. It is imperative that you remain boundaried while doing this. If you're flooded or triggered with too much information, the healing cannot happen. Make your request to your guide considering the actual space you have to witness at this moment. Remember that your guide can easily translate the information in a gentle way you can understand.

Once you have a sense of what happened, ask your guide for the next ritual step. Do they wish to pursue healing at this time? If so, what would that look like?

After they share with you, assess your own capacity. Are you willing and ready to move forward? Do you need an integration break? Either way is fine.

If you would like to continue the healing ritual, rely on your guide to lead the way forward.

If it is time for a break, close out with gratitude for your guide and allies.

Say a prayer for your own good life.

Make notes of the information you receive.

Dissolve the circle while keeping the protection intact.

NOTE   *If any information you have received during this ritual feels heavy, overwhelming, or confusing, please seek out support quickly. That could be a good friend, a therapist, or an ancestral lineage healing practitioner. Sometimes bearing witness can have quite an impact on your heart. This is also a good moment to do some spiritual hygiene for your body and your space.*

# Month 6
## *Justice Moon*

It's true, no healing without justice.
But justice is an inside job.
Not retribution nor collapse.
Not forgiveness nor punishment.
Some moments, violence seems warranted
But at what cost, in terms of your good life?
Justice as Belonging, as Dignity,
Joy as justice.
Not rising above, nor sinking beneath,
Instead, dwelling warmly alive, you all present tense.
A living tribute to what happened.
A breathing testament to what can happen next.
Proof that healing is real, like magick.
Here's your opportunity for agency, do it.
Make your own life beautiful and Just.

## *Moon of Justice Practice*

*Breathing in,*
*I am healing,*
*breathing out,*
*I am justice.*

Make of your body a home for justice. Train your attention to feel what justice is, as you live it. Not waiting for others to change, to heal, to do or say anything. Claim your justice like the treasure it is.

Let your lineage ripple, echo, tremble with this new shape of rightness.

# MONTH 6

# Justice Moon

Reaching Month 6 means you're almost halfway through this process. Congratulations! You have been slowly building an excellent foundation for doing the work of healing sexual trauma in your ancestral lineages and yourself.

This Month is about justice. Complete healing is impossible without justice. Harm must stop before justice can manifest. Part of healing is creating a definition of justice that matches who you are right now, and this is a piece of your work this Month.

## What Is Justice?

The concept of justice is complex and nuanced. Because most of us have learned that justice equals retribution and punishment, let's start with what justice is not.

Any of the following ideas can be part of justice, but none of them holds the entirety of justice.

Justice is not a state. Justice is not a cosmic or karmic achievement. It is not legal punishment for perpetrators. Justice is not retribution, nor is it forgiveness. It's not vengeance or retaliation, either. Denying what happened is not justice.

Justice is not holding bad thoughts and feelings in your body while waiting for someone else to do their work. You do not need to be the accountability police, and seeing yourself that way does not serve your good life. Your healing is not dependent upon the actions of others.

Justice is not developing competency despite whatever happened; that is, you don't just build competence over collapse and call it good. Justice isn't a magickal time machine that takes you back to before the hard thing happened and restores life to a preimpact state.

When folks consider justice, a lot of times what they're hoping for is a return to the time before the impact happened: "I want it to be just like it was." "I want to erase what happened." "I want to go back in time to before it happened so I can live and have an experience that is free of this impact."

When you say or feel these things, you have more work to do with acknowledging. Take your time.

What happened, happened.

Everything that happened to you, happened to you.

What happened to your ancestors, happened to your ancestors.

Everything your ancestors did, they did.

Acceptance that something happened is a necessary step before justice.

## What Is Embodied Justice?

Justice is self-created and self-defined. What I love about holding justice in this way is that you don't need to wait for someone else to get right in order for you to have the justice you need. You get to figure out what it means for you, and then create that set of circumstances.

We know we can't go back in time and make something unhappen. So the question becomes: How do you live your best life? When your life is what you want it to be—when you have the capacity to have the relationships you want, and to accept into your life the good stuff that you choose—justice lives inside of you, and you live inside of it.

**Justice is alive.** What feels like justice to you will change as you grow and heal. The shift in focus from placing attention on perpetrators (and what you hope happens to them) to paying attention to what you want for yourself and your communities is huge.

**Justice is embodied.** Acknowledgment is an embodied process. It is slow work to come to the point where you say, "Yes, that happened," and to feel your feelings about that. Healing is not linear, so there may be layers of emotion as you spiral deeper into acknowledging all the everything. You may admit one layer of what happened, only to come back later to acknowledge another deeper layer.

**Justice acknowledges what happened and the impact.** How do you find peace with what happened? I hope I've convinced you of the necessity for acknowledgment. After that happens, things are usually quite stirred up. Coming to acceptance and peace is another stage of the healing process. Coming to peace does not mean you tacitly approve of what happened; it does not mean you forgive or condone. Rather, it means that your internal state can bear to say "yes, that happened" without feeling flooded.

When you acknowledge what happened, you must feel the feelings that come with it. Grief, rage, impotence, powerlessness, regret, loss, overwhelm, despair, longing, disbelonging . . . all the impact and the emotions that come with it.

**Justice supports your good life.** Embodied justice includes feeling safe with yourself and your emotions inside your body and experience. You get to feel calm, relaxed, and easy. You have permission to be at peace, even though those fucked-up things happened. Justice is you getting to live a good life. You can practice joy as justice. You get to consciously create your own life as art, as pleasure, as happiness—whatever you want to spend your life doing.

**Justice is accountability.** You allow those who have done harm to bear the weight of their choices without you having to hold them accountable. Justice means you are unburdened from this labor unless you want it. It takes a lot of work and effort to hold someone accountable for their choices and actions; justice means you are the only person you need to hold accountable.

When you wait for someone else to become accountable so you can heal, you are not a safe person with yourself. You outsource your safety if you link your healing to someone else's process. Any time you outsource safety to someone else, meaning someone else's behavior has to look, sound, or be a certain way, you deny yourself sovereignty. It's great if someone who has done harm wants to repair and make amends; but even if they never do, you still get to heal. That's justice. You get to live your good life, regardless of what others choose.

## Justice Is an Inside Job

There may well be some things that haven't been resolved or repaired, and perhaps they never will be. For example, maybe the person who perpetrated those actions has died. Does that mean you have to live without justice? Not if you can create justice for yourself.

When violations happen, it can feel like an equal and opposite reaction should happen to the person who did that, but that's not necessarily how it works. It is a paradigm shift to consider that justice lives inside of you, not outside. The paradigm shift here is engaging a different question by turning your focus from the external (What should happen to that person?) to the internal (What do I want for my good life?).

Ironically, this is the ultimate "Fuck you!"

There is a moment in healing where you may realize that the people who acted against you or your lineage did not determine the outcome of your life. You become informed by what happened, rather than being defined by it.

Consider this for a moment; really take a breath into it: What if, just for one breath, your good life is your justice?

The act of sexual violence is threaded with an attempt to take power. Often the intention can be to break and shatter another person. You do not need to be complicit in this. You can, with loving support, gather the pieces of yourself back.

Violence or violation happened to you (and/or your ancestors). While there may have been an attempt to break you, it did not succeed. Changing your perspective from victim to survivor is powerful, and there are many survivors who live lives of love, brilliance, and connection. Your trauma need not define you.

Jyn—a persona who stands for a composite of my clients—is a survivor of childhood sexual abuse. For a long time, they waited for their perpetrator to take responsibility for his actions. He never did. Jyn started on a healing path, only to find themselves afraid that if they healed, their perpetrator would get off without justice. This is something that can happen too: we hold our wounds close, afraid that healing means erasure of the violation. Jyn had to learn to trust that their own healing did not exonerate their perpetrator.

It's important to understand that causing harm and being unwilling to repair it has huge internal consequences for the person who does that. Talk about feeling unsafe inside oneself and disconnected from one's own goodness! It is impossible to do a horrible thing and then live a wonderful life. There is a price.

You get to embody the glittering expression of your destiny that you are here to fulfill. Suppose you are willing to do justice work for yourself and, by extension, in your communities. In that case, you are practicing the opposite of reactionary or retributive justice.

I once heard that the opposite of love isn't hate; it's apathy. Likewise, the opposite of harm isn't vengeance or retribution; it's beauty. When you create justice for yourself, you are centering yourself in your own life. You are creating a beautiful life.

I'm going to say it again. When you create embodied justice for yourself, you are centering yourself in your own life. You're not an observer. You're not on the sidelines. You're not a victim. You are the central agent. This is so beautiful, and it's the first thing that I invite you to consider this month.

What is justice for you?

What does it feel like?

How does it look?

What are the criteria that you set for yourself to be able to really say that justice has happened, and therefore healing can happen?

## PAVINI'S STORY

Here is part of my own story and exploration of justice. I share it to provide an example.

My ancestors told me there is no healing without justice. What is justice? I will never live in a body untouched by sexual violence. No matter how much healing I do, no matter how much I practice embodiment, erotic liberation, boundaries, and consent, I will never, never live in a body that has not endured things that no body should have to endure.

This body holds multiple truths. It holds the truth that I am grateful for who I am, and I would not prefer to be different. It holds the question of who I would be had these acts of violation never occurred. In this latest wave of the sexual trauma healing process, I have questioned what healing is and if it is even possible to do.

How can I be with what is, while I also move toward healing? How do I accept and also change? How do I accept what has happened—that this is the body I live in—and how do I also change my body to be one of strength?

I long for steady, quiet power that is embodied and just. I long for the wide view—the acceptance that healing happens in degrees, that some wounds take more than one lifetime to heal, and that that is okay. I long for acceptance of the degrees of healing I have accomplished, rather than constantly focusing on all that remains unhealed.

Here's what I believe about healing. Two things are required: acknowledgment and justice. Wounds cannot fully heal without these two medicines. They can partially heal, and heal enough for those of us bearing them to be able to survive and even do good work; and yet, though they are clean, they remain painful.

What is acknowledgment? Everything that happened to me, happened to me. This has been my mantra for months. It's taken so much work to even get here, to be able to say this. There is space in me to acknowledge the entirety of my experience: the childhood sexual abuse, the incest, the spousal rape, the transgenerational trans-mission of sexual trauma that I carry from my ancestors. Everything that happened to us, happened to us.

The starkness of this acknowledgment feels clean. There is no justice that can make what happened unhappen. There is no way to ever answer the question of who I would be without these violations. What is, is. Sometimes that makes my stomach wrench and my skin crawl. Sometimes there is a quiet widening into the fullness of my embodied form, which brings the awareness that this is a source of great power for me.

Acknowledgment as a practice is personally and culturally challenging. Denial has been a steady friend, but one who rarely returns what it borrows: my memories. I want all of me back. I'm ready to open all of the doors of all of the locked nightmare rooms because I deserve to have all of me, and all of me deserves to belong. Fuck that familial pattern of turning attention away from the wound, hoping it will go away. It hasn't, and I'm not passing it on.

Acknowledgment is the practice of turning my attention to the wounds, to truly see the monsters, the train wrecks, and the rape and abuse from once-beloved men in my life. Even as I identify these men, I worry. What ramifications will I face for breaking silence? What further violence is heading my way? To acknowledge the existence and brutal impact of these three men is to acknowledge my own powerlessness and the ownership, possessiveness, and disregard all three had for my personhood, even as they "loved" me.

The dismissal of my dignity as a human being who deserves choice; the invasion of my body, even when I voiced my choice; the blatant lack of care they all displayed for the impact they created in my body, my relationships, my capacity to trust, my capacity for pleasure and erotic freedom, and even my ability to feel love, to give and receive love.

How many times have I asked my sweet partner, "Are you loving me right now? How do you know?" Because I cannot feel it. Can you look at this, fathers, uncles, husbands, can you merely see without turning away what you have done? I bear witness: those things happened. Can you bear the load of your transgression without collapsing into worthlessness, shame, or aggression? Was your dignity lost when you violated mine?

Acknowledging that these men took what was not theirs to take and gave not one fuck while doing it breaks my heart so completely that it is difficult to imagine repair is indeed possible. Acknowledgment is expensive because it means examining my role, my silence, my terror, my anxiety. At least I've broken free of this terrible idea that somehow I could have been complicit. I was not complicit in anything other than my own survival, fuck you very much.

The feeling of powerlessness is beyond unbearable. To acknowledge these perpetrators is to acknowledge that this is a true thing in the world. Humans violate other humans and don't give a damn, and there is no justice system in the world that could ever undo the harm, ever.

I'm sick as I write these words, and I write them in honor of my ancestor burned alive by her husband. I write them in honor of my mother. I write them in honor of my own sweet self who has survived the ashy, trauma-filled wasteland of these violations. I write these words in honor of my children so they may be free of these abusive patterns. I write these words in honor of the black heart of innocence, the rose that grows from the bombed-out rebel, my heart.

## WHAT IS JUSTICE FOR ME? (AN EXAMPLE)

Writing this is me providing justice for me.

In doing so, I claim rank among all the victims of sexual violence who blessedly will never understand the impulse and follow through to intentionally perpetrate sexual harm upon another.

¤ Justice is getting to be soft instead of brittle.

¤ Justice is marrying my sweet partner with all of our cherished chosen family as witnesses in a sacred oak grove in the California hills.

¤ Justice is professional success.

¤ Justice is creating financial well-being and security for myself.

¤ Justice is a sexuality that I inhabit exactly how I want.

¤ Justice is choosing movement and dance.

¤ Justice is vulnerably opening, again and again, to receive support for healing my deep wounds.

¤ Justice is choosing transparency about what happened to me.

¤ Justice is my thirteen-year-old child understanding transgenerational trauma and naming my role in healing it in our bloodlines.

¤ Justice is knowing without a doubt that I belong to my loving ancestors, and feeling that when I die, they will welcome me home.

None of these things alone is justice, but when I put them all together, and I hold the weight of the life I live against the violations that occurred, I see that there is some balance here.

Somehow, I thought justice would be more assertive, louder, more definite, more precise. I thought finding justice would be about the righting of wrongs, the undoing of harm, but it's not because it cannot be. What is, is.

Instead, I find justice in the quieter moments of my life, the moments when I can accept the goodness I have.

Justice finally is how I place my attention on love, the feeling of it, the giving of it, and the receiving of it.

I get to feel worthy of love. I get to be here. I get to be well in all the ways. This is my justice.

## Last Thoughts for Month 6

Justice requires your participation, body and mind. In your body, you learn to create internal safety. In your mind, you discern what you need to live your good life regardless of what others choose. You choose you. Say it out loud: "I choose me." You get to prioritize your wellness over the comfort of others.

**In conclusion, this Month you will:**

¤ Complete the Month 6 worksheets in the appendix. You can also download this month's worksheets at www.pavinimoray.com/ttb-bonus.html.

¤ Daily breath practice: "Breathing in, I am Healing. Breathing out, I am Justice."

¤ Add something to your healing altar that represents justice to you.

¤ Complete Ritual 6: Justice.

# Ritual 6: Justice

## Preparation

¤ The purpose of this ritual is justice to heal the trouble.

¤ You can do this at your healing altar or in another place where you will not be disturbed.

¤ You will also need a notebook or voice recorder.

**Begin by setting a container of prayer as you read this aloud:**

*Ancestors, I pray for embodied justice.*
*I pray for justice for all people.*
*Black people*
*Brown people*
*Indigenous people*
*Trans people*
*Fat people*
*Disabled people*
*People with less access to resources*
*People in prison*
*Marginalized people of all experiences*
*Colonized people*
*People living under oppressive regimes*
*People who have faced historical trauma*
*People who are currently in harmful situations*
*People who have committed harm*
*I pray for justice for all people.*
*I pray for justice for my good life.*
*I pray for justice for my ancestors.*
*I pray for justice for anyone harmed by my ancestors.*
*I pray for justice for the Earth.*
*I pray for justice for me.*
*I pray for justice for all of my descendants.*

**Next, cast a circle of protection with the help of your allies.**

Call out to the trusted spiritual sources of protection you already have. This may be deities, guardians, the elements, or relationships with animals, stones, holy places, herbs, or anything from the green world. Invite each to come toward you, and pause until you sense they are present.

Then, with their support, imagine a layer of protection that goes all around you. You can visualize it if you like, or feel it.

Drop in and create connection with your ancestral guide.

Check in and ask if there is anything they would like to share.

Check in about the offerings, those received and those requested.

Check in on the cocoon of prayer. Are any dead ready to transition?

Let the guide do that work before continuing.

Next, ask your guide if they are ready to do ritual justice work for this line. If so, what do they recommend?

Allow your guide to lead this ritual.

When they have completed what is necessary, ask if they would be willing to offer healing to you, so you can update and reflect any healing that has occurred in the line.

Receive healing from your guide, and notice what happens.

Make notes of the information you receive.

Close this ritual with a prayer for your own good life, and thank your guide and the allies who showed up.

End the ritual while keeping the protection intact.

# Month 7
## *You Know*

Healing beats wilder and wider
Thrum-ta, thrum-ta, **thrum**
Ribs rattle the cage
Heart refuses jail
But your thorax is not outfitted
to fight shame, smoking in through cracks
"Don't outgrow your edges, stupid child,
stay here" shades mumble,
that poison chorus
Something deeper rumbles,
low murmur of ancestors
Quiet, beneath the anxious jangle

Remember
Here
Come down
To go low you have
to get under your diaphragm's stranglehold,
deep breaths, sighs and moans
Let your shoulders collapse,
no need to prop yourself up
You need
to get down to the Earth of you
Your true god, Belly
Your ground, fallow and rich
You know.
Your knowing knows.
Be from here.
Say
*"I am."*

## *Moon of Knowing Practice*

*I know.*

Who would you be if you trusted your own knowing?

What does knowing deep down in your belly, in your core, feel like?

This month, spend moments each and every day feeling into that deep body sensation of your knowing.

Opening a channel of listening to your depth, your viscera.

# Freedom Moon

This Month is about freedom. Welcome to your liberation!

Take a moment to appreciate all the work you've done, all the ways you have shown up for your healing, and all the sovereignty and foundational work you have accomplished.

This Month addresses two big blocks to your liberation: shame and disembodiment. Also, you will investigate choosing presence and adopting a practice mindset. Freedom involves learning to place your attention where you want it and trusting your knowing.

## Shame

"Talking about shame is my favorite!" said no one ever. However, talk about it we must, so you can start seeing how it keeps you bound. There is a high possibility (as in 100%!) that you feel some degree of shame about where you are. This is in terms of your life, your sexual expression, and your personhood. Shame is such a common experience, and it turns out that there are several excellent reasons why you experience it. When there is trauma, shame is always present. Shame is a by-product of trauma.

It's important to realize that shame is not something you are born with. Shame is something that was put on you and your ancestors. However, you do have a choice about how you interact with it. The problem is that shame prefers to remain hidden and is often invisible. When you turn your attention toward it, poof! It vanishes. At other times it is driving the bus, with you unawares.

Shame is a miasma. It's like a wafting cloud that prohibits your freedom. You feel it but can't see it. Shame is born from a good strategy gone sideways. Shame actually has a protective function. Although the particular signature of shame may vary slightly between individuals, at its core shame is a somatic mechanism insulating you from powerlessness. That's the thing that no one wants to feel. It's better to feel shame than it is to feel powerless.

The primary way that shame keeps you from experiencing powerlessness is by having you take responsibility for the situation that is catalyzing the shame. If you are somehow responsible, that means you're not a helpless victim. Clever, huh? It bounces you out of feeling powerless because now you're responsible.

However, shame also acts as an electric fence for your freedom.

Once you get zapped by the electric fence of shame, you probably don't venture near there again. The sensations of shame are often so uncomfortable that many people veer widely away from the perceived source of those sensations. This is where aversion comes in. We become averse to things that make us feel a certain yucky way.

The electric-fence metaphor works well in the realm of sex. For example, if you express a desire to a lover and they say no, you may feel shame about having that desire. And your shame may keep you far away from ever asking for that thing again.

The sensations of shame can also get wired with arousal. For example, I've had many clients who struggle because they fantasize about nonconsensual sex, even though they don't really want that. In some cases they have been survivors of sexual abuse who experienced arousal as part of the abuse. Neurologically speaking, this is a challenge to unravel, but it is doable.

The somatic strategy that links feeling shame with feeling arousal goes like this: if I can be turned on by something I have or had no power over, I retain my power. My wise monkey brain has devised a solution. I figured out how to flip the out-of-control thing into something I desire.

We can look at rape fantasies through this lens. Many people have shame about having rape or incest fantasies. They feel confused about why this feels hot. However, making something you probably don't want in real life into a fantasy is a somatic strategy to make the powerless situation more manageable. And sometimes we long to give up our power, our responsibility. As an adult, there are many safer ways to explore this consensually.

There are other things shame takes care of. One is toxic loyalty. Shame keeps you loyal to a broken system, such as a dysfunctional family. Shame's unconscious mechanism understands that if you heal your shame, you will no longer belong to that dysfunctional system. But if you also feel that you need to belong to that system, you have a problem because those things feel incompatible. You cannot be shame-free and belong to the system. Shame solves that problem by keeping you connected, at least in theory.

Healing from sexual trauma often raises the topic of loyalty. When you speak a thing aloud, you are violating a loyalty that demands silence and complicity. You step out of belonging in a system guarded by shame. Even if you are stepping out of your dysfunctional family dynamics for the sake of your healing, you will likely still feel grief. They are *your* fucked-up dynamics, after all, which are likely familiar and comforting in certain ways.

The narrative of shame is about belonging. It goes like this: "If anyone knew this secret, this story, this thing, this thought, I would be rejected. I wouldn't belong anymore." And some part of you understands "rejection" to mean you would die, forsaken by your pack, alone on the frozen tundra. Your life force would be ebbing away. You would be completely abandoned and utterly alone. Of course, none of this is happening at the conscious level.

Still, this is where shame is an electric fence. It says, "Don't go there. Here are those uncomfortable sensations. Don't share that, don't reveal that; stay hidden, stay secret." You can see how this is a protective system. It's designed to keep you safe and belonging.

However, the strategy of remaining in shame has a high cost. You can see that cost if you think about shame as a burglar alarm in your home. Let's say you decide you need a home security system, so you shop around and choose one advertised as the best on the market. It costs $100,000 a month, but hey, at least it's keeping you safe. If anything happens, it'll go off. You'll hear the alarm and get to safety. The problem is that you're spending so much money all the time for a system that rarely needs to go off. How often are burglars trying to break into your house? Hopefully never.

It's like that with shame. The price you pay for shame's "protection" is believing you are broken, flawed, and unlovable. Parts of you never get to show up and are always alone because they can never be shown without suffering the consequences.

This is all invisible, which is why it's an invisible electric fence. It can be very, very difficult to see where you're being affected by shame because it feels like, "Oh, that's just the way it is."

An electric fence just looks like a piece of wire until you get zapped by it. Afterward, you're like, "Holy shit. That's an electric fence. I know exactly where that is, and I'm going to stay far away from it."

For folks who have any kind of marginalized or oppressive experience—folks with disabilities, fat folks, folks of color, trans folks, queer folks, or anyone else who doesn't fit into the "normal," cisgender, heterosexual, white, able-bodied, young Protestant center—all of you are going to have an extra dose of shame put on you by the dominant culture. You are going to have to address shame at the personal and the identity levels. Personal shame is shame you hold about your unique personality. Identity-level shame is shame attached to any identities you hold. Fun times!

For all these reasons, it is an important healing step to consciously seek shame out by asking yourself: "What are the things I'm ashamed of? Am I ashamed about my body? Am I ashamed about things I've done? Am I ashamed about the way I show up in a relationship? Am I ashamed about my selfishness, my greed, my whatever?"

You start to name your shame. Shame wants to keep you silent, so you start to break your silence. When you break that silence, it interrupts the process. As we have learned from Brené Brown, vulnerability is how to get out of shame.

If there is some part of you that you're deeply ashamed of, you start to claim it by naming it out loud. For example, you say, "I have shame about my belly." "I have shame about the way I eat food." Whatever it is, you start to tell people about it. You start to refuse to be complicit in it.

Get to know the sensations of shame. For me, shame is hot. It's gripping. It's smoky. It's a spiral that goes down my body and casts me plummeting into worthlessness. It's terrible, but not unbearable. It's not very pleasant, but here's the thing: it only consists of sensations, emotions, and narratives. It's not real outside of you.

How do you want to be with yourself when you feel those things? You have lots of choices here, because you could join in with that chorus of haters inside your head. Or you can bring in your wise older self who can say, "Oh, sweetheart, you're feeling shame right now. Let's gently interrupt it."

You can also develop a fierce protector part of you who fights internally on your behalf when you feel shame: "Get the fuck away from me, shame." You can also just start to get good at being with the sensations of shame without following whatever story they are telling. This sounds like, "Yes, this is just that sensation of falling into the pit of my stomach, cringing inward, and collapsing. I'm just going to follow it." You can get good at being with it on a sensation/body level.

I know I'm making it sound really easy. I don't think it's really easy, but it is doable. I do it, and I invite you to do it. I am no longer willing to be complicit with shame in order to protect myself from powerlessness. I'd rather just deal with the powerlessness and say, "Okay, here's the place where I feel really powerless. This sucks. What are the sensations? How can I be kind to myself here? How can I make vulnerability one of my practices?"

How can you make vulnerability one of your practices?

What shame hates most is being seen—especially being seen with compassion. In fact, when shame is compassionately witnessed, it often deflates just like those blow-up used-car lot roadside Santas or dinosaurs that are inflated from the bottom. Once the blower is turned off, the creature just collapses. Well, that's what happens to shame. Shame cannot exist in the light of love and acceptance.

## Understanding Dissociation and Disembodiment

There are three D's that help humans manage overwhelming experiences: denial, dissociation, and disembodiment. You cannot choose presence if you don't understand the value of all three. We discussed denial in Month 5, so now let's take a closer look at dissociation and disembodiment.

The sensations and emotions of life can only be experienced from within a living container: your body. Your body is the site where you experience life while you're alive.

Of course, life's sensations and emotions can be overwhelming. Your nervous system is there to help you meet each situation, but life has sped up until it's moving faster than ever. Human nervous systems have not evolved quickly enough to keep up with the pace of modernity. Many people are often overwhelmed with information or stimuli.

The human brain can process eleven million bits of information every second, but our conscious minds can handle only forty to fifty bits of information per second. That means real life often moves too fast for us to attend to consciously. To survive, we need to have strategies that help us react automatically. Much of daily life is automatic because it needs to be.

Sometimes there is too much information coming into your system. Your system gets flooded, and you experience overwhelm.

## Dissociation

Humans have various strategies for dealing with that overwhelm. One of the automatic strategies humans have developed to help us deal with overwhelm is dissociation. Dissociation means removing association, or your attention, from a situation. Whether or not we realize it, everybody dissociates from time to time. Basically, you draw your attention away from whatever is causing you distress, and place your attention elsewhere.

Dissociation is cool because you can move your focus and place it outside your immediate dire situation. When I realized I could do this, I was seventeen. In a restaurant work accident, I cut my finger to the bone and went to the emergency room. They didn't give me anything for the pain. I remember lifting up and out of my body and watching them sew up my finger. I thought, *Oh, I have a superpower.* When you dissociate, the intensity of everything suddenly lessens.

Every strategy we use is effective in some sense of the word, which is why we use them. I want you to hear how valuable dissociation is, because it helps you survive. It helped me get through that emergency room visit without shrieking, screaming, hitting, or kicking.

Some common ways that we all dissociate without realizing it include:

¤ Daydreaming

¤ Binge-watching a TV show

¤ Doomscrolling on the socials

Dissociation is indeed a gift from nature that helps us survive tough situations. However, I like to imagine that eons ago, when someone handed out the blessings of humanity, this one had a big orange warning label: "Only to be used when absolutely necessary." Like the anarchists we are (ever ripped off a mattress label?), humans ripped off that warning. Watch out, world: here comes a species with the unique ability to check out of life whenever they want!

When you dissociate, you take your attention and slide it quickly away from your center, away from your feelings and sensations. You move your awareness elsewhere. Some people dissociate outside of themselves, above, behind, or beside their body. Some people go deeply inward, hiding their awareness in the very core of their being.

Dissociation is not a problem in and of itself. Giving yourself a mental break isn't inherently bad. However, disconnecting from feeling yourself and being present in your life can be costly for you and your relationships when dissociation is the only tool you have for dealing with hard situations.

To be clear, most of us are not consciously choosing to move our attention away from our bodies. It just becomes easier and easier. We even have stock phrases that promote dissociation, like "Just don't think about it." "Oh, forget about that." "Sounds like you need a drink."

Dissociation as a way of life has huge costs. Let's say you're driving on the highway dissociated. All around you are other people who are also checked out and not in their skin. They're not feeling their sensations; they're not attending to what's happening. How many fatal accidents happen because someone is on their phone, distracted, not attending to the life-or-death task of driving?

## Disembodiment

Disembodiment is the term for chronic dissociation from feeling and sensation. It's when you live outside your experience. It's possible to disembody from a part of your body or from all of your body.

Dissociation means you move your attention away from being present for a little while. Then you move your attention back to center. Disembodiment can mean you live outside your body full time. It means you're steering your skin suit around, but where is the you who is doing the steering? Are you on autopilot? Are you ten feet above your body? Are you twenty miles behind? Are you a year in front of you, or maybe buried deep inside?

Although the strategy of disembodiment may have served you well historically, and may continue to serve you well sometimes, let's look at some potential costs you may experience. Studying a particular region of your body helps highlight the costs of chronic disembodiment. For this example, let's talk about the pelvis, since this is a book about healing sexuality.

The pelvis is a fraught body region for many folks. It's a locus of sexual stimulation, so a lot is happening down there, so many nerves and structures. There are few good support spaces to discuss your sexuality, receive care for it, and understand it. There's no operating manual that comes with your pelvis.

So many things exist within the physical structure of your pelvis: sensation, emotion, longing, fear, disgust, contraction, craving, shame, pleasure, pain, arousal, taboo, and confusion, to name a few. For example, many people believe the genitals are dirty, which comes from shame.

Those who are overwhelmed by this region of their body will disembody from their pelvis. They pull their attention away and keep it away. Sure, they may have sex or even pleasure, but they also may have a significant absence of sensation in this part of their body.

Many factors contribute to disinhabiting the pelvis, and often there are good reasons for doing so. But perhaps you get to a point when you again want access to your pelvis. You want to inhabit the lower part of your torso. You want to feel your genitals more deeply or explore your sexuality. You want to play, you want to learn, you want to connect. However, after years of disembodiment, your pelvis is asleep. It's numbed out. It's off limits, it's painful, or it's absent or blank. You find that reconnecting with the deep and sacred wellspring of your pelvis isn't easy because you've been gone so long. It takes time.

Suppose you extrapolate that level of disembodiment from your pelvis to your entire body. Disembodiment, or global dissociation from feeling and sensation, is a problem. You don't have access to your body, which is where you spend your life.

From inside your body you can connect with your humanity. It's where you can make good, heartfelt decisions with conscience and kindness. You can feel the impact you create, negative and positive. You feel the impact you experience. You feel love. Being embodied is how you make good, connected whole-body decisions that honor everyone's humanity.

Also, when you're connected with the Earth of your body, you're connected with the Earth itself. Thus, if you disembody, you also disconnect from the Earth. Then it becomes so much easier to extract, to strip-mine, to pollute, to poison. This is because you cannot feel.

How do you become aware of disembodiment? How do you learn to feel what you do not feel? Luckily, disembodiment has some tells. Symptoms of disembodiment include:

¤ Numbness

¤ Lack of sensation

¤ Chronic muscle tightness

¤ Forgetting to pee, eat, or drink

¤ Very few or no orgasms

¤ Being disconnected from your emotions

¤ Difficulty accessing playfulness

¤ Lack of access to desire

¤ High tolerance for pain, either emotional or physical

¤ Lack of access to creativity

You can become more aware of the places where you are not fully inhabiting your body and your life through embodiment practices. These can include meditation or any number of mindful body practices like dance, weightlifting, or martial arts. Remember, embodiment is the medicine for disembodiment.

To be clear, trauma creates an absence from our bodies. Trauma tells us that we're broken beyond repair and unworthy of love and pleasure. Trauma says the only safety is somewhere else instead of here and now in our bodies. Trauma tells us that our suffering is our due, that muddling through the tangle of our supposed "brokenness" is the real work.

This is not the way things are supposed to be. We are not damaged goods. We can learn to choose presence.

One more note on disembodiment. I am not suggesting that you must be 100 percent embodied at all times or else. As mentioned, dissociation is helpful as a way to take a break from overwhelm in your system. But make it a conscious practice rather than a constant way you live your life.

## Choosing Presence

Becoming present is a choice. When you become present, you choose to embody. You develop an awareness of your disembodiment. It also means committing to developing your capacity for your feelings and sensations. It means making conscious choices about when you need to check out and when you need to drop in.

Choosing presence means you feel everything you feel. It's not some blissful, enlightened state where you're like, "I am so present. I am so mindful." It's often deeply uncomfortable to be present. You feel everything: the good, the bad, and the ugly.

In healing, you decide to feel your feelings—all of your feelings—because the alternative has become too expensive. As one of my teachers, Richard Strozzi-Heckler, writes: "If we are capable of experiencing our sensations it's possible to laugh, cry, yell, demand, desire, protest, accept, and love. If we anesthetize ourselves from feeling sensation, our emotional range will shrink and with it the capacity for effective action, passion for life, and the ability to sustain meaningful relationships."

Choosing presence is a practice. What does it mean to be present? It means that you're here, now, with your body and your attention. You're in the now, you're feeling, you're attuning. You're listening to yourself and the needs of your organism. You're paying attention when you have to go pee. You're feeding yourself when you need to eat.

Relationally, you are deeply with others. I'm sure you've had experiences where you've been sitting with someone who is looking at you and nodding as you speak, but you do not feel they are present. You have the sense that their attention is elsewhere.

When you're present, you are here and now. You choose this because it feels good to have your attention here. To be fair, it doesn't always feel good in the short term. There are many situations you would rather not attend to. But in the long term, it feels good because you feel your life, you are present for your aliveness.

I love this quote from Henry David Thoreau: "I am alarmed when it happens that I have walked a mile into the woods bodily, without getting there in spirit.… It sometimes happens that I cannot easily shake off the village. The thought of some work will run in my head, and I am not where my body is—I am out of my senses. In my walks I would fain return to my senses. What business have I in the woods, if I am thinking of something out of the woods?"

I love his commitment to presence. When you are present, you give yourself the gift of being in your life. This is a practice that you choose to do repeatedly.

# What Is Sexual Freedom?

Author Susie Bright had this to say about most people's attitude toward freedom: "Not many people are actually looking for sexual liberation, at least not until they get to the end of a very weary road of dissatisfaction. That usually takes a decade or two. Liberation, per se, is not the sort of thing people count as tops on their to-do list."

Regardless, every person on Earth is born with the potential to feel erotically free. Sexual liberation is available to those who place their attention on it.

Sexual liberation is a process, not a goal. For the rest of your life, you will (if you so choose) be freeing yourself from all the rules you have swallowed, whether they are culturally constructed or self-imposed. For the rest of your days, you will be calling yourself home to erotic wholeness.

When I first started to learn about sexuality, somatics, and embodiment, one of my teachers said, "Sexuality is a road to freedom. It's not the easiest, but it's one of the most direct." Because sexuality is so core and central to our being here on the planet, it makes sense that it can become a weighty, charged topic. I speak with folks all the time who feel stuck in their sexuality, their relationships, their lives.

Sexual freedom matters because it is a place to gauge the importance you place on freedom in your own life through your practices. For most, sexual freedom is *not* super easy. Sometimes each breath, each moan, is hard won.

Each day you must choose to traverse the challenging road back to your body, back to your breath, back to your pleasure, back to trust and vulnerability and intimacy. Just as a path quickly becomes overgrown without traffic, this liberatory road of the body must constantly be trod and reinforced. You must continually reinforce the neural wiring you are consciously choosing for the sake of sexual liberation.

And yet we all feel and acknowledge the pull of liberation as an imperative of being human. We feel it. We deny it. And we get ourselves stuck, with the very purpose of later being able to set ourselves free.

Sexual liberation can be understood not as a state, but as a series of practices. It's the work you do to liberate yourself every day from the norms, narratives, oppressions, violences, and contractions that are constantly moving against a free, open, and flowing experience of embodied freedom.

# Practice Paradigm

Richard Strozzi-Heckler says, "You become what you practice, and you are always practicing something." There are conscious practices and unconscious practices; practices you have decided to explore, and habits enacted on autopilot. When you choose what you practice consciously, you decide how you allot your attention in your life. What you practice determines the results you get.

Were you forced to practice anything as a kid? If so, your relationship with practice probably got damaged. As an adult, you may need to relearn the value of practice that is not coercive. You can practice anything you want.

If you want to make a personal change, practice is imperative.

The steps of change are:

- Awareness
- Choice
- Practice
- Integration

Personal change happens through developing awareness. You learn to pay attention to your survival responses and the internal landscape of your body, including your subtle sensations and emotions. You develop somatic awareness; you become aware of what's happening inside you.

Once you know what's happening inside you, you can make choices. For example, you become aware of your body and notice you are always holding your shoulders tightly. You get curious about that and notice that tightness happens when you're around certain people. Let's say it happens when you're around your sister.

You notice your narratives. You become aware of them. What is your story about your shoulder tightness? "Oh, my shoulders help keep me safe. They help hold me together so I don't fly off the handle with my sister."

Then you can start making current choices. Perhaps you think, "It's true my sister was a bully when we were kids. But she's changed. I want to feel more relaxed around her."

Now you begin to attend to your practices. Your practice in this situation becomes, "When I'm around my sister, I'll practice noticing the tension in my shoulders. If it feels safe, I'll relax."

As you do that practice over time, relaxation around your sister becomes integrated into who you are. Your new narrative is, "It's safe to relax around my sister."

Holding a practice paradigm for your life is how you can get the good stuff. For example, if you have a narrative that you're unlovable, you've likely been practicing that tired old bone for years. At this point let's say you have become aware of the narrative. You've done enough healing work that you are ready to move on, ready to practice something else.

What will you practice instead? Maybe you decide you want to feel lovable. First, decide why. Knowing the reason why you're doing something keeps you committed to your practices. You decide, "I want to feel lovable so I am no longer distracted by these narratives of unworthiness and so I can just get on with what I'm here to do."

That's a great reason.

Now, how will you know when you have made the change? What will be different in your life? How will you act and think differently from the way you act and think now?

"I'll be satisfied that I am lovable when most of the time I'm not saying shitty things to myself in my head anymore."

What are the practices for feeling lovable? Here are a few sample practices:

¤ Whenever my partner says "I love you," I will try to feel it.

¤ Each night, I will rub rose oil on my heart and say the names of the people who love me out loud.

¤ I will look at myself in the mirror and say, "I love you."

## Resistance to Practice

Did you get brainwashed about practice? If so, you won't be surprised that resistance often rears up when you choose a change practice. For example, you decide you want to be a person who moves every day. You choose to go on a walk every morning. You get off to a great start, but then you go out of town and miss a day. When you return, you find it difficult to pick your practice back up.

Unfortunately, many of us have had negative experiences with practice. If we were forced to practice a musical instrument or didn't establish solid self-discipline when it came to something we wanted to learn, practice becomes fraught.

We know we should practice; we know learning requires repetition. And yet we still get in our own way by resisting practice. This resistance can show up in a variety of ways. Some narratives that accompany resistance to practice include:

¤ I don't want to.

¤ I don't have the time.

¤ That's boring.

¤ I'll do it later.

Resistance is a protector. It is there to protect you from failing by ensuring that you pre-emptively fail. You'll never know what could have been if you don't practice. Resisting practice often means holding on to control. If you don't practice, you will surely fail, and that way you remain in control of the outcome, even though it's negative.

Different parts of you want different things. There is a part that wants to learn to play the guitar, and there is another part that worries if you know how to play the guitar, you'll want to perform, which is terrifying. All of this is to say that resistance to practice is perfectly normal. It should be expected. So what do you do about it?

First, acknowledge the protection your resistance is trying to offer you: "Thank you for taking care of me, resistance." You don't even need to know what it is taking care of.

Next, discern what information your resistance is offering about the practice in question:

- ¤ Is it the wrong practice for you?

- ¤ Is there another practice that would be more useful?

- ¤ Are you scared of what will happen if you engage in this practice?

- ¤ Do you need more support?

Almost no practice is the right practice forever. Just because you start a practice does not mean you have to do that practice until you die. You do a practice until you have achieved what you need from it. If you stop a practice, you can always return to it later.

If you start a practice and then your resistance gets the better of you, you may feel shame. Here's a simple solution for that: just tell someone. This sounds like, "I had a practice that I was going for a walk every day, and I stopped, and I haven't done it for three weeks. I'm telling you because I want to start my practice again."

Then do that practice once, and see what happens. Your friend may even go with you to offer support!

Sometimes you get resistant and discern that it's time to say goodbye to a particular practice. It's important to acknowledge the end of it. Don't just trail off. You can say, "Okay, I'm not going to practice that anymore," and then feel gratitude for what you've gained from that practice.

Find the practices that light you up, the practices you want to do. If and when you get resistant about a practice, stop and discern before giving up on that practice. It's surprising how little you sometimes need to practice to have something shift in your life.

You can date a practice before you marry it. I often will start a practice and say, "I'm going to do this for the next seven days," or "I'm going to do this for the next three weeks." Give it a short time container you know you can complete. Completion builds self-trust.

NOTE *Even the smallest life transition, like a weekend trip, can disrupt your practice, so go gently here. Add structure, add support.*

## Writing Your Liberation Story

Did you know you can write your story of sexual liberation, even if you don't feel erotically free yet? Begin by envisioning where you want to be in terms of your sexual freedom. The purpose of this narrative is not to map out the exact path to your liberation, since we've established that liberation is an ongoing journey, not a fixed destination.

Instead, create a narrative arc that demonstrates your commitment to sexual freedom throughout your life. Craft the story as if it has already happened. By doing so, you open a space for this reality to exist in the world. This narrative will serve as a path, affirming that your erotic liberation is not optional but necessary and inevitable. Understand that the unique journey to get there will likely differ from person to person.

Here's an example of how writing out history before a thing occurs can be helpful. During my second pregnancy, I wrote a narrative for my daughter's birth before it happened, detailing the ending I desired. Although her birth didn't precisely match the story, it bore similarities in key aspects. This exercise involved envisioning and manifesting the desired outcome without being overly attached to specific details.

I encourage you to write the liberation story of your sexuality, creating the path in your imagination and affirming its inevitability, even if the methods may vary. This exercise is about manifesting the commitment to your erotic liberation.

## Last Thoughts for Month 7

I don't believe it is presumptuous to say that shame exists at the root of all stuckness. That means liberation is the antithesis of shame. Liberatory practices that confront shame help it shift to spaciousness and freedom. Your freedom matters, and it's worth doing the hard work to excavate shame in order to live freely and openly.

**In conclusion, this Month you will:**

- ¤  Complete the Month 7 worksheets in the appendix. You can also download this month's worksheets at www.pavinimoray.com/ttb-bonus.html.
- ¤  Write your erotic liberation story.
- ¤  Daily practice: Spend a moment daily listening for what your body says. Ask to feel your own knowing.
- ¤  Add something to your healing altar that represents your freedom.
- ¤  Complete Ritual 7: Freedom.

## Ritual 7: Freedom

### Preparation

- ¤  The purpose of this ritual is to find embodied freedom by choosing presence and attention.
- ¤  You can do this at your healing altar or in another place where you will not be disturbed.
- ¤  You will also need a notebook or voice recorder.

**Begin by setting a container of prayer as you read this aloud:**

*Sweet and powerful ancestors of my blood,*
*I come as your beloved child, your descendant.*
*I am seeking freedom for me, for all descendants of this line, for you all.*
*Help me know freedom as I have it.*
*Help me feel free in the best possible ways for my life.*
*May all of this line be free.*

**Next, cast a circle of protection with the help of your allies.**

Call out to the trusted spiritual sources of protection you already have. This may be deities, guardians, the elements, or relationships with animals, stones, holy places, herbs, or anything from the green world. Invite each to come toward you, and pause until you sense they are present.

Then, with their support, imagine a layer of protection that goes all around you. You can visualize it if you like, or feel it.

Check in: Do you feel protected all the way around? Can you feel yourself?

Drop in with your guide.

- Check to see if there is anything they want you to know.

- Check in about offerings received and requested: Anything they need?

- Check in about the justice ritual that was conducted: Is there anything else needed here?

- Check in on the dead who remain in the cocoon of prayer: Anything needed here? Are any dead ready to transition to the realm of the ancestors?

Allow your guide to do any ritual work that needs to be done.

Once that is complete, ask your guide what ritual work needs to be done to create freedom for this line of ancestors, for you, for any other living descendants, and for any yet to come.

You can ask your guide to bring healing to any stuckness you embody from the line. Receive the healing they give you.

You can also ask your guide to show you or help you feel an embodied feeling of freedom.

It can be useful to notice how the results of acknowledgment and the creation of justice combine to create a felt sense of freedom. This may be a new feeling you have not experienced.

Pay attention to the nuances of sensation and emotion, and if needed, ask your guide to turn up the volume so you can have a full experience of what freedom feels like in your body.

Do this for as long as is interesting.

Thank your ancestral guide and the allies who showed up.

Make notes of the information you receive.

Close this ritual with a prayer for your own good life.

Dissolve the circle while keeping the protection intact.

# Month 8
## *Transformation*

When finally it is safe
To let love in

Shed the skin of
"Unloved," "unlovable."

Over and over

Say to yourself
I love you. I love you.
I love you so much.

Say, You are precious.
You are valuable.
You are needed here.

Over and over.

Watch the shadow voices of despair,
How they flail, flee, slide back across
Walls, to dusty corners.

Stand in your kitchen.
Feed yourself.

Locate yourself
At the center of your life.

Newly soft, trusting heart
Built for loving. Here to love.

## *Moon of Transformation Practice*

Each day, bring yourself to your best and
sweetest mirror.

Fold your hands under your chin for balance.

Staring into your own eyes, first right, then left,

*say aloud,*
*"I love you."*

Watch your lips move as you say it.

Wait patiently, still gazing, until you feel
different.

MONTH 8

# Transformation Moon

The work of Month 8 is transformation. This includes creating new ways of living in your body and transforming historical pain into current pleasure.

## Having a Body

To be alive, you need to have a body. You are made of flesh. You are made of spirit. You are made of Earth, of water, of fire, of air, of all the elements and minerals and chemicals. This is what makes up your body. Your body is made of Earth. You are Earth, and you will return to Earth. Right now, you have this Earth in a particular form.

Depending on your spiritual beliefs, you may believe that you have chosen to incarnate, that you decided to put spirit into flesh, into human form. You can also think that you were just born and are now a living skin, a breathing animal. No matter what you believe, if you are reading this, you have a body.

Perhaps there are moments when you feel at ease inside your skin. At other moments you may not be able to bear being in a body. Physical pain, emotional pain, or trauma may preclude pleasurable experiences and sensations.

Animals don't obsess about having a body, but many people struggle with it. If you have difficulty having a body, it's likely a cost of human intellect and culture. There is so much cultural toxicity and pathologizing of bodies. Bodies that exist outside the cultural norm of the North American beauty standard are pathologized. Racism and white supremacy are closely linked with fatphobia and ableism. The medical-industrial complex pathologizes bodies deemed "other."

There are many types of challenging body experiences, which can include:

- Having a congenital disorder
- Having a disability
- Feeling body dysphoria or dysmorphia
- Feeling a sense of wrongness about any part of your body
- Aging
- Being injured or ill
- Experiencing uninvited body changes caused by illness or injury

- ¤  Having complicated feelings about intentional body changes like plastic surgery
- ¤  Having an invisible disability
- ¤  Experiencing chronic pain or having a chronic illness
- ¤  Having a fat body
- ¤  Being trans or nonbinary
- ¤  Having any kind of nonnormative body or queer body
- ¤  Being visually or hearing impaired

Conversations about bodies are not happening in the broad public discourse. For example, body acceptance, body shame, societal norms about bodies, oppression and projection onto certain bodies, Femme bodies, highly melanated bodies, fat bodies, old bodies, trans bodies, and disabled bodies are not being widely discussed. The lack of public awareness and empathy can produce suffering for folks who have any of those experiences.

Suppose you have any of these experiences and are interested in developing a different experience of having a body, free from pathology. In that case, body hatred has to be interrupted. You can practice radical body acceptance instead of joining with the haters. Below are several suggestions for how to do it.

## Situate the Problem outside Yourself

What does it mean to situate the problem outside yourself? If you want to practice body acceptance, it's helpful to contextualize the shame you experience in the broader societal arena. You have to become well acquainted with that shame. You have to know its sneaky ways. You have to talk about it in a way that doesn't create more of it.

Personally, I want to love myself and all my parts. I want to love the part of me that loves this body. I want to love the part of me that hates this body. I want to love the pleasure, the discomfort, the preoccupation, the pain. I want to accept all the experiences of having a body.

If you are very preoccupied with these different body experiences, here are some questions to consider: Who benefits? Who stands to gain if you are locked into these internal shame dialogues? If you are constantly pathologizing your body, who's benefiting from that?

Let me share a personal example. Years ago, I was doing some healing work on loving my body, my stomach in particular. I constantly sucked my stomach muscles in to appear thinner. I was just beginning to ask myself, "What would it be like if I didn't suck my stomach muscles in?"

Back then, I was married to a white, straight, cisgender man. One day I asked him, "Do you ever suck in your stomach?" He looked at me bewildered and said, "Why would I do that?" I was shocked. He had not been socialized to think of his body as something that needed fixing or changing. He had not been required to expend the mental effort and the energy, the actual physical energy, that it takes to suck in stomach muscles, which meant he had all of that attention and energy to place on other things, like ruling the universe. Hello, patriarchy.

Desirability is an often unspoken part of the conversation about body acceptance. Desirability is a level of social capital you can access depending on where you are situated in the beauty-standard spectrum. The beauty standard is a construct of marketing and Hollywood to define how a body and face "should" look. At this moment in history, the beauty standard defines desirable as thin, young, able-bodied, white-skinned, heterosexual, cisgender, and flawless. All genders experience the impact of the beauty standard.

I disagree with assigning value to humans based on their appearance, but this phenomenon is prevalent, and you no doubt experience more or less access to desirability capital depending on how others perceive your appearance.

Some people have lots of access to desirability capital. They get a lot of opportunities, attention, and privilege. You may or may not have access to that, depending on the desirability factor projected onto your body. If you have access to less of that, you might think it's your fault. You might think there's something wrong with you. That is a mistake. If you have more of that, you might worry that it will go away.

Discussing this kind of social capital is hard because it operates by remaining hidden. Until it is named, it works freely, without prohibition. When working toward body acceptance, it's helpful to name the forces invested in you feeling bad about your body.

Additionally, if you already hold a critique of the beauty standard and desirability capital but you're *still* struggling to accept your body, it makes sense. Even if you have all the language to deconstruct the bullshit put upon your sweet body, that doesn't mean you're magickally healed. We all live in a culture that places inordinate value upon appearance. While part of healing from body negativity includes being able to critique, analyze, and discuss, recovery doesn't end there.

You can choose to stop having shame about your body shame. You can also choose to have compassion for yourself when you do feel shame.

It's okay to have complicated, paradoxical feelings about having a body. You get to learn to be wide enough somatically and honest enough emotionally to hold the complexity of that experience. By placing some of the problematic parts of having a body into the correct context, you can situate the problem outside yourself. You are not the problem. Society is the problem.

## Practice Embodiment

Embodiment means placing your attention inside your body and noticing feelings, which are both emotions and sensations. You can choose to be embodied. It's the practice of switching the focus from thinking to feeling. You feel within your body instead of thinking about your body. When you notice your inner critic starting to wind up, ask yourself, "What am I feeling?" Later in this chapter we will present several tools that will help you practice embodiment.

## Practice Radical Self-Love

The third suggestion is to take up radical self-love as a practice. You do not need to know what "self-love" means when you start. You can live inside the question, "What would I do right now if I loved myself deeply?"

Radical self-love and self-care mean confronting that voice inside that says shitty things about you, that is mean and self-flagellating. You can attend to that internalized voice of hate.

Although doing sweet things for yourself is essential, being nice to yourself on the inside is even more critical. This is how you become a safe place for your soul to live: noticing the voice of criticism and challenging it.

One of the most important things I did in my healing was commit to being sweet to myself inside of myself. My process went like this: First, I made the commitment. Then, I wore a jade heart around my neck. It was my "I love you, Pavini" reminder. Whenever I noticed I had a mean thought, I would grab the heart, hold it, and say, "I love you, Pavini."

I did this for eighteen months. In the beginning, I grabbed that heart all the time. With practice and attention over time, the negative self-talk lessened. The comparative thoughts, inner critic, and punitive voice got much quieter.

Now it's rare for me to say a mean thing to myself. When I do, it's immediately apparent. My radical self-love means I will not participate in that paradigm of being mean to myself. I invite you to try this on.

## Embodiment

Many survivors of trauma live chronically disembodied lives. As you heal, one of the things you can choose is to become more embodied.

When you practice being embodied, you practice bringing your attention to your body. You place your attention on your sensations and your emotions, your internal processes. You learn to feel yourself in ever more subtle ways. Basically, embodiment is about feeling your aliveness and life happening inside you.

Embodiment helps you learn to trust your own knowing. You are returning home to yourself. If you have lived a life of dissociation or disembodiment, part of this return is to feel what you could not feel before. You build a new capacity for emotion and sensation. You left your body for good reasons. Now you are coming back and learning to trust yourself again.

Your body speaks through sensation and emotion, which are linked but different. Emotions are feelings like sadness, joy, grief, fear, and excitement. Sensations are body feelings like fullness, hunger, exhaustion, pleasure, and itchiness.

Sometimes if you ask someone what they're feeling, they'll tell you how they're feeling instead. They'll say, "I feel good," or "I feel tired."

Emotions are chemical experiences that pass through your neurons. Remembering that emotions have a beginning, middle, and end is important. Often, strong emotions can rock through your body very powerfully. They can make you believe that this moment is how you will feel forever. They feel so true and real. For example, when you are angry it can feel like you will always be angry.

Sensations are typically more subtle than emotions, at least in the beginning of an embodiment process. Some sensations can get really loud, such as hunger, thirst, needing to go to the bathroom, and tiredness. There are also subtle sensations. For example, pay attention to the sensation in your sacrum, a bony structure located in your lower back. What do you notice?

Sensations are often created inside you, in your inner landscape, through muscular contraction or relaxation. We often use the language of "energy" to talk about sensation. Maybe you feel a buzziness or a tingle in your diaphragm, or you may feel energy in the large muscles of your legs.

With an experience like nervousness, it's a combination of emotion and sensation, and the same is true with joy. Sensation and emotion combine to create an internal experience.

The process of embodiment takes a while. It is a lifelong practice, like learning a new language. It takes time to learn the language your body speaks, to get fluent in the feeling state of you.

Embodiment comes and goes. Your access to your felt state is dependent on your attention: What are you attending to? Also, you build your capacity for feeling a little at a time. With embodiment practice over time, you learn to start feeling more of yourself, more of the time.

As that process continues, it opens up access to the wisdom of your body. Your body has an innate intelligence that is always trying to take care of you. Your somatic wisdom can help you get more in touch with your needs, your desires, and your boundaries.

## Five Tools for Embodiment

### Breath

Breathing brings oxygen into all the tissues in your body. It revitalizes everything. Breath is a tool that helps you place your attention. It enables you to focus. It allows you to feel pleasure more deeply. When you breathe consciously, you're paying attention to that inner world of your body. If you want to feel more, breathe more.

There are various types of breathing you can choose, some of which we discuss below. All of these breaths are an exploration. Nothing is "supposed" to happen, only your personal experience. Each one of them supports your embodiment differently. You are your own authority about breathing. The guidance offered below should be measured against what your body actually wants. Feel free to try these breaths, but know there is no dogma about breathing.

If you feel dizzy or uncomfortable at any point while doing these breaths, or if you don't like how you feel, stop, lie down, and breathe normally. Conscious breathing brings more oxygen into your bloodstream, and most of us are not used to that. You are in charge.

## Belly Breath

Often we breathe very shallowly. Belly breath helps you start to breathe lower into your body. It helps to lie down the first time you do this. Breathe fully into your soft belly. Imagine your belly has nostrils.

Track your belly moving up and down with your breath. Your shoulders are not moving. There is a gentle rise and fall of your belly, soft and expansive. You can see your belly move. You can feel your belly moving as the breath enters and leaves.

## Genital Breath

As with belly breath, breathe into the fullness of your belly, and bring your attention to your genitals. That's it! Breathe, and notice your genitals. There's no way you can get this wrong. Just breathe, and notice the tissues between your legs. You don't need to be able to explain it or put it into words. Genital breath is a feeling breath that increases your embodiment by helping you focus on your genitals.

Try it now. Full breath, genital awareness. All of the effort in the genital breath is on the inhale. During the exhale, allow your breath to fall out. See if you can do ten genital breaths and then notice what's happening in your body.

## Ecstasy Breath

You can use the ecstasy breath during erotic encounters with yourself or others to create more arousal and pleasure.

Breathe in through your nose and out through your mouth. Again, only expend effort on the inhale; the exhale is easy. Now imagine that air is coming in through your genitals, as if your genitals are doing the breathing.

If it helps, you can contract your pelvic floor muscles a bit on the inhale, and relax them on the exhale. Inhale more quickly than usual. Your exhale needs to be no longer than your inhale.

This breath encourages erotic sensation to be present in your genitals by inviting it: "Hey, Eros, come on in, I'm here!"

Release expectations for what will happen. Just start with the invitation and breathe with your genitals.

After some time of breathing in through your genitals:

**1.** Imagine exhaling through your heart.

**2.** Imagine that breath looping back to your genitals.

**3.** Run this breath like a cycle.

**4.** Slow down or stop if you get dizzy or don't like how it feels.

When you breathe consciously, there is a different quality of internal sensation. Many people chronically constrict their breath. Usually we're using about a third of our lung capacity. There's a good reason for that. When you breathe less, you feel less. Constricting your breath helps you manage. It helps you not become overwhelmed with sensation so you can get through all of the work and other things you need to do. When you start breathing more, you start feeling more.

## Sensation

Sensation is what you feel. It can be pleasure, pain, temperature, pressure, or movement. Sensations can be internal or external. You feel your heart beating in your chest. You feel the cool water on your skin.

You have visceral sensations. These are the organ and body sensations, like rumbling in your tummy. If you've ever been constipated, you know this sensation. These are the inside sensations, which provide information about the insides of your internal organs. The neuroscientific word for this is interoception.

The language of sensation is not the language of the mind. It's not rational. It doesn't explain itself. It doesn't justify itself. Sensations are not emotions, but they can accompany emotions. Sensations are part of the language that your body speaks. It's how your body communicates with you.

Sensations are the most basic body communications: thirst, hunger, satiation, pain, arousal, temperature, nausea, and the need to void the bowels or bladder. There are so many more subtle layers of sensation available.

Neuroscientists classify sensation according to function. You have your somatic, tactile sensations. These are touch, pressure, vibration, thermal, and pain. You have your proprioceptive sensations. These sensations allow you to know, even if your eyes are closed, where you are in space, where your hand is. You've probably seen a drunk driving test on television, where the cop says, "Close your eyes, touch your nose." Proprioception is what allows you to do that.

As an embodiment practice, ask yourself, "Am I feeling all I can right now?" This question allows you to pay attention to what you're feeling. It helps you recognize what's happening inside, attune your attention, and get even more nuanced.

Another practice to track sensation in your body is the body scan.

During a body scan, you scan your attention through each part of your body in a slow and methodical manner to notice what is happening there. The point is awareness, not relaxation. You are not necessarily changing any internal experience, but rather paying attention to what is.

Body scanning works best in a quiet location where you won't be interrupted. If this is your first time, allow at least ten minutes. Once you get more skillful at this practice, it can happen quite quickly.

Starting at the top of your head, move your attention down through each part of you, slowly.

As you notice what is, what happens next?

- Does the sensation increase as you pay attention to it?

- Does it decrease?

- Does it change?

- Does it shift?

- What else do you notice?

As you begin paying more attention to your sensations, make an effort to expand your repertoire of what you can describe in your experience. Expanding the vocabulary you use to talk about your internal experience will help you put the more subtle sensations into words, which heightens your embodiment.

## Movement

Movement is a characteristic of life. When you move mindfully, you are cultivating embodiment.

The goal of mindful movement is to inhabit your body. It's different from moving for a different goal, such as catching a bus. When you move mindfully, you're paying attention to life happening in your body. The more you move, the more you breathe, which is another way to support your embodiment.

What are the ways in which you love to move? For anyone steeped in diet or exercise culture, love of movement may be interrupted or may have overlays of shame as a motivator. When you move as an embodiment practice, you are moving to experience more in your body. This can happen from any position.

Many people move but are not mindful or embodied while moving. You can be a marathon runner and not be embodied. Or you can be someone who cannot use your legs and be incredibly embodied in your movement. Embodied movement is about intent and attention. You intend to move, and when you do, you are present to the experience, really feeling it.

What does it mean to move your body as a form of activism? What does it mean to be deliberate in a practice of movement that feels good to you—not movement that you "should" do or that is intended for a utilitarian purpose, but movement for pleasure's sake? You can seek pleasure in how you move your hips, for example, or how you stretch or undulate, or how you allow movement to guide your attention back into your body.

Movement can be a turn-on. Movement is generative and life-affirming. There are no wrong ways to move. I often move my hands while sitting at my desk. All movement counts!

## Vocalization

Your voice is a tool for your embodiment. When you speak, make sounds, and vocalize, this connects you to your animal self. You're moving air across your vocal cords, which creates vibrations in your body. You can feel those vibrations, especially if you drop down to the lower registers of your voice.

Many people habitually constrict their throats. They have learned to be silent as a way to be safe. They may be worried about saying the wrong thing or getting into trouble by using sound and vocalization. Many experience shame around singing, speaking publicly, or making noises that are considered rude.

Silencing your voice is deeply linked with white supremacy and patriarchy. It is also linked to gender and race socialization.

Using your voice through humming, moaning, singing, ululating, or speaking can bring your attention to your thoracic cavity. If you pay attention, you can feel the vibrations reverberating inside it.

To start using the tool of vocalization to practice embodiment, I suggest a simple practice I learned from Dr. Peter Levine. Find a place where you are alone and no one will hear you. Your car is perfect. Once you're there, take a belly breath, and on your exhale, make a *vooooooooooo* sound low in your abdomen. Feel the movement of the sound inside of you. Get curious about it.

## Senses

The final tool for embodiment is your senses. We've talked about breath, sensation, movement, and vocalization. Your *senses* are different from your *sensations*. Your senses are how you conduct information from the external world into your brain. You do this through your eyes, your ears, your nose, your sense of touch, and your sense of taste.

Placing full attention on any of your senses will immediately increase the sensation level you are experiencing. You immediately sense more if you decide to smell the proverbial roses and focus on breathing in that beautiful scent.

Interestingly, we can only smell in the present tense. The same is true with your other senses. They are present-moment ways to experience the world through your body. Through the senses, embodiment can be quite playful: you can feed your senses delightful things and allow that experience to unfold.

What are your practices of offering beauty and surprise to your senses?

To use this tool, you can deliberately choose to experience things through an embodied lens. Listen to a piece of music you love, while feeling your body. Smell something gorgeous, and feel. Taste something delicious, and close your eyes. Allow something soft to caress your body, and be present for it. Gaze at a beautiful vista with the intention to feel your body.

Breath, sensation, movement, vocalization, and your senses are tools for embodiment you can choose. They become more powerful when layered. For example, you are listening to music while intentionally breathing and dancing. Maybe you even sing along. Using these tools in combination supports increased levels of feeling and emotion. Give it a try.

## Last Thoughts for Month 8

As you heal from trauma, you learn to inhabit your body in ways that are free of the constriction trauma creates. You give yourself permission to feel more. You learn how to feel safe in your body, and beyond that, how to create pleasure through breath, movement, sensation, singing and vocalizing, and using your senses to receive the world.

**In conclusion, this Month you will:**

- ¤ Complete the Month 8 worksheets in the appendix. You can also download this month's worksheets at www.pavinimoray.com/ttb-bonus.html.

- ¤ Daily practice: Look in the mirror. Say aloud, "I love you."

- ¤ Add something to your healing altar that represents your personal embodiment.

- ¤ Complete Ritual 8: Transformation.

## Ritual 8: Transformation

### Preparation

- ¤ The purpose of this ritual is to claim your body and allow it to be transformed by healing.

- ¤ You can do this at your healing altar or in another place you will not be disturbed.

- ¤ You will also need a notebook or voice recorder.

**Begin by setting a container of prayer as you read this aloud:**

*Beloved ancestors, sweet elders,*
*you who have already learned what can be learned from having a body,*
*I invite your gentle support as I lay claim to the Earth of my body,*
*as I claim the space of me,*
*as I learn to feel myself and live inside my skin.*

*Help me to know my sensations, and help me to be easy in my form.*
*Help me find pleasure in good ways.*

**Next, cast a circle of protection with the help of your allies.**

Call out to the trusted spiritual sources of protection you already have. This may be deities, guardians, the elements, or relationships with animals, stones, holy places, herbs, or anything from the green world. Invite each to come toward you, and pause until you sense they are present.

Then, with their support, imagine a layer of protection that goes all around you. You can visualize it if you like, or feel it.

Check in: Do you feel protected all the way around? Can you feel yourself?

Drop in with your guide.

¤ Check to see if there is anything they want you to know.

¤ Check in about offerings received and requested: Anything they need?

¤ Check in on the dead who remain in the cocoon of prayer: Anything needed here? Any dead ready to transition to the realm of the ancestors?

Allow your guide to do any ritual work that needs to be done.

Next, communicate to your guide that your intention for today is to learn more about the blessings this line can offer around embodiment. What wisdom can they offer you about having a body? How can they support your embodiment process? What positive support can they offer about pleasure?

If you have other questions about having a body and enjoying it, bring them to your guide. Bring your confusion, your complicated feelings. Remember that if you are feeling it, they have also felt it. Let yourself be welcomed with the nuances of being incarnate.

Stay with this for as long as feels good to you and your guide.

Make notes of the information you receive.

Close this ritual with a prayer for your own good life.

Thank your ancestral guide and the allies who showed up.

Dissolve the circle while keeping the protection intact.

# PART 3
# Savor

The last part of this book is about savoring. Savoring is the act of enjoying after you have worked and worked. All of the efforts you've made are taking root and beginning to come to fruition. You are tired but in a good way. Now is the time to relax and savor. You enjoy the languor of the fruiting garden.

During times of languor, you are present with yourself. You have clarity around who you are, who you are becoming, and what you want to practice—the pleasant tiredness of lounging. There's an active quality to your relaxation. You are feeling. You are more aware of the aliveness inside of you.

# Month 9
## Sovereign Moon

I only own myself,
but all of me is mine.

All fur, glitter,
raven feathers

Stuck with moon blood,
I AM this Earth

Fucking with abandon,
mountains thrusting into sky.

Not what you think
nor what you see

But a sumptuous galaxy
guiding heavens, morning Venus

Orbiting, bucking,
twining through velvet moss, fine sheets, easy.

Reckless,
I take myself, again, again

Writhing on forest's floor,
arching against the sprawling stars

Moaning, self-luminous
I claim pleasure

To get to the core of it
the sparking come of it.

That singular moment
when "I" dissolves

That cracked open
All.

## Moon of Sovereignty Practice

Become present more and more in your life. A moment, and another:

*I am here.*
*I am fully present.*
*Feel my heart.*

Meet the next moment, no agenda. Again and again. Try it now.

To become sovereign is to trust your edges, trust your gut, and trust the sacred world. As you are more present, you trust you can let go of what you cling to. Try it now.

As you cling less, trusting the letting go, more and more peace is available. Try it now.

# Sovereign Moon

Welcome to Month 9, where we'll discuss erotic sovereignty and sexuality, including erotic role models, the triangle of your sexuality, and creating a vision board for the erotic self you are constructing.

## What Is Erotic Sovereignty?

You will find your own definition of erotic sovereignty through this work, but let's start here: erotic sovereignty is the confidence and agency to know what you want and don't want, to make requests and declarations, and to inhabit your sexuality on your terms.

Part of finding justice for yourself is claiming erotic sovereignty. Your sexuality is *informed* by all the experiences you've had, rather than being *defined* by them, including experiences that were nonconsensual or traumatic.

Being erotically sovereign means you relate with Eros on your own terms. You define your pleasure. You choose what you want to do and what you do not want to do. How you want to be touched and to touch others, or not. When you are erotically sovereign, you fully hold your sexual power. You are no longer coercible. You have boundaries. You are attuned to your own needs. You are proud of your desire. You continually weed out shame.

Another way to talk about erotic sovereignty is to use the language of sexual liberation. You create your own experience of how it feels to be sexually free.

Here's a practice that will allow you to experience what I'm describing.

Imagine a moment in your life, whether alone or with someone else, when you feel genuinely relaxed and open, receiving the goodness of life, the blessing of aliveness.

You may have experienced this in real life, or you can create this moment now in your imagination.

Feel into this moment. What happens if you breathe more deeply and allow a slight expansion of your breath? Don't force; allow. Permit yourself to be as you are in this moment. No need to analyze, fix, or judge. Feel for a moment into the felt sense of safe-enough freedom.

Whatever you feel is right. The point is to focus on allowing goodness and pleasure, whatever that means to you.

If you like, you can try saying this phrase aloud or in your head: "I create my sexual freedom."

Notice what happens.

# Sexuality

Your sexuality is yours to curate. You get to define it on your terms. Your experience of your sexuality changes and fluctuates throughout your life. You get to participate in who you want to be erotically. If you aren't familiar with Rachel Pollack, who wrote *Seventy-Eight Degrees of Wisdom*, she was a great taroist, queer elder, and trans creator who passed away in 2023.

Here's Rachel's description of the Justice card in the tarot deck: "We must accept the justice of our lives. What we are, we have made ourselves."

I take this to mean that we all get dealt a particular hand regarding our gender and sexuality. How we respond to that hand is our self-making and self-becoming process.

You get to have a responsive sexuality. It is not a given that your sexuality only reacts to negative stimuli. Reactive sexuality means that traumatic things have happened to you that become defining features of your sexual self. An example of reactive sexuality would be, "I've experienced sexual trauma, and that limits my sexuality for the rest of my life."

In contrast, responsive sexuality considers all that has happened and then says, "This is what I'm working with. Where do I want to go with this? How do I want to experience my sexuality moving forward?"

Erotic sovereignty includes deciding what's good for you in your life. How do you want to feel? We are what we have made of ourselves in response to the hand we've been dealt. Discerning is a lifelong practice of continual self-making.

We don't have to do this alone. It's challenging to do alone, and it's easier to do in a community. It is also easier to do when you have positive erotic role models.

# Erotic Role Models

Whom do you admire? Who has a sexuality that inspires you to consider what might be possible for you? Erotic role models give us the opportunity to see what we want embodied in action. You see someone's outsides and model your behavior after them until you feel confident. Through their pure beingness in the world, they give you permission to want what you want, to like what you like. Erotic role models offer representation, showing that people like you get to have a fully expressed, confident, wholesome, connected, alive sexuality. It is remarkable to see ourselves reflected in someone who's slightly ahead on the path.

For folks with any marginalized experience, it's vital to have erotic role models who show that these people get to feel erotically alive. These people get to be sexy and feel sexy. The presence of positive erotic role modeling is crucial. A role model can be anyone: someone you know, alive or dead; a real person or a character in a book, a film, or a TV show. It could be a living relative; it could be an ancestor; it could be your best friend. It could be someone you see walking down the street, and you're like, "Ooh, they got it."

One of my erotic role models when I was growing up was Miss Piggy from the Muppets. This fierce, fat femme had an unadulterated desire for Kermit and expressed it unapologetically. Another was Prince. Note that there's a difference between walking in someone's tracks in the snow and actually aspiring to be that person. I'm not trying to be Miss Piggy or Prince. I'm letting them walk in front of me, and I'm trying it on. I'm trying it on the outside until I get confident on the inside.

It's crucial to find role models who make you feel good about yourself, rather than people who make you feel like you're failing when you compare yourself to them. That's why this piece around representation is so important: when we see it out there, we can be it in here.

Sometimes our ancestors make fantastic sexual role models for us. One of the people I interviewed talked about her grandmother:

*My grandmother was a very sexual being. I think of her riding her horse, coming up over the crest of a hill, her red hair flying behind her, and being free on the back of that horse. She was an artist. She was a bohemian. She traveled a lot.*

Someone else I spoke with about her grandmother said:

*She went to the German part of New York City, and she partied and was known to sleep around. I remember her getting dressed up to go out and wearing red lipstick and a red coat, and fixing her hair. We knew Nana was going out. You know what I mean? She loved her sexuality. She was beautiful. I know she was sexual. She had a number of lovers.*

Sometimes there is erotic role modeling from within your family line as you look back and see an ancestor who embraced their sexuality. Another piece of role modeling is getting to see sexuality changing across a life span or getting to observe a role model's sexuality as it changes, as it grows, and sometimes as it continues beyond death. One of the folks I interviewed spoke about the change in her grandparents as they experienced dementia, and the role of nudity in that change. She also mentions feeling her grandfather's vital erotic energy even after he died:

*I think of my mom's dad, my grandpa, who was very in his body. Then he had dementia for several years before he died. He would just show up naked on the steps regularly. My grandma had dementia too. I was often in her presence when she was fully naked. That was the first time in my life that I experienced my grandparents naked or had exposure to their genitals directly, and it was so healing and humanizing to me to remember the vitality and the sexualness of my grandparents. They were alive then during the stories that I'm telling, and I feel like I have more context of them now that they're ancestors. My grandpa, I feel his erotic vitality.*

# The Triangle of Sexuality

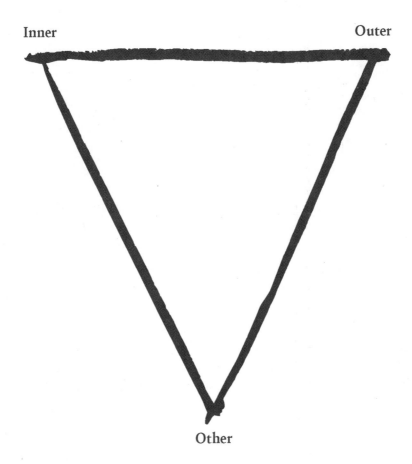

Inner            Outer

Other

Your sexuality is composed of three types of experience—inner sexual experience, outer sexual experience, and other sexual experience—that together form a triangle. You can also find this exercise in the appendix on page 226, but first let's discuss each type of sexual experience separately.

## Inner Sexual Experience

This type of sexual experience is your inner experience of knowing your own sexuality.

To begin exploring this concept, I invite you to recall your first memories of uncomplicated feelings of sexual arousal, of desire or pleasure. Notice what comes to mind as being the earliest memories that belong solely to you of your inner sexual experience. I know this can be complicated if you experienced early violations, so go gentle here.

This is a feeling state—your inner experience of your sexuality. It may have words; you may be able to put some of it into words, and some of it may be wordless. Your inner sexuality is how it feels to be a creature with a sexuality. Your inner sexual experience also includes your deep beliefs, past experiences, and any secrets you have, whether positive, neutral, or negative, about your sexuality. Your inner experience includes what pleasure feels like to your brain's nerves.

Your inner experience of sexuality includes horniness and the readiness to notice that impulse, that urge toward sexual release.

Your inner experience includes your attractions, your turn-ons, your fantasies, and the sexy dreams you have when you're sleeping. How it feels when you move your body like this and like that, the desires you have, all the pleasure your body has experienced and can experience. Your unspoken wants and needs, your urges, and your confidence level. Your felt sense of being desirable, feeling sexy.

Your inner experience of your sexuality includes your kinks. These things turn you on: anything that's "nasty" that you like. But your inner sexuality also houses inadvertently internalized yuck from the outside, like shame, especially religious guilt, religious conditioning, and gender roles.

Sometimes porn can influence your inner experience, especially at a young age. Your inner sexuality is an entire vast universe inside you. Maybe you've never given voice to some of this. Perhaps it's always just been at the experience level, and you've never contextualized it as "This is my experience of sexuality." Everyone's experience is unique to them.

This inner space contains all of the inside stuff: your attractions, your sexual orientation. Who you want to have sex with, how you want to have sex, when you want to have sex, and where you want to have sex—or *not* have sex! All are part of your inner experience of your sexuality.

## Outer Sexual Experience

The outer experience of your sexuality is where your skin meets the air, meaning how you express sexuality in the world. One way to think about your outer sexuality is what is visible to an observer. Another way to think about it is that while your inner experience of your sexuality is the being, your outer experience is the doing. How do you bring your sexuality out to greet the world?

You express your sexuality in a variety of ways. You have a lot of choices in how you express your sexuality. (*Note:* The following list assumes that you value and practice consensual sexuality. Nonconsensual instances of outer sexual experience are not on this list.)

Expressions of sexuality include:

¤ When, where, and how you prefer to connect sexually with other people

¤ How you hold your body in public spaces

¤ How you dress when you want to be sexy (i.e., what makes you feel hot)

¤ Your flirting style

- ¤ Your sexualized behavior in the world
- ¤ Your methods of announcing your attractions
- ¤ How you initiate sexual activity
- ¤ Who you have sex with
- ¤ Sex with yourself
- ¤ How you perform your sexuality
- ¤ How you talk about desires
- ¤ How you negotiate consent with your partner/s
- ¤ Kinks you express in the company of others
- ¤ Sexual activities you partake in

There is another layer of how you *see* yourself as a sexual being in the world, as you express (or don't express) your sexuality. It's important to mention here that representation—seeing people who are like you represented as sexual beings in the media—can greatly shape your experience. Where do you see people like you represented as sexual in the world?

If you don't see people like you represented in the media as sexual, how does that affect your outer experience, or your inner experience?

## Other Sexual Experience

The final part of your sexuality is about others and how they experience your sexuality. You have less control over how others perceive your sexuality. For example:

- ¤ What assumptions or judgments do others make about your expression of your sexuality?
- ¤ What level of desirability do you have access to?
- ¤ How do others gender you?
- ¤ How do others label your sexuality?
- ¤ Do others perceive you as gay, straight, queer, asexual, or are you even visible as a sexual being?
- ¤ What do others project onto you?
- ¤ What stories do others make up about you?
- ¤ What stories do others make up about your genitals, your sexual history, and your sexual identity?
- ¤ How do others desire you?
- ¤ How much social capital do you receive based on your perceived level of desirability?
- ¤ What level of validation do you receive as a sexual being?

The "other" part of your sexuality is about how the world validates you or not. The "other" part includes the projections of societal gender roles, the projections of porn, and the "shoulds" of how you're supposed to be. The dictates that get put on you that are not yours, whether you want them or not.

## Assembling the Triangle of Your Sexuality

The three corners of this triangle constitute your sexuality. These three different aspects interact in interesting ways. While we rarely tease all of this apart and categorize it this way, doing so helps you understand the complexity of your sexuality.

"Inner," "outer," and "other" are tools to help you understand your experience more deeply. Through this thought exercise, you can understand the pain and pleasure associated with sexuality more clearly, both physically and emotionally.

You can break it down and tease these apart by asking yourself, "What is my inner experience? What is my outer experience? What is my other experience?"

Then, you can notice how they interact. Here's an example. Perhaps your inner experience of sexuality often includes asking, "Am I sexy?" If you then notice little to no sexual capital from others, you can piece together these factors. This might sound like, "Oh, this internal experience that I'm having is deeply affected by this external experience I'm having."

In another example, if you used to feel quite sexy, but lately you notice you feel blah, you might track that to your age. When you were twenty-five, your inner experience of sexuality was quite confident, and you received a lot of social validation about your sexual value. Now you're fifty-six and not receiving that same level of external validation. In this case, you can notice that ageism in the "other" realm affects you in your "inner" domain.

When you tease it apart, you start to notice what's causing you pain, what's causing you to feel bad. You become aware of shame and how it prohibits your sexual expression.

For example, let's say someone grew up in a fundamentalist Christian family where they received the message that only heterosexual attraction is permissible. This message lands solidly in the "other" corner of their triangle of sexuality. But if they are a person who is deeply fluid in their attractions, meaning they like lots of different people, this presents a conflict.

Notice how shame moves from the "other" to the "inner" in this example. The religious mandate tries to control sexual attraction and behavior. The person on the receiving end accepts that this is their experience of sexuality: "This is just the way it is. I feel bad when I'm attracted to people my faith tells me I'm not supposed to be attracted to. I feel bad about myself." Others put shame on us.

In this example, what comes from the "other" corner significantly affects the inner experience of sexuality.

Unfortunately, most of us do not get to have an experience of sexuality that is untouched by the "other" corner of the triangle. The forces around you shape you. However, you can begin to deconstruct what your sexuality is on your terms. You can start to work with that in a very gentle way.

## Vision Board for Your Emergent Erotic Self

When setting out on a course of healing and change, it can be helpful to take the time to visualize what you're going for. Visualizing is like setting visual intentions. You can do that with a vision board.

You've probably heard of vision boards before. A vision board is something you create that captures the visual essence of an idea or intention. Before I did my first one, I had judgment about them, but when I was setting out to create the erotic self I wanted, I found a vision board to be very helpful. So even if you have feelings about vision boards, try this anyway. There's something about seeing a representation of the erotic self you are curating that is quite powerful.

Before beginning to work on your board, consider your desires and what you want to embody. For example, my erotic vision board includes an image of a tiger. The tiger represents power, virility, grace, agility, and embodiment, which I want to cultivate in my sexuality.

The tiger doesn't mean that I want to shape-shift into a tiger. It means that tiger energy exists within my inner experience of sexuality, and I want to invite it to the outside more. I've placed it in a central location on my vision board because this is how I want to feel about my sexuality. I want to feel confident. I want to feel radical. I want to feel free, playful, and creative. I want to wear fun outfits and to physically express my erotic energy. I want to feel good about my body.

I found images to represent all of these different concepts and energies. I didn't just surf the internet to find pictures of cool things and stick them on my vision board. You could do that, but what do you really want?

Consider the triangle of your sexuality. Here are some questions to think about:

¤ What are some words that describe your ideal inner sexuality? How about your ideal outer sexuality?

¤ What longings can you let yourself feel?

¤ What do you want that is more than you would ever let yourself ask for?

¤ What do you envy in the sexual expression of others?

¤ What is your wildest dream for your erotic self?

As you feel into these questions, start to find images that represent your answers. It might take you a while to find the right images.

The image does not have to depict a human, nor does it have to have the same gender expression as you. It does not have to be a natural feature; it could be something that's constructed. For example, if you saw a picture of a beautiful fountain and thought, "Oh, I want that overflowing, abundant sexuality," you might include that image.

What are the things that are calling to you? What do you want to nourish, feed, and become with regard to your sexuality? For instance, you may want to:

¤   Connect with others more easily. What image represents that desire?

¤   Be more available for actual pleasure. What image represents that? Is it a flower opening?

¤   Be clearer with your boundaries. What image of a boundary works for you and feels sexy?

Creating this map or this vision is one way of working with erotic role modeling. Have fun with it! Permit yourself to be bold.

## Last Thoughts for Month 9

Your sexuality is a powerful piece of the experience of being human. The big takeaway for this Month is that you get to design a sexuality for yourself that feels powerful, sexy, and pleasurable. It does not have to follow anyone else's rules (other than consent!).

**In conclusion, this Month you will:**

¤   Complete the Month 9 worksheets in the appendix. You can also download this month's worksheets at www.pavinimoray.com/ttb-bonus.html.

¤   Daily practice: Become present in the moment. Say to yourself: "I am here. I am fully present. I feel my heart."

¤   Create a vision board for your erotic self, and situate it in a place where you can see it.

¤   Add something to your healing altar that represents your sexual sovereignty.

¤   Complete Ritual 9: Sovereignty.

## Ritual 9: Sovereignty

### Preparation

¤   The purpose of this ritual is to embody sovereignty.

¤   You can do this at your healing altar or in another place you will not be disturbed.

¤   You will also need a notebook or voice recorder.

**Begin by doing belly breathing.**

Do the belly breathing for as long as you want, but at least one minute. Notice when you feel present in your body.

**Next, set a container of prayer as you read this aloud:**

*Sweet bright ancestors of my blood,*
*Sweet body I live in,*
*I call back my power*
*to this human frame.*
*I call back my power*
*so that I may live well.*
*I honor my sexuality.*
*I make space for my pleasure.*
*Please witness and support my healing*
*as my body becomes my temple*
*and pleasure my worship.*

**Then cast a circle of protection with the help of your allies.**

Call out to the trusted spiritual sources of protection you already have. This may be deities, guardians, the elements, or relationships with animals, stones, holy places, herbs, or anything from the green world. Invite each to come toward you, and pause until you sense that they are present.

Then, with their support, imagine a layer of protection that goes all around you. You can visualize it if you like, or feel it.

Check in: Do you feel protected all the way around? Can you feel yourself?

Drop in with your guide.

¤ Check to see if there is anything they want you to know.

¤ Check in about offerings received and requested: Anything they need?

¤ Check in about the justice ritual you conducted: Is there anything else needed here?

¤ Check in on the dead who remain in the cocoon of prayer: Anything needed here? Any dead ready to transition to the realm of the ancestors?

Allow your guide to do any ritual work that needs to be done.

When all that is complete, ask your guide to help you understand the gifts of sovereignty in your blood that you have access to.

Ask if there is a well ancestral guide on this line who during their life embodied gifts of erotic sovereignty, and if your guide can introduce you to that ancestor.

After meeting them, you can ask them to give you a blessing for your sexual sovereignty. This may be something your guide wishes to offer.

If you want, you can ask your guide to help you feel an experience of sovereignty in your body.

You can ask them to do ritual with you or on you so that you can experience your power and agency on a regular basis.

When it feels complete, close out with your guide and any allies who supported you.

Take time at the end of this drop-in to savor the experience.

Take notes on the information you receive.

Dissolve the circle while keeping the protection intact.

# Month 10
## *Instructions for Blessing the World with Your Eros*

Before self-pleasure,
pray.

Pour the cream and honey
over the copper murti.

Holy elixir,
mix in the bowl.

Ruby tongue
flick the rim.

Sip consecrated nectar,
imbibe sweet blessing.

Prayer done, move to the bed,
slide hands down sheets.

All smooth skin,
snakey strokes.

Put mouth to skin.
Let time surrender to presence.
Make universal sound.
Cruise and seduce
the god who dances
on the riverbank.

With your pleasure,
**bless the world Erotic.**

## *Moon of Blessing Practice*

Bring yourself to yourself, and invite in the
knowing of your own deeply profound beauty.

In every mirror, every day, say the following:

*"I am beautiful.*
*I am so beautiful."*

Mean it, and don't look away from receiving it.
This practice will change your life if you let it.

# Blessing Moon

This Month we'll be talking about ancestral sexual blessings and embracing your erotic gifts, as well as some self-love pleasure practices.

When you were born, you received an inheritance from your living family and from your ancestors. Your inheritance includes a bundle of beliefs, practices, traditions, and values. This inheritance bundle is full of both good things and challenging things. It's full of burdens and blessings.

As you grow up, it becomes incumbent upon you to unpack this inheritance bundle. You have likely asked yourself, "What part of my inheritance is in alignment with who I am?" and "What are things I've received that I do not want to embody or pass on?" As an adult, you can consciously open your bundle and discern. What are the burdens? What are the blessings? Although you were handed all of it, you can choose which parts to accept.

## Blessings

Let's talk about some of the erotic gifts you may have received from your people.

Ancestral sexual blessings support you to enjoy, savor, relax, and feel good. They include sexual freedom, sexual self-esteem, pleasure, and feeling connected to the Eros of your ancestors (which you came from!).

Other blessings include queerness, sexual libido, sexual creativity, erotic connection to the Earth, and sensual aliveness.

### Sexual Freedom

One of the powerful blessings that can come our way is sexual freedom. If our ancestors embraced sexual liberty, it could be a precious gift passed down to us.

During my doctoral research, I interviewed a person who had a unique perspective on sexual freedom because of her ancestry. She spoke about how she holds her ancestors' sexual repression in her thoughts. For her, it's a way of staying mindful of the privilege and freedom she enjoys in her own life, especially when it comes to her sexuality. She said:

> *Because of the repressive culture I grew up in, a traditional Chinese family, some of my ancestors may not have had the same access, rights, or freedoms. I'm aware of the fact that I'm very privileged. I live a life that probably very few people in my family, alive or dead, have experienced.*

*I'm really aware that my current existence didn't just happen by chance. I'm certain there were many people like me, who were kind of wild, curious, or strong. However, they probably didn't get to explore or express themselves in the same way. I often reflect on the blessing and privilege of my life. It's easy to see when I compare it to my parents; they didn't have the same freedom.*

This unique perspective allows her to understand how her own sexual expression relates to that of her parents and her cultural background. In her experience, living life the way she does is a way of honoring those who didn't have the opportunity to experience such freedoms. It's about recognizing the concept of sexual freedom as a gift from one's ancestors.

She also emphasized the importance of acknowledging ancestral sexuality. Speaking about sex within families can often raise concerns about the taboo of incest. However, my interviewee doesn't believe it has to be that way. After all, each one of us is here because of the sexual acts of our ancestors. That's how we came into being. Discussing our ancestors' sexuality in a more complex manner is a way to honor their humanity, recognizing that they were complete individuals leading rich and intricate lives.

## Nurturing Sexual Self-Esteem

Another remarkable blessing that can be bestowed upon us is sexual self-esteem. This is all about feeling a sense of self-worth and attractiveness as a sexual partner.

Another person I interviewed shared a fascinating perspective. He talked about receiving a lot of validation regarding his level of attractiveness and sexual well-being through his mother; from her, it traced back to his grandfather. He said:

*It's not just about sexual attraction; it's about having a certain charisma or a special quality that I inherited from my mother. It felt right, not crossing any boundaries. She made me feel attractive, and she connected it back to her father. So, if we're talking about sexual well-being, it's about feeling like a valuable person.*

In this case, the grandfather had a certain level of sexual self-esteem that his daughter observed, and it was a healthy, respectful connection. She passed on this gift of sexual self-esteem to her son, making sure he knew he was attractive and valuable. The person I spoke with embraced this blessing and stepped into it.

## Inheriting a Sense of Pleasure

Another blessing we can inherit from our ancestors is how we perceive and embrace pleasure. Another person I spoke with emphasized the importance of erotic pleasure in his family's lineage:

*I believe it's a good idea to consider that some of your ancestors may have had incredibly fulfilling sexual experiences and genuinely enjoyed them.*

It's entirely possible that our ancestors had delightful experiences that they might not have shared with anyone, including us. Although the person I interviewed may never have firsthand knowledge of his ancestors' pleasure, he told me that thinking about their enjoyment enabled him to experience more pleasure himself. This concept of letting our ancestors' pleasure guide us in our own pursuit of pleasure was a recurring theme in several conversations.

Interestingly, some individuals I spoke with mentioned having ancestral guides who appear as spiritual sources of wisdom in matters of sensuality and pleasure. These ancestors actively pray for a good and pleasurable life, offering support in embracing pleasure. This isn't done in any strange or unnatural manner but rather from a desire for their descendants, both in blood and spirit, to relish the sensations of pleasure in their bodies and lives. After all, who wouldn't wish for their loved ones to experience joy and well-being?

## Ancestral Connection to Erotic Energy

We've been exploring the idea that there can be a unique connection with our ancestors' erotic energy. Some of the individuals I interviewed described feeling linked to their ancestors' erotic energy, experiencing this connection as a blessing in their own lives. What's particularly captivating is that for those I spoke with, the positive impact of a loved one's sexual energy could persist even after that person had passed away.

One interviewee expressed immense gratitude for the erotic energy blessings she received from two ancestors:

> I feel so thankful to have these two ancestors who are a part of my spiritual family. They possess such vibrant and active energy, and they continue to bestow their blessings upon those of us who are living, as well as those who have passed on. It's like they're still so full of life and erotic vitality.

## Connecting with Queer Ancestors

Another positive aspect of ancestral sexuality concerns queer and marginalized identities. The perceived blessing of being in connection with gay, lesbian, queer, and transgender ancestors emerged in many of the interviews I conducted. Individuals spoke about feeling a greater sense of permission, sexual freedom, and support for their sexual well-being as a result of these connections. They found strength and grounding through this ancestral link. Additionally, connections with the present-day queer and LGBTQ+ community allowed some people to establish connections with their LGBTQ+ ancestors, drawing on the spirits' struggles, suffering, and successes for strength and grounding.

It's important to note that I didn't specifically inquire about my interviewees' sexual orientation, but many chose to discuss it. A pervasive theme that emerged was how a connection with queer and LGBTQ+ ancestors empowers individuals in owning and embracing their identities.

For instance, one individual I spoke with recounted the oppression he faced as a queer male, but he linked his ancestral connection with gay and queer ancestors to his sexual well-being:

*Homophobia doesn't hold power in the face of our grand histories. I see that when I'm around people who carry pride and righteousness. Having a sense of LGBTQ+ ancestors is crucial to my sexual pleasure, which is deeply tied to my sexual well-being. The ability to connect with ancestors who shared those identities and took pride in them can significantly enhance one's access to pleasure.*

## Embracing Your Erotic Gifts

In addition to the blessings already discussed, numerous other ancestral gifts can play a pivotal role in supporting sexual wellness. These include having ancestral role models who validate your sexual identity and serve as guides in navigating your changing sexuality throughout life. Ancestors who exemplify the capacity for committed and nurturing relationships can also have a profound influence.

One individual I spoke with shared a unique example of her mother giving her a vibrator when she was a young woman, effectively granting permission for sexual freedom and self-love, along with the capacity for pleasure. These connections with living, spirit, and queer ancestors are all part of a bundle of erotic blessings.

We will now delve deeper into ways to connect with your unique bundle of ancestral blessings. It's important to realize that even in the face of what may seem like burdens, blessings are waiting to be uncovered, offering you a source of strength and support.

## Self-Love Practices: Nurturing the Erotic in Daily Life

Let's talk about self-love practices. "Self-care" is often viewed as a buzzword, and conversations on the topic can sometimes be superficial. However, there's genuine depth to explore when we delve into self-love and self-pleasure. How do you wish to integrate pleasure into your daily life? How do you want to weave the erotic into your everyday experiences?

Eros is not sex. Eros is the holy life force that moves through you and through all beings. It sparks all creative endeavors and acts of creation. Inviting the erotic more fully into your life is an invitation to feel your full aliveness more.

When you feel in touch with your erotic self, do you also feel more connected with life? With spirit? What if the erotic wasn't something you relegated just to the bedroom, but rather you curated it in your everyday actions? Another way to understand this idea might be *presence*. When you are truly present, you are aware and noticing. You feel the wind and the sun; you notice the details of your environment with more clarity and awe. You are simply more available for the beauty of life. To focus on inviting in the erotic is to focus on how you live your life.

The "how" is what truly matters. How present are you in these activities? This focus on presence can transform almost anything into an erotic experience. I often find something as mundane as doing the dishes to be a sensual experience: the warm, soapy water, the weight of the china, and the simple act of gazing out of the window while feeling my feet on the floor.

Bringing attention, mindfulness, and presence to your actions is critical to unlocking the erotic potential in your daily life. Part of embracing self-pleasure is saying yes to the erotic, which involves being present. Self-pleasure is more than masturbation. Self-pleasure can be a wide range of sensory delights and experiences that feel good. That said, masturbation is a wonderful way to know your sexual self and make yourself feel great.

## Presence and Self-Love in Masturbation

Masturbation can be a profound form of self-love, allowing you to experience that deep, warm, and abiding sense of presence and care, much like your love for someone else, be it a loved one, a pet, or a close friend. In this case, instead of giving your love and touch to someone else, you give it to yourself. It's a surreal experience because you are both directing love toward yourself and receiving it from yourself simultaneously.

When it comes to the practice of masturbation and experiencing pleasure, presence again is key. There are lots of ways to masturbate, all of them valid. There's the I-just-need-to-get-off quickie, and then there are the lengthy self-love sessions, where you spend an afternoon exploring your body and paying full attention to your touch and sensations.

There are lots of doorways to enter into sexual arousal. You probably have your well-tested favorites: the right porn, the most potent fantasies, or the reliable ways of touching that always do the trick. However you enter arousal is fantastic!

Right now, I want to focus on touch. There is a distinct quality that emerges when touch becomes the focus of your masturbation practice, and it's rare for most of us.

Receiving touch is crucial for our well-being. But our need for touch doesn't have to be met solely by others; your own self-touch is essential. As you grow from being a baby into a toddler, you become coordinated enough so you can touch yourself intentionally. Nor does self-touch negate the need for touch by others. Instead, you learn that the touch of another has different qualities of sensation.

Self-touch allows you to feel two things at once: the touch you give, and the touch you receive. When you start masturbating, the act of touching yourself sexually, you come into a lifelong sexual relationship with yourself. Masturbation is about more than sexual release;

it's a way to establish or reclaim a touch relationship with yourself. When you touch your own body with love and care, as you would a lover's, you can feel love coming from and toward yourself. In this way, masturbation is a practice of self-connection.

## Awakening the Whole Body and Encouraging the Erogenous

People have diverse self-pleasure rituals. Some have performed their masturbation practices the same way ever since they were teenagers. Some people believe they should only masturbate while they are single. Some think masturbation should be private, while others love masturbating in groups. Some people masturbate frequently, some rarely, and some multiple times a day. It's an entirely personal experience, and there's no wrong way to do it.

In this perspective, masturbation isn't just about reaching climax; it's about engaging in active self-touch infused with love, awakening your entire body, and encouraging your erogenous tissues to fill with oxygen and blood. Many people wonder, "What do I like sexually?" Through this practice you can learn more about your preferences and desires. A slow, present, mindful exploration helps you discover the treasures of your body.

Masturbation presents an opportunity for you to express self-love, compassion, pleasure, and care. In self-touch, you become an explorer and scientist of your body, discovering the perfect ways to touch yourself. This practice benefits not only sexual health but also pelvic-floor muscles, stress relief, energy release, relaxation, creativity, general well-being, and so much more. Your touch holds a remarkable capacity for healing and connecting.

When we discuss masturbation, we've got to talk about shame. Masturbation is a beautiful, powerful way to give ourselves comfort and pleasure, yet it has been overlaid with shame. If this is a burden you carry, interrogate it. Why is pleasuring yourself shameful? Whatever answer you get, go to the next deeper layer and ask again: And why is that shameful? Keep asking until the house of cards collapses. Shame is indoctrinated, not innate.

But shame taints self-touch, and people may rush through the experience. Unsurprisingly, many people spend less time exploring their own bodies than they would spend on a lover's body. But this practice is a gateway to a deeper exploration of how you want to connect with your own body, discovering your body's unique erotic gifts and talents.

In cases of trauma, individuals may believe they are broken beyond repair and unworthy of love and pleasure. However, self-touch and self-love practices can help you challenge these narratives, offering a path toward healing. In this practice, you get to choose how you place your attention on your body, how you move, how you breathe, and how you care for yourself.

You can anoint yourself with oil, speak kindly to your body, and discover the secret places of joy that are uniquely yours. This self-touch practice can help you remember who you are, why you're here, and what truly matters. It doesn't have to be a lengthy, drawn-out ritual; it can be woven into your daily life in shorter moments of self-care and self-love. It's about blessing yourself and honoring the gift of life that has flowed through your ancestors and into your body. Your self-touch is not just a blessing to you. It can also serve as an offering to your ancestors and descendants, a profound practice of reverence.

Begin by touching your own body intentionally, speaking kindly to it, and treating it with care and reverence. In effect, you are participating in an ancestral reverence practice. You honor the gift of life and sexuality passed down through the generations. You honor the body that houses your essence.

## Embracing Your Erotic Talents

Let's dive into the concept of embracing your erotic gifts. By this, I mean the unique blessings and talents you possess, some of which you inherited, and others of which are innate gifts of your being. In every aspect of life, we carry talents, and this holds true for your erotic life as well. These gifts may manifest as curiosity, creativity, a playful spirit, skill in giving and receiving touch, a vast capacity for pleasure, intense orgasmic experiences, a connection with the divine through pleasure, the ability to direct erotic energy for magickal or healing purposes, or simply a knack for embracing your wild, dirty, funky side.

Sometimes these gifts can be so ingrained in your being that you might take them for granted, assuming everyone possesses similar attributes. You may not even consider them as remarkable or unique. However, I invite you to reflect on your erotic gifts and talents. How are you an erotically gifted individual? In the worksheets for this Month you'll have a chance to explore your erotic gifts.

We live in a culture with a negativity bias, so many of us have gotten pretty good at focusing on what needs "fixing." Sure, you can focus on areas where you have sexual and intimate challenges, working to improve them. But you can also dedicate your time and attention to nurturing your erotic talents! Just like someone might have the natural capacity for playing the piano but may or may not choose to develop it, you can decide whether to embrace and express your erotic gifts or let them lie dormant. This is an invitation to reflect on how you want to engage with your erotic gifts and where your curiosity leads you.

Where you place your attention is where growth occurs. If you identify an aspect of your erotic life where you'd like to excel, dedicating your attention to it can lead to significant progress. Embracing your erotic gifts is about practice, and practice is something you are not obliged to do; rather, it's something you are privileged to do. It's through practice that you become more skillful in the areas you choose to focus on. Remember that practice doesn't need to be regimented or daily; even small, mindful practices can yield significant benefits.

I invite you to explore your erotic gifts, recognize your talents, and decide what you want to embrace and practice. Your unique erotic gifts are a treasure waiting to be discovered and celebrated.

## Last Thoughts for Month 10

Embracing your ancestral blessings of sexuality is a gift you give to yourself, your descendants, and your ancestors. Just as you want your descendants to live lives of pleasure, consent, connection, and beauty, you can assume that at their core, your ancestors wanted those things for you and still do. These bodies are temporary and are capable of great pleasure. When you begin to increase your capacity for experiencing pleasure, your capacity for receiving goodness into your life also increases. Through self-touch, you can offer freedom and joy to your neurons, which has a positive impact on your overall well-being. Just as your sexuality evolves over your life span, so too can your masturbation.

**In conclusion, this Month you will:**

- ¤ Complete the Month 10 worksheets in the appendix. You can also download this month's worksheets at www.pavinimoray.com/ttb-bonus.html.

- ¤ Daily practice: Look in the mirror daily and repeat, "I am so beautiful. I am so beautiful."

- ¤ Add something to your healing altar that represents your ancestral sexual blessings.

- ¤ Complete Ritual 10: Blessing.

## Ritual 10: Blessing

### Preparation

- ¤ The purpose of this ritual is to receive erotic blessings of your line.

- ¤ You can do this at your healing altar or in another place you will not be disturbed.

- ¤ You will also need a notebook or voice recorder.

**Begin by setting a container of prayer as you read this aloud:**

*Blood of my blood, ancient bright ancestors,*
*through whose passion and pleasure I exist,*
*I long to connect with the erotic blessings of my lines, no matter how long ago.*
*I pray for your support and love*
*as I seek to embody my sex and my power*
*to embody the energy of Eros*
*to allow my sexuality to be fully mine*
*just as I want it to be.*

**Next, cast a circle of protection with the help of your allies.**

Call out to the trusted spiritual sources of protection you already have. This may be deities, guardians, the elements, or relationships with animals, stones, holy places, herbs, or anything from the green world. Invite each to come toward you, and pause until you sense they are present.

Then, with their support, imagine a layer of protection that goes all around you. You can visualize it if you like, or feel it.

Check in: Do you feel protected all the way around? Can you feel yourself?

Drop in with your guide.

- ¤ Check to see if there is anything they want you to know.

- ¤ Check in about offerings received and requested: Anything they need?

- ¤ Ask your guide to help any remaining ancestors in the cocoon of prayer to transition to the ancestors, unless more time is needed.

Allow your guide to do any ritual work that needs to be done.

Ask your guide to help you understand the sexual blessings and erotic gifts you have inherited.

Working with your guide, touch a different part of your body as you welcome each blessing. For example, if a blessing you inherited is lustiness, you may wish to hold your genitals as you feel for that gift in your body.

Go through each blessing and let it land in your body, with the intention of blessing your embodied sexuality.

When this feels complete, thank your guide and allies.

Dissolve the circle, but keep the protection.

Take notes on the information you receive.

# Month 11
## *Pleasure*

Hold this image in your mind:
Your tombstone, lichen and moss,
chipped rock.

Your name,
and inscribed by your descendants below:
"Healed by Pleasure."

What life was that,
lived to savor wind, water, and sun?

Moving as you were moved.

Releasing to the river
so you could flow.

Thank you.

## *Moon of Pleasure Practice*

### Play? Sure!

Go on an impulse walk. This means allowing your impulses to make decisions for you, for a period of thirty minutes.

Notice how quickly the inhibitors arrive, acknowledge them, and move on. What does your kid self want to do?

*Allow pleasure to be whatever it is. Follow your curiosity and delight.*

# Pleasure Moon

Welcome to the Pleasure Moon, a time dedicated to exploring and understanding pleasure. As we begin this new chapter, take a moment to reflect on your journey thus far. Congratulations on your commitment to self-discovery, growth, and transformation over the past ten moons. Your dedication is commendable!

## Understanding Pleasure

What exactly is pleasure? The concept may seem straightforward, but the reality is more complex. A more academic definition of pleasure is to say that pleasure arises when an enjoyable activity (the stimulus) activates neurons that send messages to the brain, which releases neurotransmitters such as dopamine, oxytocin, serotonin, and endorphins. This release causes that feel-good sensation and a feeling of reward, evoking the desire to repeat the pleasurable action again and again.

Certain stimuli trigger consistent responses in our brains. For instance, consuming sugar is enjoyable for many people, and it consistently activates pleasure.

But pleasure is more than neurochemicals! The pursuit of pleasure and avoidance of pain are driving forces in our lives. Pleasure is physical, emotional, relational, and political. Pleasure can be directed toward healing as well as toward resistance. Pleasure can be personal and private, and it can be shared and collective. Pleasure can support liberation.

## Society's Views on Pleasure

In many cases, when we hear the word "pleasure" our minds immediately veer toward thoughts of sexuality and the erotic. During this month, we will aim to broaden our understanding of pleasure beyond its sexual connotations. In Western culture, we grapple with a paradox. On the one hand, our society judges and stigmatizes those who indulge in pleasure excessively, labeling them as hedonists, gluttons, lazy, or unmotivated. On the other hand, society also condemns those who struggle to experience pleasure, branding them as workaholics, uptight, prudish, or unable to feel pleasure.

In reality, many of us experience pleasure to some extent at various points in our lives. It may appear that those who embrace pleasure are hedonistic pleasure-seekers, but this is a commodified perspective of pleasure. Capitalism has commodified and packaged pleasure as something to be bought and consumed. It suggests that you can purchase joy and happiness. Yet beneath this commercialized layer lies a fear of what authentic pleasure truly entails. Most of us are well versed in sitting with pain and suffering, and North American culture often reinforces that this is morally commendable.

However, what I've learned from two decades as a somatic sex therapist is that when it comes to feeling pleasure (during sex, for example), many people resist it. They clamp down on these sensations, cease to breathe deeply, and focus intensely on genital pleasure. We embody the pursue/deny pleasure paradox by seeking pleasure while also resisting pleasure.

## Distinguishing between True and False Pleasure

False pleasure provides immediate gratification, but the long-term impact is detrimental and unsustainable. True pleasure, on the other hand, offers immediate gratification *and* a lasting sense of goodness. True pleasure doesn't evoke guilt, shame, or regret.

A typical example of false pleasure could be the excess consumption of alcohol, which might bring temporary pleasure but leads to a hangover, dehydration, and regret the next day. True pleasure is sustainable and wholesome, nurturing your body and well-being. True pleasure feels good both now and later.

Somehow we got confused. Material gratification and consumerism got conflated with embodied pleasure. When you widen your lens, the situation doesn't make sense. Why would we think a new phone or gadget would provide the deep contentment and satisfaction of a good warm hug, for example?

In the 1950s, researchers James Olds and Peter Milner conducted a series of experiments on rats in which they inserted electrodes into different parts of the rats' brains, seeking to stimulate the rats' pleasure centers. They then gave the rats a lever they could push that would send a signal to the electrode to trigger the good feelings. Eventually, the rats were removed from the experiment because they spent all their time pushing the reward lever, neglecting to eat, drink, or rest.

This early research has become a foundation of neuroscience, and many have used this model to theorize about the nature of addiction. We can become addicted to things that feel good and yet are not truly good for us. Any exploration of pleasure needs to include the muscle of discernment.

## Decolonized, Rewilded, and Feral Pleasure

We're here to unpack what decolonized pleasure, rewilded pleasure, and feral pleasure are. You won't find a one-size-fits-all definition here. You get to craft your own. This is your opportunity to break free from the narrow definitions of pleasure we've been spoon-fed.

Have you ever asked yourself, "What is my pleasure? What does my nervous system crave right now?" It's essential to recognize that your pleasures can shift and evolve as you move through life. What once lit your fire might not do the trick anymore, but that's all right, because new sparks await you.

So, here's your mission: commit to defining pleasure on your terms. Throw away the rule book that dictates what you should like or what others say your pleasure should be. This is all about what feels good to you at this very moment. And remember, it's okay if what feels good to you today isn't the same as what felt good yesterday. Your ever-changing desires and sensations deserve to be acknowledged and celebrated. That's what we call feral pleasure. That's also what we mean by rewilded pleasure—being intimately present with yourself in real time, listening to your body and what it craves in the present moment. You don't have to know what you like; you have to tune in to what would feel good right now, without being shackled to the past.

Let's liberate ourselves from the pressure of confining pleasure to our genitals. Pleasure is a vast landscape, not a one-stop destination. Maybe your genitals aren't the center of your pleasure universe, and that's perfectly fine. The most exquisite pleasures can come from the sun's warm caress on your skin, the gentle breeze embracing you, the cool embrace of water, the passionate kiss of a lover, or the indulgence of eating your favorite food. These, too, are pleasures, and they should count.

If you seek embodied liberation, you'll need to dismantle the notion that pleasure must align with the commodified depictions we see. Your pleasure might not resemble a scene from a movie, and that's more than okay. It's about allowing your genuine pleasures to be recognized. Basking in the sound of the crickets from your front porch? A profoundly erotic pleasure. Shed the expectations, unhook from other people's definitions of pleasure, and reclaim what's genuinely pleasurable for you.

## Play

Let's revisit the concept of play. Play isn't just about having fun; it's about innovation and spontaneity, both antidotes to the frozen stuckness of trauma. When we immerse ourselves in playful states, we dance with the unknown. We don't have a script; we make it up as we go along, and there's incredible freedom.

Now, think about this: What if we swapped out the word "pleasure" for "play"? Pleasure = play? Sure! What if the hallmark of pleasure for you was feeling playful and good, and having fun? Your ability to be neuroplastic comes in handy here. Yes, you do have the capacity to deal with suffering and endure it, but developing the capacity to feel lasting pleasure on your terms is a revolutionary act that takes time and practice.

As you explore this realm, you'll realize that pleasure is a potent medicine. It's where you show yourself you are worthy, good, and valuable. When you adopt play as an ethos, you acknowledge that feeling good is about safety. It's not "extra" to feel good; it's necessary. When you feel good in a playful, ethical, and self-care-focused way, you're allowing in goodness.

Embracing goodness is a hallmark of your healing. It's like saying, "I've done enough healing to feel safe enough to accept kindness, blessings, goodness, care, love, and safety. I've done enough healing to lower my armor and let these good things in."

So how do you get back to play? When we've been locked in trauma, play can feel foreign, distant, or even scary. When you play, you don't know what comes next.

At one point in my own healing from sexual trauma, I realized I had lost the capacity for silliness and playfulness. I was so serious all the time. I remember watching friends burst into a spontaneous dance party in the middle of a forest road, and I felt unable to access that playful spirit.

One tool I found enormously helpful was to take improv classes. Improv is, at its heart, deep play—the kind of play where you immerse yourself in another world and have to be totally present. Although I initially felt embarrassed to play improv games and take part in the exercises, with practice over time I experienced a great liberation. I could throw myself into a scene and not know what would happen. I came to trust my ability to show up.

The dance floor was another place where I relearned how to play. Thanks to a thousand dances with many partners, I learned it was okay to move unexpectedly and spontaneously. I could respond to what was offered in the dance and not take it too seriously.

But I'll be honest: I was serious about remembering how to play. Play is the most significant tool of my healing, and my capacity for silliness and humor is a tremendous sign of my healing.

While improv or dance may not be the kind of play that's right for you, there is a kind of play that will make your heart sing. Roller skating? Costumes? What did your kid self love? If you read this section and feel called out, that's fantastic! Now you get to remember how to play or learn for the first time, which is fun! You may need to do some digging or try a few different practices to see what delights you, but your goofball self is waiting for you.

## Types of Pleasure

Let's consider some of the many facets of pleasure. Pleasure isn't just confined to the realms of genitals and erotic sensations, even though that's where most people's minds gravitate. We'll certainly start there, but we will expand and explore much further. What follows is a noncomprehensive list of pleasures.

### Erotic Pleasure

First, let's delve into erotic, sexual pleasure. It originates from nerve endings in the erogenous tissues of your body, which include the genitals, lips, nipples, anus, and even the fingertips. These tissues are rich in nerve endings and often in erectile tissue too, like the genitals, lips, and nipples. Erotic pleasure can be highly focused in one of these areas, but it's not limited to them. It can spread across your entire body, possibly showing up in unexpected places like your feet, shoulders, or wrists. The fascinating thing is that with some training, any part of your body can become an erogenous zone. You could even experiment with erotifying your left elbow.

Erotic pleasure is connected to sexuality, to desire and arousal. While sexual acts are often erotically pleasurable, there are kinds of erotic pleasure that do not involve sexual touch. Many different kinks deliver erotic pleasure. For some, pain is erotic. While erotic pleasure is often connected with sexual arousal and orgasm, neither of these needs to take place for erotic pleasure to occur.

## Sensual Pleasure

My favorite kind of pleasure is what I call "sensual aliveness." It's the pleasure that awakens your senses, reminding you that you're truly alive. It occurs through your senses.

- ¤ Sight: gazing at a breathtaking landscape or a beautiful piece of art, or watching your cat play.
- ¤ Smell: a botanical material like pine or roses.
- ¤ Taste: something delicious like a perfectly ripe strawberry or peach.
- ¤ Touch: the silk of a violet leaf.
- ¤ Sound: your favorite song.

Anything that engages your senses has the potential to bring you sensual pleasure. It's the pleasure of feeling your aliveness in the moment, not just intellectually but in your whole being. Sensual pleasure can be relaxed and savoring.

## Intellectual Pleasure

Intellectual pleasure is the thrill and delight that comes from engaging your mind. It's that rush you feel when you discover a creative solution to a complex problem, you grapple with a new idea or concept, or you immerse yourself in a late-night philosophical debate with an intellectual companion. There's an undeniable pleasure in forging new pathways of thought, and it's like your big brain is firing on all cylinders, turning you on to the world of ideas. A great book can deliver this kind of pleasure.

## The Pleasure of Connection, Collaboration, and Attunement

Another source of pleasure lies in connection and collaboration. It's the joy of being in a harmonious relationship, reveling in the company of good friends, embarking on a road trip adventure with your bestie, or collectively working toward a shared goal. This type of pleasure is found in attunement and synchronization, like when you sing in four-part harmony, engage in line dancing, or perform synchronized swimming. Collaborating on a substantial project or cocreating an immersive experience such as a play or a show can also ignite this sense of pleasure.

## The Pleasure of Vigor

Have you ever experienced the exhilaration that follows a fantastic dance session or an intense workout? It's like an electric current surging through your body, leaving you feeling invigorated and alive. This pleasure arises from the sheer delight of moving your body, whether through dance, exercise, weightlifting, running, or a thousand other ways. It's all about reveling in the vitality and dynamism coursing through you.

## Creative Pleasure

Another facet of pleasure comes from the act of creation. It stems from deep focus, concentration, and the experience of bringing something new into the world. This could manifest in various forms: crafting poetry, creating art, composing music, or even inventing a groundbreaking idea or product. When you're absorbed in the creative process, the parts of your body that you're using become instruments of pleasure, and the act itself is a source of profound satisfaction.

## Ritual Pleasure

Ritual pleasure takes us into the realm of the sacred and the unseen. It's as if you're in sync with a greater force in the world, working in harmony with the invisible, the elements, magick, spirits, or even deities. Engaging in ritual can lead to profound and transformative pleasure. Whether it's a grief ritual that provides a deep sense of rightness and purity, a healing ritual that involves offering or receiving healing, or a movement-based ritual such as dance, each kind of ritual can be intensely pleasurable.

## Ecosexual Pleasure

And then there's the remarkable realm of ecosexual pleasure. This is the delight we find when we engage in an erotic relationship with the Earth. After all, you're made of Earth, and the Earth is an integral part of you. Ecosexual pleasure entails a profound recognition that our bodies are intertwined with the natural world. It's not just about human sex but the myriad forms of sensuality and sexuality that play out in the world. It's a way to creatively and erotically connect with the Earth, much like you instinctively did as a child—feeling the smoothness of acorns, savoring the sensation of rain on your skin, or dancing and playing in harmony with the changing seasons. This, too, is a form of ecosexual pleasure that resonates deep within us, connecting us to the heartbeat of the Earth.

## Complicated Pleasure

Let's delve into the landscape of complicated pleasure. Marketing teaches us that pleasure should be effortless, a sensation we should relentlessly pursue because it offers us an escape from pain. This promise of pain relief and pure pleasure is a cornerstone of commerce, regardless of the product or service sold. Yet, for many people, pleasure is not always straightforward.

There are moments when pleasure flows effortlessly, embracing you fully, expanding your sense of self until your entire body feels at home. However, there are also those times when pleasure becomes challenging. It requires your full attention to remain present or focus on the aspects of the encounter you wish to engage with. At times, it isn't easy to connect with your arousal. Distractions make it hard to feel your own body.

For many people, pleasure is a multifaceted experience, marked by simplicity on some occasions and complexity on others. Perhaps the most complex relationships with pleasure are experienced by those who have a history of sexual trauma. In such cases, pleasure may be deeply entangled with shame, creating a challenging web that needs patient untangling.

Sometimes, trauma results in a disconnection from certain regions of the body, where unawareness or numbness masks muscular contractions or even pain. In these instances, pleasure can feel uncomfortable or even unbearable, often causing dissociation or triggering traumatic memories.

This complexity might be amplified by negative emotions experienced after pleasure, such as feelings of shame, remorse, or guilt that creep in once the moment of pleasure has passed. Unwanted thoughts, intrusive memories, or unwelcome associations can also emerge, further complicating pleasure.

For individuals who have experienced sexual trauma, it may seem unfair that you bear the responsibility of working through these complications. However, despite the lack of fairness, the reality is that it's up to you to navigate this thorny terrain—but only if you want to.

There's no universal blueprint for experiencing pleasure. As I've said many times, you get to define pleasure for yourself. Most individuals yearn for simple pleasure, the kind that doesn't lead to tears or interruptions during sex or having to explain to a partner why certain areas of your body are off-limits.

But after working with hundreds of people healing from sexual trauma, I can tell you there is a silver lining. When you choose the path of embracing complexity, you delve into the beauty and nuances often missed by those seeking an easier route. Despite the twists and turns, healing reveals your pleasure is truly yours.

## Orgasm Is *Not* the Defining Feature of Pleasure

Why is so much fuss made about orgasms? How did orgasms become the sole destination for the pleasure train? Defining pleasure by the number of orgasms achieved is another form of sexual colonization. When there's only one acceptable outcome, there's no room for choice or freedom. Orgasms are merely a biological and neurological process that can occur in the body, much like any other process, such as digestion, respiration, or muscle contractions. The fixation on orgasm as the ultimate goal of all sexual experiences comes from a capitalistic, goal-oriented mindset, where only the pinnacle is worthy of attention. But what about all the pleasure you can have with or without orgasm?

Have you ever found yourself chasing an orgasm, straining to increase arousal through muscular contractions, or trying to reach orgasm as quickly as possible? Do you feel pressured to have the best or biggest orgasm for a partner? The relentless pursuit of orgasm often involves a great deal of effort. What's even more peculiar is the time pressure surrounding orgasms. When you're on your own, you may want to hurry and get it over with. But in the presence of a partner, you may also feel the pressure to climax quickly to avoid disappointing them, or feel that you are taking too long.

Let's acknowledge the weirdness surrounding orgasms. How can we rewild ourselves and decolonize our perspective on pleasure? We can unlearn our societal conditioning around what orgasms are supposed to be like, how they should look, how long they should last, and when they should occur.

Start by considering what you believe about your own orgasms. Have you internalized any "shoulds"? How has porn influenced your expectations of orgasm, for yourself or for a partner? How is your face supposed to look when you come? What is it supposed to feel like?

When you redefine pleasure that may or may not include orgasms—that may or may not even include genital stimulation—you are finding what feels good to you. Many of my clients have found that removing pressure around orgasms has increased their capacity to be present for pleasure.

Your body is capable of wonders. It is up to you to find your unique sweet spots. Don't let someone else's definition of what pleasure is become yours; and if it has, let's change that.

While we're on the topic of orgasms, there are many different types of orgasms you can have. There are many different types of sexual release you can cherish. If you are struggling with having orgasms, not having them, or how you have them, the whole idea can become fraught—so show yourself some compassion. In your masturbation practice, you can explore what happens when you don't have an orgasm, or don't try to have an orgasm. What if you investigate arousal without coming?

## Pleasure and Following Impulses for Healing

Feeling good is healing! The math is simple: the more time you spend feeling good, the less time you spend suffering. I want to go gently here; I'm not saying there is some hierarchy in pleasure or that pain is bad. Many folks struggle with chronic pain. The intention of prioritizing pleasure is not to stigmatize other experiences. In a culture highly focused on superficial pleasure, stating that somatic pleasure is healing is, in fact, radical.

Pleasure is vital for your physical and mental wellness. The inability to feel pleasure, a condition known as *anhedonia*, is one of the most recognized symptoms of many mental illnesses, including depression. As I've said before, part of practicing liberation is choosing where to place your attention. Putting your attention on your own ethical pleasure is a self-loving act.

**Life hack:** You can set an intention to follow your impulses toward pleasure. Learning to pay attention to your tiny impulses toward pleasure is one way you can engage its healing power. Whether you call it play or spontaneity, it's a spark that arises from within, an intuition, a desire, an impulse that asks you to do something: to wiggle, to stretch, to yawn, to move this way, to put your hand here, to get a drink of water, to say this thing.

Impulses that arise in the body are organic and natural. Impulses often come from our deep knowledge of what is needed at any given moment. However, we have been socialized to inhibit our impulses, which has both costs and benefits. Suppressing the impulse to yell "fire" in a crowded theater = good (except when there's really a fire in the theater). Suppressing the impulse to comfort a grieving loved one = bad.

Let me share an example of when I suppressed an impulse and regretted it. When my best friend and I were in the Peace Corps in the early 1990s, she found out that her best friend at home had been killed. I was with her when she found out. We were sharing a hotel room that night, and we were sleeping in the same bed because there was only one.

Later that night, I woke up, and I could feel her sobbing next to me. Everything in me, all the impulses, said, "Reach out and take her into your arms. Just do it." But I inhibited that impulse, and I didn't do it. I didn't want her to think I was coming on to her. I didn't want her to think I was invading her space. I wanted to give her privacy for her grief. Blah, blah, blah. So I inhibited that impulse.

If I could do the situation over, I would take my friend in my arms and hold her. I would pay attention to my life-affirming impulse toward care and comfort. It would have benefited both of us. Imagine how healing it could have been if I had followed that impulse.

Our impulses guide us in good directions most of the time. Most of the time, our impulses are healing impulses. Our pleasure impulses are healing impulses. They often lead to greater nervous system regulation when we follow them. When you follow a pleasure impulse, your brain releases many great chemicals.

My teacher Steve Hoskinson, founder of the Organic Intelligence framework, says that healing your nervous system involves learning to increase the amount of time between having the impulse and inhibiting the impulse. For most of us, the impulse/inhibition cycle is automatic. We don't even recognize that we have the impulse; it happens so quickly. If you can lengthen the cycle's duration, you have more space for choice. Instead of automatically stifling a healing or pleasure impulse, you give it a bit of breathing room. You become more aware of the impulses. Then you can discern if that impulse is something you would like to pursue.

Most of us have excellent intuition about what would feel good and what could be helpful at any given moment. We must reclaim our capacity to feel and acknowledge our impulses. In doing so, we again become capable of play.

As you relearn to follow your impulses, one practice is to ask yourself, as often as you remember, "What would feel good right now?"

If the answer you get is "Having some water would feel good right now," go ahead and drink. You practice following the pleasure impulse.

Once you've gotten into the habit of asking yourself what would feel good, you can layer on the practice of savoring. When you savor, you bring yourself to the present moment to enjoy what is happening. In the example of drinking water, if you were to savor, you would notice things like the coolness of the water as it moves down your throat or the satiation of thirst. Savoring gives you more bang for your pleasure: you extend the enjoyment of a particular event or experience.

You can savor in the moment or after the fact, or both. Reflecting on pleasurable experiences optimizes the feel-good benefit.

Neuroscientist Rick Hanson shares a perspective worth considering:

*Sometimes joy is a sustained experience. Your child is born, you hold her, and your day is filled with a stunned and solemn joy. But I've found intense joy usually comes in brief pulses. You smile, and there is joy for a few seconds. One practical approach to evoke joy is to value opportunities for spontaneous joy that occur in daily life. Perhaps reminisce about a beautiful mountain meadow at sunset. With a simple shift in your mind, you can focus directly on joy. The more experiences of joy you embrace and incorporate into yourself, the easier this process becomes.*

Hanson's insight suggests a practice to optimize the benefits of pleasure: recalling a pleasurable experience to mind after it has passed. This is a readily available resource. Try it for a few days. Savor and revisit moments of past authentic pleasure. This practice contributes to building a repository of joyful experiences you can use—a library of your happiness.

Many of us have a habit of revisiting our "pain book" and dwelling on things that went wrong. You can learn to recognize your human tendency to focus on pain. You can also choose to change the channel and decide where to direct your attention. When you sense yourself veering toward darker emotions or heavier energies, intentionally switch to the "joy channel" or the "pleasure channel" and reflect on the positive aspects of your life.

Let me be clear that I am not advocating for toxic positivity or bypassing more challenging emotions. I want you to have the capacity to feel the full range of your emotions and sensations. However, I am suggesting that you have agency in how you focus your attention. If you are giving your pain more airtime than your pleasure, it's worth considering why.

You can increase the frequency with which you notice your impulses toward pleasure and follow them. You can deepen your capacity for pleasure. Doing this practice does not mean that everything else that's happening in your body suddenly stops happening. If you are a person who experiences chronic pain, this doesn't mean, *woo-hoo, no more pain*. It's just choosing how you place your attention and what you're putting it on. You can give yourself the gift of starting to believe, "I deserve to feel good." Say that right now. "I deserve to feel good. I deserve to feel good. I deserve to feel good." Take a breath. "I deserve to feel good. I deserve to feel good."

# Ecstasy and Ecstatic Practices

My teacher and friend Barbara Carrellas says ecstasy is necessary. She writes, "Ecstasy is the human reset button. It shakes you up, reboots your system, and opens your eyes to a whole new world of possibilities. Ecstasy introduces you to your deepest, most authentic self, while simultaneously offering freedom, intimacy, connection, and spiritual awakening."

I used to think that ecstasy was about drugs or sex cults in the desert in the time of the Greek philosophers. But really, when we're speaking of ecstasy, what we're talking about is a state of embodied emotional clarity. Hallmarks of ecstatic states are profound presence and a sense of connection with the divine, whatever that means for you. Ecstasy is notably free of inhibition and shame. Ecstatic states are typically expansive.

Ecstasy is the essence of a feeling state in your body. It's not stagnant. It's like sensual aliveness on steroids. It's the capacity that we all have to be wide awake and fully present in deep joy and connection. Ecstatic experiences often involve movement, breath, sound, music, or embodied practices like dance or sex. Ecstasy can be loud and big! But sometimes ecstasy is quiet, a sense of pure contentment. Again, you get to decide what ecstasy means for you. There's no wrong way to do ecstatic practice, but there are tools and practices for cultivating ecstatic states that have been time-tested by other practitioners of ecstasy through the ages.

Ecstasy is not about just being in joy. Many deeply profound states can be ecstatic, such as grief, longing, reverence, and catharsis. When you allow what is alive inside you to move in the way it wants to move, states of ecstasy can occur.

Although a full exploration of ecstatic states and practices is beyond the scope of this book, others have done much great research and writing on the topic. I point you toward Barbara's work, found in the "Resources" section at the back of this book.

I believe that the goal of embodiment is to feel the full range of our sensations and emotions. Ecstasy may be a rare state, but it is well within the realms of what humans can experience. Sexual pleasure is one road to ecstasy, but there are many others.

What is ecstasy for you? How do you know it? How do you feel it?

Since calling a past experience of pleasure to mind can help you feel those feelings again, let's try it with an ecstatic experience. At what moment have you felt alive, exhilarated, present, or even holy? Have you had a moment when you felt you were a part of something much larger than you?

I experienced this moment on a river in Oregon. I had spent the previous week at a spiritual retreat for queers and anarchists. Like almost everyone at the retreat, I had just finished experiencing the deep purge of the norovirus. The day I was leaving, I went to a nearby river where the water had carved out the river rock, making pools and cups of stiller water. As I sat in the river with water rushing over me, my perspective shifted, and suddenly, I was the rocks, the river, the sky. I felt a tremendous sense of merging with the world, being part of rather than separate. This state lasted for ten minutes, and I sobbed through the entire experience. It felt so right, like home.

This was an ecstatic experience that I had without drugs, sex, ritual, or any other structure. When I think of what ecstasy feels like in my body, this is a hallmark moment that comes to mind. When I recall it, it helps me feel that deep, sensual belonging.

Ecstatic experiences can be spontaneous. The experience I describe is one of grace, but in some ways, the context around it supported it. My heart was open. My body had been violently ill and then returned to good health. I felt connected with my community.

In looking at the conditions that contextualized my experience, I can notice the elements I need in place to feel that kind of pleasure: rest and retreat, connection with aligned humans, time in nature.

What's cool is that you can actually practice ecstasy. In Barbara's book *Ecstasy Is Necessary*, she offers a series of practices you can do to cultivate ecstatic states. Holotropic Breathwork, ice baths, singing, dancing, and drumming with others are all tools humans use to achieve states of embodied ecstasy.

## Genital Mapping

The practice of genital mapping comes from an educational modality called Sexological Bodywork. Genital mapping is a process of deepening your awareness of your genital area. Often this area remains vague and undefined to us, described simply as "down there." But what happens when you develop a more profound awareness of the tissues, structures, and nerve endings in your genital area? What is it like to have an embodied understanding of this part of your body?

Genital mapping is a form of exploration, a curiosity-driven practice that allows you to investigate what's happening between your legs. It is not inherently a sexual practice, and ideally you would explore it on your own or with a practitioner who can provide a supportive space.

The "Resources" section at the back of this book provides a URL where you can access an online recording that will guide you through this process. When you decide to engage in this practice, try it first as a solitary experience. To begin, allocate about an hour of uninterrupted time for yourself in a comfortable, private setting where you can be at ease while naked. This could be a bedroom, a massage table, a couch, or even outdoors. The key is to get curious about your genitals.

Lie down and initiate some deep breathing and relaxation techniques, allowing your body to awaken. You might engage in gentle self-massage, tapping, patting, or other actions that feel right for you.

When you're ready, gently cup and hold your genital area with tenderness. At this point, it's not about seeking pleasure or arousal; it's about simply being present with what is. Maintain this posture and observe until it no longer piques your interest. Be aware of moments when you think, "This is uninteresting," because that could be a smoke screen for

"I can't remain here." If you find it challenging to stay, that's okay, but don't label it as "dull." Acknowledge that this space may be too intense or overwhelming for the moment.

If you're comfortable with the cupping and wish to delve deeper into this practice, next you can create a mental map of various points around your genital area. For this part of the practice, many people find it helpful to imagine superimposing the image of a clock face on their genitals. Begin at twelve o'clock. Touch that point on your genitals with whatever pressure you prefer. Hang out and notice what happens. Stay with it until it feels complete.

Next, move around the clock an hour at a time, stopping at each hour. At each point, apply a bit of pressure, whatever feels right. The amount of time you hold each point depends on you; it could be just a minute, or it could be much longer. Your job is to stay present with your touch and to notice your sensations. Continuously tune into the subtle shifts in your experience. Remember, there is no wrong way to do this; it's a personalized journey. Some of the points on your genitals may feel intensely alive; some may feel numb. Sometimes people feel nothing; some people experience emotions or have memories emerge. Go slow and tender here. You are not trying to make anything happen.

There is nothing you are supposed to be experiencing. This is important to understand. You are in a process of curiosity about your own body. Genital mapping can be an uncomfortable learning edge because we often engage with our genitals only for sexual sensation, elimination, health care, or procreation. To extend kind attention to this part of your body without expecting anything is a return to innocence.

Initially, the focus is on external genital mapping. However, you can conduct subsequent sessions to explore internal genital mapping if that's applicable to your body. Anal mapping is also a possibility.

Should you wish to involve a partner, make it clear that this is not a sexual or arousal practice but rather an exercise in presence and awareness.

It's helpful to record what you notice at each point. An hour-long session can bring about substantial changes in your state of consciousness, making it difficult to recall all the details later. Consider using a voice recorder to document your experience, as it can be challenging to toggle your attention between writing and holding your genitals. Recording your observations allows you to revisit your experiences.

This practice can be particularly transformative for those who encounter resistance to genital touch or have a hard time staying present with pleasure. If, when you read this, you initially hesitate or dismiss the idea, pay attention to your response. Is this not the right time for you? Or are there deeper reasons for your reluctance? Trust your instincts, and remember that you can always take a break. This practice is not about pushing boundaries. It's about being present with your body's tissues.

The more attentive you become to your body, the more you can bring that presence to your sexuality. This self-exploration is valuable, and I encourage you to undertake it this Month.

# Last Thoughts for Month 11

It can be challenging to release the narratives of what we think our pleasure should be, especially when it once brought us joy. Here's an invitation for you: take the time, dive deep into your sensations, and express, with authenticity, what *is* pleasure for you at this moment in your life right now.

Track the path of true pleasure versus false pleasure. True pleasure lingers, leaving you with a sense of goodness long after the moment has passed. Learn from those experiences so you can make mindful choices in the future.

Your healing and your ability to feel pleasure aren't just about you. There's a misleading narrative about selfishness and pleasure, and it's utter nonsense. When your pleasure is deeply connected to your well-being and joy, it becomes a blessing to your community. It's a healing force in the world. You're not just doing this pleasure work for yourself; you're doing it for your descendants, for those with you right now, and for the world.

There's a secret to this process: it's better when you work for it. Erotic expressions that require effort, practice, and a willingness to traverse the terrain of emotions such as grief and anger are like a treasure hunt. It is through this process that the core story of unworthiness begins to heal. In your quest to find a pleasure that genuinely resonates with you, it's vital to cultivate a sense of worthiness.

It's essential to acknowledge that the process of sexual healing might be slow to yield results; for many, it's a lifelong project. You deserve the pleasure you desire.

**In conclusion, this Month you will:**

- Complete the Month 11 worksheets in the appendix. You can also download this month's worksheets at www.pavinimoray.com/ttb-bonus.html.
- Daily practice: Go on an impulse walk. You can do this as many times as you like.
- Explore the practice of genital mapping.
- Add something to your healing altar that represents pleasure.
- Complete Ritual 11: Pleasure.

# Ritual 11: Pleasure

## Preparation

- The purpose of this ritual is to increase the amount of pleasure you are available to receive.
- This ritual will require a bit more preparation and time than others.
- You can do this at your healing altar or in another place you will not be disturbed. You may wish to create a nest of pillows and blankets.

- You may wish to have some essential oil or beloved perfume, or a lush body product of your choosing. You can also use water.

- Have a delicious beverage and/or yummy snacks at hand, to give pleasure to your insides.

- You can also have some music or an instrument to lovingly vibrate inside your ears.

- You will also need a notebook or voice recorder.

**Begin by setting a container of prayer as you read this aloud:**

*Sweet and blessed ancestors of my blood and heart,*
*I pray to know the holiness of my body,*
*the sacred nature of my pleasure.*
*Help me feel the lush swirl of natural rhythms as they move through me.*
*Let me know the dance of the fire and starlight as they shine on me.*
*May I dissolve as the flow of water courses in and around me.*
*Give me subtle safety and sublime honey of what is good.*
*Give me welcoming waves of pleasure and bliss.*
*I say yes to all of this:*
*Please harmonize my body, sweeten my nervous system, let my pleasure make me whole.*

**Next, cast a circle of protection with the help of your allies.**

Call out to the trusted spiritual sources of protection you already have. This may be deities, guardians, the elements, or relationships with animals, stones, holy places, herbs, or anything from the green world. Invite each to come toward you, and pause until you sense they are present.

Then, with their support, imagine a layer of protection that goes all around you. You can visualize it if you like, or feel it.

Check in: Do you feel protected all the way around? Can you feel yourself?

In your imagination, run a blast of clean water, air, earth, and/or fire through your entire line. Things should be flowing freely.

Invite in your connection with your guide, and the ancestors of erotic wellness who bequeathed to you their blessings.

With their boundaried and appropriate presence, bring your own loving touch to your body.

You can begin anywhere that feels right. You may wish to use a body product, oil, or perfume. You can also use clean water. Touch that part of your body. Bring the intention of offering pleasure to yourself. Remember that Eros is not always about sex and genitals and orgasms. Eros is about sensual aliveness.

Bring the blessing of pleasure to each part of your body. If you don't know what to do, just hold a loving touch until it feels complete. If that part of your body wants to be stroked, massaged, held, kissed, gentled . . . do that. Ask what each part of you wants and needs to feel pleasure in this ritual. Explore to find out what you want.

This ritual creates new neural pathways of body sovereignty through intentional pleasure.

Anoint and bless your body. Notice what else is wanted, and pay exquisite attention to what is enough. Nothing should feel forced or pressured. Truly consider your own consent.

If you would like to bring genital pleasure and arousal into this ritual, it is welcome.

At the end of your time blessing and honoring your pleasure body, bring yourself to stillness for some minutes. Savor any reverberations in your system. Offer deep honor to yourself for engaging this ritual.

When things feel complete, make notes of any important information.

Thank your guides, allies, and ancestors for their compassionate and boundaried presence.

Keep the protection intact as you end the ritual, and make any notes you wish.

# Month 12
## *Ancient Pleasure*

Where you put your body,
your body is.
Is it a garden, a temple, a rave?
A lover's rumpled bed?

Where do you feed your pleasure
a full meal?

Make offering of your spiraling delight?

Because.

The rise and fall of day's light
cares not for your struggles, your joys.

Two years will pass
no matter what you allow, or don't.

Soft shining body,
you can set your true to here.

## *Pleasure Offering Practice*

Drum up some good breathing, good feeling,
good aliveness. Do it now.

Build it like a boiling pot, covered and
steaming.

When you are ready, send it hurling through
the night sky to nourish something you love.

*Magick is real.*

# Ancestor Moon

This month we discuss elders, ancestors' sexual liberation, erotic offerings, and sharing your sexual self.

Before we dive in, I invite you to consider your work of the last eleven Months. All of the showing up for yourself. All of the attention. Every narrative you've worked to change. Every belief you are actively shifting. All. The. Healing. You've done so much, and you have so many tools in your toolkit. Honoring all of that work is part of integrating a new way of being in your body and your sexuality.

## Elders

When we talk about ancestors, we talk also of elders. Each one of us is moving toward becoming an elevated ancestor. We can practice being loving ancestors by being wonderful elders.

In Western culture, because of ageism, eldership and the somatic and intellectual wisdom that lives in the bodies of older people are minimized or dismissed. Younger generations may pay lip service to our elders, but ours is not a living tradition that values what elders have earned. Therefore, we must interrogate the ageist beliefs we have internalized so we may learn from those ahead of us on the path.

Who are your elders? Who do you honor for the depth of their lived experience?

One of my elders, Joseph, is in his late seventies. He is a queer, white man who survived the AIDS epidemic, started the profession of Sexological Bodywork, and has been a huge influence on somatic sex education. We have worked together for years as collaborators, boss and employee, and friends. He was my dissertation mentor. I worked for him helping him with his writing for eight years. While there are many things I've learned from him, the most important is how to be an elder who changes.

I've watched as he allows himself to have his beliefs confronted, again and again. When we started working together, I felt strongly that the binary gender pieces of his professional training needed to be updated to a more inclusive model. Despite it requiring months of revision of an entire curriculum, he was joyfully willing to learn and change, not just the material but his own understanding. I've watched him open his heart repeatedly to the suffering of others as he works to understand and dismantle white supremacy. Something special about him is his lack of defensiveness and fragility. He truly wants to live in an equitable, just world, and he's willing to do the internal work necessary to help get us there.

Joseph shows up, organizes, teaches, and remains a learner who is dedicated to cultivating more empathy. This is who I want to be as an elder: heart open, mind open.

While every person who survives to old age has learned many things and has gifts to offer, just being older does not, in my opinion, make you an elder. The role of elder is earned through commitment to empathy and continual learning.

Elders I respect are willing to engage new beliefs and challenge old ones as conversations about complex cultural topics emerge and evolve. They're willing. They're not resistant. They're excited to be in this learning process to improve continually. They haven't gotten to a certain point in their learning and development and then stopped and said, "Now I have finished learning. I will rest on my laurels."

The role of elder is by nature an erotic role—erotic because of their softened skin, both literal and metaphorical, and because of their seasoned body, which has survived and lived to tell the lessons learned. An elder can speak to the importance of the sensual because they've tuned to it for many years. They can talk to it because they are someone who has experienced sexuality firsthand across their entire life span. They know intimately the changes and transformations of healing and of time. They know what works and what does not in intimate relationships because they've learned through trial and error. Their knowledge is not theoretical but lived. An older role model can articulate what you need to hear.

The role of the elder is erotic, but unfortunately, older adults in Western culture are stripped of their sexuality. Think about it: When was the last time you saw a scorching sex scene in the public discourse involving older people? The embodied knowing that they have accumulated from a lifetime of navigating being in a body, being a sexual being, goes unrecognized. It's made obsolete or even taboo because older people in our culture are desexualized, which is part of cultural amnesia.

Cultural amnesia means that most of us have never known intact lifeways wherein the wisdom, grace, and guidance of elders are offered to us consistently. Intact lifeways include connection with elders, ancestors, and older ways of knowing, feeling, and being; connection with the big, ancient powers of the cosmos; reverence for the Earth; and attunement and care for descendants more than two generations away from us.

Without a cultural value of eldership and the role of elders in our communities, we flail about. We age out of our activist communities. Marketing tells us youth should be our standard, and we've likely all seen pretty twenty-three-year-old life coaches preaching on social media.

But without elders to hold cultural memory, we must navigate each new situation from scratch rather than relying on accumulated wisdom to guide us. You have to figure it out each time because no one's there to guide you. No one's there to guide groups through conflict. There's no cultural or institutional memory.

# Elders, Intergenerational Relations, and the Necessity of Community for Healing

Intergenerational relationships are a healing resource. You can create them by finding folks older and younger than you and sharing stories, memories, and guidance from them, and seeking support from them. Mutual aid is sexy! And it can flow up and down the generations in a nonhierarchical sharing of information. The young need the elders, and the elders need the youth.

Healing does not happen in isolation. It happens with a supportive community that includes elders.

One person I spoke with told me about a relationship she had developed with an elder and spiritual mentor:

*Well, there's the part that's community, and there's the part that's elders. Having elders around you who understand what's happening with you and what you need. I feel lucky after getting to my mentor because I was able to incorporate that part that I didn't even know I needed to be healing. Because she could see my life, she was like, "Okay, you got to work on this, and you got to work on that. You definitely got to work on this over here."*

One corrective to the transgenerational transmission of trauma is to seek the transgenerational transmission of wisdom. Especially for folks living in any kind of marginalization, there is so much goodness in our roots, in the shoulders that we're standing on. Who could you turn to for stories of solidarity and resistance?

One of the people I talked with said:

*We're in such an amazing time. There were very few people in the seventies who had a sense of their ancestors. There was this notion of a break between generations. Now, whether it's faggots or hip-hop or trans people or trans hip-hop faggots, there's really a different attention paid to elders. In these kinds of communities, people give props not just to their parents but to the people who struggled before them. To the people who created these spaces.*

(*Note:* The word "faggots" is an intentional reclamation of a historical slur, spoken by someone who uses the term to self-identify.)

The concept of feeling worthy to receive support from the community was discussed by someone I interviewed who was an elder herself and who talked about the deep gratitude she had for one of her teachers:

*Teachers came into my life and helped me, and made me feel whole and good and worthy. Because that's an important element that can get lost as we work on our healing. It's important that we feel worthy of receiving the help that we're getting.*

Someone else I spoke with talked about how having relationships with living elders helped her with the secrecy and shame that were preventing her sexual healing. I asked her if spiritual healing includes relationship with ancestors, as well as living community elders, to break secrecy and shame:

*Yes. Community, we need each other. We need each other to heal. We need containers, we need other people, we need those who have gone before us so that wisdom isn't lost.*

I want to share with you an amazing email that I received years ago from a queer elder of mine. She was eighty-three when she wrote me. I had written a blog post about erotic energy, and she reached out with a reply:

*My response to your blog post is to tell you that sex keeps getting better and higher though with different nuances, and it somehow always feels new or at least slightly different, even with the same partner, no matter how old you are, in my case, how old I am. I will reread some of your stuff and try to incorporate some of the things that you mention that I'm not aware of doing or being, but I must admit very little mind is involved at this point. Possibly, thinking ahead may nudge me in some direction I'm curious about.*

Isn't that amazing? I want to be able to write that email at eighty-three. Do you? Being the person who writes an email like this becomes possible when we commit to evolving our sexuality across our life span and not desexualizing ourselves or our elders or ancestors. You are here because of the sex of your ancestors. Many, many, many people had sex for you to be here.

## Learn about the Historical Conditions Your Ancestors Lived In

NOTE *We are moving into a conversation about ancestors and sexuality, and ritual safety is paramount. You may wish to review the content in Month 1 that speaks to safety.*

Likely you know where your ancestors lived, but what conditions did they live in? What historical events did they experience? Having a context for your ancestors beyond just knowing their names and dates of birth and death helps you to connect with them more fully.

Just as your identities are important to your life, so were theirs. What specific cultural identities did they hold? Were your people at the center of their times, or the margins? What oppressions and privileges did they experience? Especially for folks of European ancestry, or anyone with colonizer predecessors, knowing your people's circumstances can help direct your attention to what needs healing. For example, I know that my ancestors were early white colonizers who participated in genocide in Ohio. That means I can direct my healing attention toward repair and reparations with the Indigenous people of that land, and with the land itself. Knowing the stories of my ancestors allows me to do work to heal what was wounded. For me, this is a way for my lineage to get right, both externally and internally. When I know the work is done, ritually and in this realm, I can find pride in the strengths of my people without being mired in the shame of their actions.

I must acknowledge here that limited information is often available through genealogical records about blood ancestors for people who come from marginalized identities like people of color, queer folks, and gender-blessed folks. Often there are no records, or the information you seek is not presented in the genealogical record that does exist. Researching and knowing the history of marginalized and oppressed peoples means you can track the technologies they used to get free. Learning whose shoulders your work rests on and knowing the lineage of liberation you are continuing helps you feel your belonging to a lineage of folks who fought for freedom.

These stories may not be easily available, but they are there. They can be hidden in plain sight sometimes. But if you have living elders, and you can get them talking, they can be a tremendous source of information.

## Understand Your Ancestral Sexual Legacies

We've spent a lot of time understanding your ancestral sexual inheritance. Some people decide to heal with ancestors precisely because they understand the sexual legacies that they've inherited from their ancestors.

You have been making a concerted effort to understand the ancestral sexual legacies you embody and how they live in you. Understanding both the sexual burdens and the erotic blessings you've inherited from your ancestors offers awareness and choices about how you continue to either embody or change these traits and behaviors. Without doing the work to develop this understanding, it's possible to replicate unhelpful or even harmful patterns of behavior unconsciously.

As we've discussed extensively, discernment is of the essence when deciding how you wish to engage with your ancestors and sexuality. Your personal boundaries serve both you and your people. You inquire inside yourself about what feels right, and you take action based on your own felt sense of what's appropriate.

For example, I interviewed one person who discussed how she initially had her ancestor altar in her bedroom, but she quickly moved it out based on her sense that this was not right for her:

*I had my ancestor altar in my bedroom for a very short time. They wanted to be in there, and they were like, "Hey, let us come in." I had them in here, and I was like, "Oh, this is not right. It's not right. It's not becoming, it's not seemly. It's not sweet."*

Another person had this to say about their discernment process:

*I am honest and forthright, and I trust myself and my ancestors, including my real boundaries about what I do not choose to share with them.*

Others I interviewed have ancestor altars in bedrooms or even invoke particular ancestors for sex magick rituals. Discernment is everything. What is right for you?

## Discernment around Ancestors and the Erotic

Sometimes people choose to connect erotically with their ancestors of heart, and some people choose to connect erotically with their ancestors of blood. I've had many clients and students who have had consensual erotic connections with their ancestors. This is an individual choice. For me and my ancestors, it does not feel right to connect in this way. However, sometimes I do offer erotic energy to one of the lineages I claim, often to a lineage that is not my blood lineage. For example, I might decide to make an offering of an orgasm to the bladesmith tradition of which I am a part. When I do this, I am clear that the offering is made to those who are entirely well, shiny, and bright in spirit.

I am not suggesting this practice is necessary for healing. This information is provided for those who have done this or who intend to do this. You can heal from trauma without this practice, so please be quite diligent in discerning whether this is something you wish to do or not.

Besides discerning what is suitable for you personally, it's also critical to determine the degree of wellness of the ancestor you want to work with. Through ritual, you've worked to develop an ongoing relationship with your ancestral guide, and they can help you with this discernment. Through them, you should have a good understanding of what a well ancestor feels like and what qualities of consent they exhibit.

You can use the questions we discussed in Ritual 1: Intention and Boundaries to ascertain ancestral wholeness, which includes discerning inappropriate reasons for connecting erotically with an ancestor. These would include things like the ancestor in question is requesting an erotic connection, you feel pressure or obligated, or it repeats and reinforces instances of sexual violation, coercion, and abuse that you have personally experienced or that you are aware have occurred in that line. For example, if there is an ancestor whom you know to have committed sexual harm, it would likely not be appropriate to connect erotically with that ancestor unless there was a very good reason.

One person I spoke with who does have an erotic connection at times with particular ancestors told me:

*I feel like I need to check in with each ancestral line and find out who's available: who's well, who's not. I don't feel like there's a blanket "yes." I don't want to have sex with all my ancestors or even share pleasure sexually with my ancestors, any more than I would with every living person. It's on a case-by-case basis.*

Sometimes people connect erotically with their ancestors of spiritual (not blood) lineage. One person I spoke with talked about the discernment process she used in having an erotic connection with an ancestor from her spiritual lineage:

*Well, I would only do it with an incredibly well ancestor. I would have no interest in this otherwise. The person I'm speaking of, I would consider—and many people would consider—an ascended master. He's high, and so that's exciting to me. I wouldn't if he was not. The first thing is, it's not a thing to negotiate unless you really know the wellness of that spirit.*

## Dangers and Taboos of Ancestral Erotic Connection

There are dangers and taboos in connecting erotically with ancestors or sharing erotic energy with an ancestral line. The incest taboo prohibits sexual contact between close relatives. Many of us have internalized this as a cultural norm. When speaking about sex and ancestors, the taboo often arises.

The danger of working with erotic energy and ancestors is mostly about predatory energies. Just like living humans, there are human dead who are not yet well. They will not respect boundaries. If you ever find yourself in such a situation, either with the living or the dead, for the sake of your own healing sexuality, move away as quickly as you can. Your boundaries and your consent matter.

Another danger of working erotically with the unseen realms is getting involved with unsavory elements who do not have your best interests at heart. If something feels off, or it's a "no" for you, listen to that. Just because something is in the spirit realm doesn't mean it's awesome or wholesome.

Many established traditions prohibit erotic contact between the living and the dead. That said, there are also traditions that encourage it and have become more skillful in ritual technology, training practitioners how to use the erotic in their ancestral healing work.

For further information, I point you toward Dr. Megan Rose's book *Spirit Marriage: Intimate Relationships with Otherworldly Beings*.

## Benefits of Ancestral Erotic Connection

Now that I've named the dangers and taboos, there are also benefits to erotic ancestral work. It can provide a nourishing offering of energy for the entire line. It can be healing for the individual experiencing it. It can be a way to connect.

Another significant benefit is that if there has been sexual wounding in an ancestral line, you can choose to create sexual wholeness for the sake of the entire line—ancestors, the living, and those yet to come. You do not need to connect erotically with your ancestors to do this, however. In Month 13 we'll discuss how you can make an intentional pleasure bundle to pass to your descendants, which is another way to create sexual healing in a lineage.

## How to Connect Erotically with Ancestors

Ultimately, the decision of whether to connect erotically with your blood ancestors or other lineages is very personal. If you do decide to do this, I would suggest moving very slowly and collecting lots of data in order to discern next steps. Working with a practitioner could also be supportive here.

If you want to try a simple and relatively safe practice, try finding a natural object like a stone, and then nourishing that object with your erotic energy. You could hold it against your body and imagine the flow of the erotic infusing it. You could kiss it. You could bless it with an orgasm. Then, you could offer the stone to an ancestral lineage. You are creating something powerful and beautiful with your Eros, which is so lovely.

Another way to engage the supportive energies of elders, role models, and ancestors is to invite them into the spaces where you practice the erotic, like your bedroom. One of the people I interviewed mentioned how he places images and photographs of his erotic superheroes and ancestors in his sexy space. Whenever he has a hookup, he pays homage to them first by making an offering. He then invites in their blessings of protection, pleasure, and sex positivity.

The best way to avoid negative outcomes is to take small, incremental steps. Approach these practices with care! Consider consulting your ancestral guide before making any offerings, and definitely do so before inviting in erotic contact with the spirit world. What does your guide suggest?

## Ecosexuality

The Earth is composed of your ancestors' bodies. You are made of the Earth, and the portion of Earth that is you was once the body of your ancestors. The Earth of your body craves care, nurturing, love, and healing. It's pulsating with sensuality. Pleasure supports life. Restoring a harmonious connection between human sexuality and the Earth is an essential form of environmentalism.

Nature is undeniably sexy. If you think back to your childhood, you might remember instinctively knowing the Earth's sensuality. You might feel it now as the sap rises in trees after winter; you might sense it as your veins pulse like waves caressing the shore. Call to mind your memories of the silky sensation of river water on your naked skin, the warmth of the sun on your body, the feel of sand against your skin, the goosebumps from a cool breeze. These are ecosexual pleasures.

If you have not yet encountered Annie Sprinkle and Beth Stevens's work on ecosexuality, I encourage you to explore their ideas. They pose critical questions: How do we hold the Earth as our lover? How can we make love with the Earth? How do we celebrate nature's inherent sensuality? How can we manifest the Eros of the Earth in our spirits and bodies? How can our erotic relationship with the Earth fuel our activism to take care of our planet?

Here's a vision of Earth-honoring human sexuality that my ancestors shared with me:

Imagine a pleasure garden, spacious and lush, adorned with abundant fruit trees and grapes hanging heavily from vines. A serene stream meanders through this place, emanating the scents of blooming roses, lilies, and honeysuckle. This garden is a sacred space for intimate connections outdoors, beneath the stars, on the Earth's body.

In this garden, there's a vital agreement held among all visitors, so subtle that it is felt rather than stated. This agreement is simple but profound: "The wellness of each is the wellness of all." Everyone who enters the garden holds this agreement as a fundamental right. The adjustments required to honor this agreement are minuscule, yet their impact is tangible and shared.

As you venture deeper into the garden, you'll discover a fountain of honey gifted by the bees that pollinate the garden. You're welcome to sip the honey whenever you desire. This garden isn't a miraculous anomaly; it's an inherent part of existence for all who come here. Its purpose is to nourish, provide pleasure, foster connections, and celebrate the beauty of life.

The law here is clear: all acts of consensual pleasure are sacred rituals. This garden is a place to experience the blessings of feeling good. It's a reminder that pleasure heals. The Earth cherishes your presence as your life pulses through its body.

The garden represents a world where everyone is their authentic sexual selves, where power is shared, desires are expressed, and deep attunement to each other's feelings is cultivated. It's a place where eroticism is celebrated, unburdened by shame. All life here, whether it's bees, streams, wind, hummingbirds, humans, or other creatures, is valued as an expression of life itself.

If this garden entices you, you are warmly invited to inhabit it. To share your sexual experiences with others, you embark on a journey of self-trust, honing your discernment. You learn to heed your body's signals, respecting your boundaries and knowing that you won't push through them.

You trust yourself to speak your truth, ask for what you desire, and listen to your partner's needs without feeling obligated. You acknowledge that you can say no or yes based on what resonates with your desires. With each successful shared experience, you develop more self-trust.

It's okay to make mistakes; they are learning opportunities. If you unintentionally harm yourself or others, you know you will initiate repair. You recognize the timing that best suits you and the people who are good for you. You understand that your ancestors support your pursuit of pleasurable sex because it's life-affirming.

When you're ready to share your sexual self, the tools you've developed accompany you. Expect some fumbles and mishaps, but also anticipate growth and new experiences. You will gather a wealth of information, and you'll have more to share as you embrace this path.

## Last Thoughts for Month 12

Having more context about the lives your ancestors lived can help you to deepen and enrich your ancestral reverence practices.

I am excited about reimagining the role of eldership in our communities and centering lived experience as a source of wisdom that can guide us to new futures.

Be really careful if you connect erotically with ancestors. Use all the safety protocols, and get support. The taboos emerged from experience. Don't do it if it's not right for you. However, if there is healing for you here, start slow.

**In conclusion, this Month you will:**

¤ Complete the worksheets for Month 12 in the appendix. You can also download this month's worksheets at www.pavinimoray.com/ttb-bonus.html.

¤ Engage this daily practice: build up some aliveness with your breath and body, and send it toward something you love.

¤ Add something to your healing altar that represents your ancestors.

¤ Complete Ritual 12: Ancestors.

## Ritual 12: Ancestors

### Preparation

¤ The purpose of this ritual is to receive healing from your ancestors for anything in your sexuality that needs support.

¤ You can do this at your healing altar or in another place you will not be disturbed.

¤ You will also need a notebook or voice recorder.

**Begin by setting a container of prayer as you read this aloud:**

*Brightest of bright, sweetest of sweet, my ancestors of bone and blood,*
*please hear my prayer.*
*Please bring me perfect healing*
*so that my heart and sex are made whole,*
*sovereign, and powerful.*
*Please tend all that needs tending with your gentle and kind attention*
*so that I am shining.*

*Please allow Eros to flow through me, in the best ways possible*
*blessing my life and my work,*
*my creativity and my projects,*
*my relationships with others and with myself.*

**Next, cast a circle of protection with the help of your allies.**

Call out to the trusted spiritual sources of protection you already have. This may be deities, guardians, the elements, or relationships with animals, stones, holy places, herbs, or anything from the green world. Invite each to come toward you, and pause until you sense they are present.

Then, with their support, imagine a layer of protection that goes all around you. You can visualize it if you like, or feel it.

With your protection in place, invite connection with your ancestral guide.

First, listen and see if there is anything they want you to know.

Next, share your intention to receive healing for any part of your sexuality that needs it.

Allow your guide to work with you in whatever way is best, knowing you only need to consent to what is right for you.

After that feels complete, thank your guide, and take a moment to feel the impact of the ritual.

Now ask your guide what else is necessary for this great healing work to ripple out from you into all of your lines. Healing can move multidirectionally throughout time. Allow your guide to work as they will.

When this is complete for now, ask if there are any offerings that would support the healing, or if there is anything else your guide wants you to know.

Finish with your guide, thank your allies, and make notes if you want.

Close this ritual with a simple prayer that Eros flow naturally through all beings.

# Month 13
## *Flow On*

Fitting together
what was apart
into some new miraculous whole,
sparklingly yours.

Whole the beginning.
You thought it the destination
final and forever.
No.
Flow on you must.

At the edge of unshattered, your heart hears
the dreams your people dream for you,
the prayers they say.
Words do echo through centuries
everything ever said still being said.

Now hear them.
Now remember,
close, just a hair's breadth from this world,
whispers:

Your pleasure brings us pleasure.

Forget anything not this.

## *Moon of Integration Practice*

*Breathing in, I welcome Eros.*
*Breathing out, I share the flow of Eros.*

# MONTH 13

# Integration Moon

Welcome to Month 13, the integration and completion moon. Congratulations on reaching this point. I acknowledge your dedication to your erotic well-being and the well-being of sexuality in your lineage. It's a significant achievement, and you deserve recognition for it. During this final Month, we'll explore topics of love as protection, blessing descendants, integration, commitment, and completion.

## Love as Protection

We begin with the concept of love as protection. Throughout this book, you've worked hard to establish boundaries, cultivate discernment, and understand what serves your highest good. You've learned to remove what doesn't align with your well-being from your life.

As you progress deeper into this work, you'll begin to notice that proper protection emanates from within. Instead of erecting rigid, impenetrable boundaries, you're protected by boundaries that exist internally. You'll become less willing to allow anything into your field that doesn't serve your highest good. It's important to note that this shift doesn't eliminate discomfort; it signifies a softening.

Love becomes your protective force as you extend love and care toward yourself. You become responsible for your life, letting go of blame and envy. Your safety rests on your shoulders. This kind of self-love integrates the love, blessings, and protection offered to you by your ancestors over generations, as well as the love you provide to your descendants.

This self-love ensures your safety and resilience. It deepens your understanding of your own love—what it means to give and receive it, and how to offer it to yourself. You become the person who can answer the question, "What would I do right now if I deeply loved myself?" This self-awareness provides profound protection.

You no longer find yourself in internal conflict, rejecting parts of yourself. Consequently, your external boundaries don't need to be as fortified because you have a solid sense of self. You understand who you are, what you stand for, and what you allow into your life. This ease allows for greater acceptance and less vigilance.

Although painful experiences may still occur, you don't abandon yourself in times of distress. Instead, you provide self-soothing, kindness, and self-compassion. The beauty of this love as protection lies in its permanence: it cannot be taken away from you.

One way to practice self-love is by praying for others and wishing them wellness, healing, and love. This type of prayer is also protective, as it prevents you from harboring hatred. I pray for the healing of my enemies daily, as well as for the healing of my own heart. Prayer like this doesn't require you to agree with or condone someone's actions, politics, or behavior, but it keeps hate from residing in your heart, which is important because such feelings are detrimental to your well-being. Forgiveness is, in essence, a selfish act of radical self-love performed for your benefit.

Who are you when you know you have yourself and don't need to hold your boundaries far in front of you because you possess the self-trust that you will *always* show up for yourself? This perspective highlights the profound protective power of love. You demonstrate love for yourself and others by clarifying what you're available for and what you're not. It's an idea to contemplate, not a mandate or a practice; it underscores how deeply love can serve as a source of protection.

## Blessing Your Descendants: Two Essential Practices

How can erotic wellness extend from you to both your ancestors and your descendants? First, let's clarify what we mean by "descendants." Traditionally, we think of descendants as those who come after us in a linear view of time. *Descendant* often refers to biological offspring, implying that having children is the primary way to have descendants. However, this perspective is limited. What if you decide not to have children? Does that mean you don't get to have descendants?

The answer is a resounding no. There are numerous ways to have descendants other than biological offspring. Your descendants can be direct blood relatives, individuals close to your heart, or even a broader community of humans who will follow in your footsteps. You can influence people, projects, structures, schools of thought, poems, pictures, and much more that continue to exist and be influenced by you after you've moved beyond this life. These are all considered descendants, not in a biological sense but as a connection of the heart.

It's crucial to bless your descendants, just as you've been blessed by those who came before you. These blessings often come from teachers, mentors, ancestors, or spiritual practices that have nurtured you. Many people in the lineages of your life have wished and prayed for your well-being. Blessing your descendants helps you recognize your place in the timeline and acknowledge the interplay of receiving and giving.

Healing operates in multiple directions. You can receive healing from your ancestors, and you can offer healing to those who came before you as well as to those who will come after you.

Transgenerational trauma and transgenerational blessings alike traverse generations. This conversation leads us to contemplate the type of ancestor we want to be. What kind of role model do you aspire to become, and how do you position yourself in the timeline so that your goodness and blessings are discoverable by those who come after you?

Your actions, thoughts, and energy create ripples that extend like rings in a pond. Just as you journeyed to find your ancestral guide, you too can leave signposts, symbols, and energies that your descendants will encounter. These markers will enable them to connect with your essence more efficiently and know you profoundly.

Praying for the erotic wellness of your descendants is a powerful way to support them. You can channel your own erotic wellness to send blessings across time. Just as you've used erotic energy to work with your ancestors, you can do the same for your descendants.

What kind of ancestor will you be? Perhaps one of sexual liberation or another embodiment of your unique essence. By being an accessible resource for those who share your curiosity about sexuality and the erotic, you leave a legacy of love and well-being.

In the final stages of this book, I encourage you to embrace an essential practice to bring everything to a meaningful close: creating a pleasure bundle for your descendants.

## Your Pleasure Bundle

Think back to when we discussed the sexual burdens and blessings you received from those who came before you. Likely, most of it did not exist in a tangible form but rather as inherited beliefs and practices.

Can you imagine if you had opened an actual bundle that a sex-positive elevated ancestor had made for you while they were alive? That's what I'm inviting you to do. A pleasure bundle is a collection of objects representing specific energies, practices, and meanings you wish to leave as a legacy. A pleasure bundle is a physical, tangible inheritance you create to be a good ancestor.

First, list the qualities you wish to pass on to future generations. Consider what you received, what else would have been helpful, and what you want to leave to your descendants. Then, find an object that represents each of these energies.

You could include a letter, a thumb drive, natural objects, or anything at all that represents thriving, boundaried, and consensual sexuality.

Once you've assembled your items, you will want to find some container to hold them, like a basket, a piece of fabric, a box, or whatever else brings delight.

The ritual for this Month will walk you through the creation and blessing of your pleasure bundle.

## Integration

Although this book concludes, your work of tending the bones continues, with the most critical piece yet to come: integration. At the end of every container, there may come some sadness, loss, or a twinge of "What's going to happen now that it's over?" These feelings might be present for you. It's been thirteen Months of diving deep into developing transgenerational erotic wellness, which is a big deal.

Integration, at its best, is an active process that you engage in. Typically, individuals integrate through reflection, and you can establish a habit or practice of conscious reflection. It may be helpful to view the work of integration as a system update. Just as you update the operating systems and software on your computer and your phone, you can update your inner experience to reflect the current version of you.

Your internal systems, like your capacity for feeling; discernment; groundedness; connections with yourself, your ancestors, and others; sharing erotic energy; and being present during sexual experiences, to name a few, can all be updated.

To clarify further, you've done the healing work, and now you'll let your system reflect a new way of being. Integration works best as a mindful practice: You tell yourself that you have updated that narrative or that behavior. You pay attention to how it feels for your sexuality to be different. You notice, you observe, you name. This is the work of integration. After a while, the new narratives and practices become second nature. They are integrated.

We've discussed that healing is a nonlinear process. That means there will be further layers that come to the surface that need attention. But for now, pay special attention to the moments when you notice you have choices. The choice points are moments when you could do things the same old way, but instead you realize you have a choice and could head down the newly forged path instead.

You are working on creating new neural pathways, and these choice points present themselves when something triggers you. You'll notice there's a choice in your nervous system between following the old path of the trigger or choosing to practice something new. Sometimes you'll clearly see the choice of two paths right in front of you, and you'll opt for the new one. At other times, you might revert to the old path, and occasionally, you may not even recognize the choice.

Over time, you'll increasingly identify these choice points and choose the new path. This shift occurs because you're more committed to your wellness than to any fleeting comfort derived from the old familiar suffering. You trust that feeling good is better than feeling resentful or hateful, and you start to have faith in your sovereignty and your inherent power.

Freedom is about making conscious choices: determining where to focus your attention and what you practice. When you don't choose the new path, it simply indicates that there is more healing to do. No judgment or self-criticism is needed. Approach these choices gently and kindly. Recognize that in those moments, you may not have had sufficient resources to make a different choice. Acknowledge it and commit to doing better next time.

While you are building and reinforcing new neural pathways, this doesn't mean the old ones disappear. Those well-worn grooves remain, and it's easy to slip back into them because they're comfortable and familiar. Choosing the new path requires a bit more effort. And remember that the old neural paths still exist. It's always a choice, and you can always return to your familiar behaviors. Be kind to yourself, and don't chastise yourself or think you've failed if you return to old patterns. Acknowledge that it's a matter of practice and resilience. It's about getting back on track whenever you veer off course.

Undoubtedly, you've encountered new ways of being and a sense of creating meaning, and you've experimented with a variety of practices. I mentioned at the beginning of the book that you would explore numerous new practices. Likely, you have embraced some enthusiastically, and others you may have found less appealing. You have been taking small steps of discovery. You don't have to adopt every practice wholeheartedly; merely tasting a bit is sufficient. As you move forward, you'll determine which practices are the best for you, and for that moment.

You can enhance the effectiveness of integration by naming it while you practice the new pathway. For instance, if you're sensing a connection with your erotic self, verbalize it by saying, "I'm practicing the neural pathway of feeling connected with my erotic self right now." As you do this, you're changing your feelings, practices, and narratives. By practicing and consciously acknowledging your practice, you reinforce the new neural pathways.

We've been exploring practices that may have pushed your limits in your heart, body, mind, and experience of pleasure. When you're expanding the edges of what's possible for you, moments of regression are to be expected. What we do is similar to stretching: we extend our boundaries, just as we stretch our muscles. We push those edges and then allow them to naturally retract a bit. This ebb and flow is a normal part of the process.

If you've ever stretched a new muscle, you know that overstretching is counterproductive. Instead, you stretch to that resilient edge of resistance; then you relax, rest, and repeat, gradually extending further. This is akin to what you've been doing with the material in this book as you increase your capacity to experience sensations and emotions, and it takes time.

It's essential to recognize the role of being well resourced, particularly in identifying new choice points and choosing new neural pathways. Making liberatory choices is much easier when you're well rested, nourished, hydrated, grounded, and connected. If you find it challenging to stay present, and you want to retreat to less demanding activities, ask yourself: "What do I need right now to be more resourced?"

Throughout this process, maintaining gentleness is crucial. How you treat yourself significantly affects your choices at these pivotal moments. Being mean to yourself, criticizing yourself, or thinking of yourself as a failure hinders your ability to forge new pathways at these choice points. The way you hold yourself and your experiences matters greatly. Embrace gentleness, tenderness, and sweetness in your journey. Understand that each expansion brings you further into your capacity, and after every expansion, there is a natural contraction. This is a normal part of the process, similar to the rhythm of breathing.

Now, in this final Month, it's a time for reflection and acknowledging all the work you have accomplished. Integration involves recognizing and appreciating what you've achieved.

I want to emphasize that you've undertaken a significant journey in these past thirteen months. When you reach the end of a successful endeavor, it's common to feel like this new way has always been the way. The new normal can make you forget where you were and how far you've come. That's why it's beneficial to revisit and recall all you've worked through.

Let's acknowledge the learning you've undergone. The work in *Tending the Bones* was divided into three parts: Build Inner Resources, Heal, and Savor.

**PART 1: BUILD INNER RESOURCES** **Month 1, Containment Moon,** offered resources. You explored intentions, altars, protection, discernment, and boundaries.

**Month 2, Grounding Moon,** delved into deeper discernment of wellness and unwellness. You focused on building relationship with your ancestral guide through connection and devotion. You practiced grounding.

**Month 3, Belonging Moon,** created a felt sense of belonging. You sang to your ancestors, learned about offerings, and deepened connection with your guide.

**Month 4, Resilience Moon,** emphasized the somatic brilliance of transgenerational trauma and ancestral survival narratives. You concentrated on building somatic resources and spiritual hygiene.

**PART 2: HEAL** **Month 5, Acknowledgment Moon,** discussed power dynamics. We analyzed the influence of sexual harm on and by your lineages, and we explored your relationship with healing.

**Month 6, Justice Moon,** continued the healing work. We explored creating embodied justice, time-travel healing, and forgiveness.

**Month 7, Freedom Moon,** focused on releasing shame and the importance of choosing presence.

**Month 8, Transformation Moon,** situated the problem outside you and practiced embodiment and breathing as tools of personal transformation.

**PART 3: SAVOR** **Month 9, Sovereign Moon,** addressed your erotic role models and introduced vision boards for your emergent erotic self. We delved into mindset work and sexual sovereignty.

**Month 10, Blessing Moon,** unpacked your ancestral sexual blessings and embraced your erotic gifts. Self-love and pleasure practices were central themes.

**Month 11, Pleasure Moon,** introduced ecstatic practices. You explored play and the importance of pleasure in your life. You practiced genital mapping.

**Month 12, Ancestor Moon,** celebrated the ancestors of sexual liberation and erotic elders. We discussed erotic offerings and practices with ancestors.

**Month 13, Integration Moon,** discussed love as protection, your pleasure bundle, blessing your descendants, and integration.

The progress made over these thirteen moons is substantial, and I'm curious how it lands with you as you read this overview. Take some time to reflect on these topics, your significant realizations, and the changes you've undergone. Consider what has been upgraded and integrated. Don't take this work for granted; recognize and appreciate your accomplishments.

## Commitment

Commitment is not merely about what you say; it's about what you do and how you return to practice when you temporarily fall off the path. My somatic coach often reminds me that we are committed to a life of continuous practice, not just to doing a specific practice. We commit ourselves to the paradigm of ongoing practice, to becoming someone who practices consistently. You have the privilege of being someone who practices consciously.

I want to suggest that, in light of everything we've acknowledged and the extensive work you've accomplished over the past thirteen Months, you take some time to reflect on your significant takeaways and aha moments, and any practices you wish to continue. Gently contemplate the journey you've been on, and gather your impressions. As I mentioned, reflection is an integral part of your integration process. It's how you deepen your learning.

As you revisit the content we've covered, you'll realize that certain practices have become an integral part of your life. While your specific practices may evolve, remember that the core of your commitment is to permanent practice, even when your methods change. Commitments may also shift. Sometimes a commitment may reach its natural conclusion, or you may need to explore new dimensions of your practice.

Most of us have experienced moments of disappointment in our personal practice. There have been times when we faltered or abandoned our routines, leaving us feeling like we've failed ourselves. Rather than viewing this as a personal failing, consider the possibility that it was an indicator that a new practice or more structure was needed.

I strongly advocate setting time containers for your commitments. For example, committing to a specific practice for six months can be beneficial. It's also important to be open to the possibility of discontinuing a practice if it no longer serves your needs. If resistance arises, investigate it, and try to understand what's happening. There's no need to carry the burden of guilt for not continuing a practice that's no longer aligned with your intentions.

Committing to permanent practice means rigorously evaluating the effectiveness of your practices and adjusting them accordingly.

## Conclusion

Now, let's explore the concept of completion, as this is where we find ourselves. When it's time to conclude, embrace it. Completion is a natural phase in the cycle of any endeavor. If there's a sense of grief associated with this ending, allow yourself to process it. Grief work is an essential part of moving forward.

Piece of advice: incorporate rest into your process. Much like the final moments of a yoga class, where you rest to allow the body to integrate the work, the same principle applies here. Dr. Montessori observed this phenomenon in young learners; after they completed a significant task, there would be a phase that appeared as if they were doing nothing. However, they were actually engaged in the essential, invisible work of integration. This underscores the importance of giving yourself time to rest as a deliberate act of integration.

Resist the urge to revisit all the content immediately. Endings are when scarcity-based thinking can emerge, making you believe that you need to return to the content right away. Instead, grant yourself at least a month, and maybe two or three months, to absorb the learnings naturally. Trust your brain to return to the content when it is the right time.

If you decide to take a break from your practices, that's perfectly fine. You can always come back later and say, "I'm ready to resume my practice." Choose your practices when you have a deeper understanding of what aligns with your current needs. Remember, it's acceptable to give the ideas and concepts time to weave into your being. This is when the work becomes an inseparable part of who you are, and you'll never be the same again.

This process is about gentle evolution, not being in servitude to your practice. In working your way through *Tending the Bones*, you have actively forged many new neural pathways. You've been creating and reinforcing these pathways. Healing happens by constructing new pathways and potential choice points. You're shaping a new somatic experience in your body, transforming triggers, and renegotiating your boundaries, relationships, and attachments. Living in your body in a new way will lead to even more new choices and greater spaciousness in your life.

As we conclude our journey through this content, I want to express my profound joy and pleasure in sharing this transformative experience with you. I'm deeply grateful for your commitment to your erotic wellness and the wellness of the planet. Your dedication matters, both to me and to the world, and I extend my heartfelt thanks.

## Last Thoughts for Month 13

Love is the greatest protection: it supports deep resilience. Expanding your capacity to give and receive love is a lifelong practice. Your freedom lies in what you choose to practice.

**In conclusion, this Month you will:**

- ¤ Complete the Month 13 worksheets in the appendix. You can also download this month's worksheets at www.pavinimoray.com/ttb-bonus.html.
- ¤ Daily practice: "Breathing in, I welcome Eros. Breathing out, I share Eros."
- ¤ Add something to your healing altar that represents integration.
- ¤ Complete Ritual 13: Integration.

# Ritual 13: Integration

## Preparation

- ¤ The purpose of this ritual is to integrate by embracing your new normal and beginning a blessing prayer for all of your descendants of blood and heart.
- ¤ You can do this at your healing altar or in another place where you will not be disturbed.
- ¤ You will need a cloth or box to contain some special items that represent healed Eros, pleasure, and sexual sovereignty, which you intend to bequeath to those who come after. These items can be representational, like a special rock to represent groundedness, or incense to represent beauty. They can also be items that represent a healthy sexuality, like some natural lube or a toy. You may or may not decide to actually give this bundle, but the point is to create it to represent the energies of blessing you will transmit.
- ¤ You will also need a notebook or voice recorder.

**Begin by setting a container of prayer as you read this aloud:**

*Bright shining ancestors of my blood,*
*beautiful tender descendants of blood and heart,*
*from my place in this line I heal, and I offer healing.*
*I feel pleasure, and I offer pleasure.*
*I find and offer acceptance for the expression of love.*
*I pray for radiant erotic wellness in my lines, past, present, and future.*

**Next, cast a circle of protection with the help of your allies.**

Call out to the trusted spiritual sources of protection you already have. This may be deities, guardians, the elements, or relationships with animals, stones, holy places, herbs, or anything from the green world. Invite each to come toward you, and pause until you have a sense that they are present.

Then, with their support, imagine a layer of protection that goes all around you. You can visualize it if you like, or feel it.

Once you are protected, invite connection with your guide. As usual, listen first to determine if there is anything they want you to know.

Then have a conversation with them. Tell them the future you envision for yourself in terms of your relationship with pleasure and Eros. Ask for their continued support as you embody the blessings and transform the burdens around sex in your life and relationships.

With the witness of your guide, stretch into your new shape, full of healing, power, and pleasure. Feel the newness of the expanded edges.

When that feels complete, turn your ritual attention to your descendants. If you have children and/or grandchildren, place your attention on them. Imagine the wellness you have created flowing toward them in the very most appropriate and respectful ways. If you do not have children, imagine the blessing you wish to convey flowing to young people in your life, or in the world. Envision a world of sensual aliveness where everyone acts with integrity, honoring the tremendous importance of Eros.

If you have collected items, place them into the cloth or box, and add your own words of blessing. You may actually pass this bundle to those who come after, or it may remain a metaphor for you being a well and bright ancestor who blesses the living.

Place your hands on top of your bundle, and allow all the prayers, pleasure, freedom, and acceptance you have to bless this legacy.

When you feel complete, thank your guide for their witness. Although this is the last scripted ritual in this book, know that you can return to be with them whenever you like.

Make notes of the information you receive.

Thank your allies for their support. Close this ritual with a short prayer for erotic wellness to bless our Earth.

NOTE *Put your bundle someplace where you can visit it and share blessings with it.*

# Acknowledgments

To Margeaux Weston, my excellent editor: your belief in the importance of this work has brought it to the world. Unending gratitude for your guidance, clear seeing, and commitment to justice.

To the many delightful, highly skilled, and professional folks at North Atlantic Books who have helped this book come into being: I offer my personal gratitude for our shared collaboration. I see you, Michelle Phan, Bevin Donahue, Janelle Ludowise, Brent Winter, Rachel Monaghan, Shayna Keyles, Joe Finlaw, Susan Bumps, Drew Cavanaugh, and all the others whose work has touched this book.

To Dr. Joseph Kramer, my beloved mentor and friend: I am grateful for your gentle, clear, embodied wisdom and practice-based guidance.

To Dr. Daniel Foor, my friend, teacher, and comrade: thank you for your unwavering support, prayer, and teaching.

To Elinor Predota, without whom this book would not exist: thank you for your hand-holding, commitment to academic rigor, and kind, magickal support.

To Meredith Broome, master somatic coach and guiding light: I am so grateful for your love and support on my path toward becoming a soft and trusting heart beating inside an erotic tiger poet body.

To all those who participated as research subjects: profound thanks for your wisdom, so generously and honestly shared.

To the students in my Tending the Bones classes: I offer so much gratitude for your willingness, your practice, your reflections, and your feedback.

To Orione and Moona, hearts of my heart and my gorgeous descendants: I am grateful for your presence in my life, allowing me to be your Oma. You continually inspire me to heal. I aspire to be a good elder and, one day, a loving ancestor to our shared bloodlines.

To Ari, my sexy Belover: I am grateful for your constancy, steadfastness, and grace. With you, I have come to know what love like honey and erotic wellness actually feel like.

To my own bright ancestors of blood and heart: I acknowledge your unseen yet profoundly experienced support. I am grateful for your love. I am grateful to embody your blessings of queerness, magick, and gender expansiveness. I am thankful for your ever-present, sweet insistence on healing for the sake of love. I am your beloved child.

APPENDIX

# Workbooks

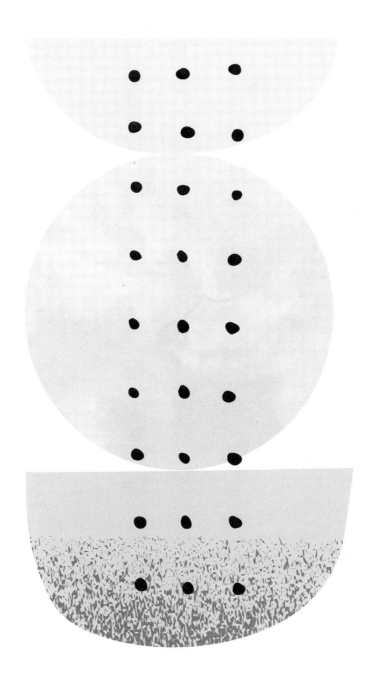

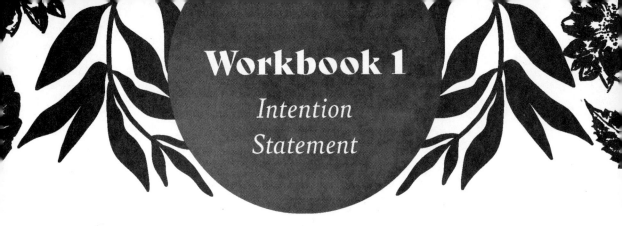

# Workbook 1

## *Intention*
## *Statement*

I, _____ , set this intention for the coming thirteen months:

(full name)

## Container Agreements

**What are my container agreements with myself? What boundaries do I set for the sake of my own wellness and the wellness of my lineages?**

# Workbook 3
## Timeline of Attachment and Belonging

Make sure to include notes about your:

- Early caregivers
- Early romantic relationships
- Friendships
- Current relationships
- Times you felt a sense of belonging
- Times you felt a sense of disbelonging
- Moments of feeling deeply rejected
- Moments of feeling profoundly connected
- Attachment to pets, places, stuffed animals, etc.
- Important attachments throughout your life, positive and negative

# Timeline of Attachment and Belonging

# Rejection Filter and Outsider Identity

**Disbelonging and belonging are both practices. Secure attachment is also a set of practices.**

**Take an inventory of your disbelonging practices first.**

What are all the ways you feel or have felt you don't belong?

What are all the things that you think make you weird or an outsider?

How do you practice disbelonging, even though it's probably unconscious? For example, what are you saying to yourself inside your head? *How* do you treat yourself internally?

There is the rejection that is yours personally, and there are also ways you are marginalized by culture. How have you been told you are "other"?

In addition, take a look at your practices of **belonging**.

Where do you allow yourself to belong?

Where do you feel satisfied with the emotional quality of your connections?

Where do you trust that others are not the enemy and are indeed allies, even if they sometimes disappoint you?

**Truly, when we speak of belonging, the questions we ask are:**

To whom or what do you want to belong?

You will not belong to every person, every place, every group. You must discern where you want to put your love.

Where do you want to put your love?

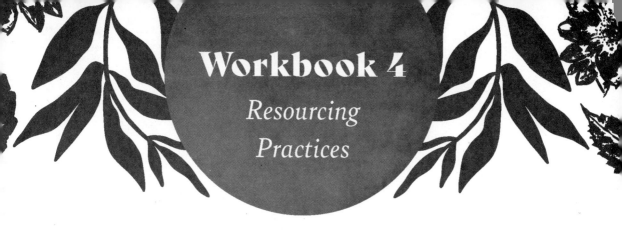

# Workbook 4
## *Resourcing*
## *Practices*

What resources you? Set a timer for seven minutes and make a list of all of the places, activities, and people who bring you a sense of greater aliveness.

# Monthly Resilience Plan

For each of the four following areas of your resilience, choose one practice you will do this month. How often you do the practice or how long you do it for are not very important. What's important is to actively practice your resilience. The smallest amounts of conscious practice can create a great benefit.

**I.** Focus on Connection

¤ Commit to regular connection in an important relationship.

¤ Show up for a group you are involved with.

¤ Connect regularly with your ancestral guide.

This month, in support of my resilience I will _____.

**II.** Focus on Wellness

¤ Choose something that supports your body/physical wellness, like drinking water or taking supplements.

¤ Engage in journaling, meditation, prayer, or another mindfulness practice.

¤ Engage in a movement practice.

¤ Avoid negative behaviors.

This month, in support of my resilience I will _____.

**III.** Healthy Mindset

¤ What new narrative do you want to practice in your life?

¤ Interrupt negative thought cycles.

¤ Visualize what you want, rather than worrying about what you fear.

¤ Focus on your resilience and your strength. Attend to what's working!

This month, in support of my resilience I will _____.

**IV.** Be on Your Purpose

¤ Help others.

¤ Move toward a particular goal.

¤ Do something that removes a block in your life.

This month, in support of my resilience I will _____.

## Okay, Now What about a Resilience Day?

What would you do in an entire day dedicated to your resilience?

What day this month is your resilience day? Write it down and put it on your calendar.

My resilience day is _____.

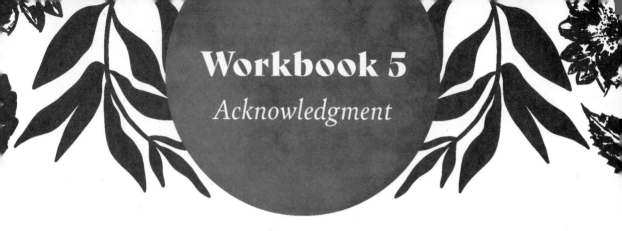

# Workbook 5
## *Acknowledgment*

**List of resources for when I am triggered:**
*What helps me come back to center?*

**What am I ready to begin to acknowledge?**

*Go gently here.*

# Workbook 6

*Justice*

What are the fractured pieces of myself I need to reintegrate?

What am I ready to begin to acknowledge?

What is justice for me?

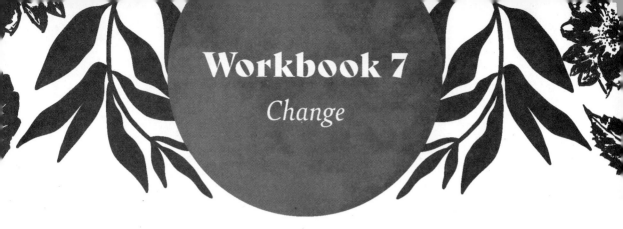

# Workbook 7
## *Change*

## Personal Commitment to Choosing Presence

1. Define your "for the sake of what." Why are you interested in making this commitment?

2. What is your personal commitment to feeling your sensations and emotions? How do you want to change? Try writing your commitment using this sentence starter: "I am a commitment to …" I learned this phrasing from my somatic coach. It feels stronger than saying "I am committed to …" because you are really embodying the commitment.

3. What are your conditions for satisfaction? How will you know when you have arrived there?

4. Brainstorm some daily practices that can support this commitment.

5. Pick one practice to try first, and give yourself some structure with it.

   When:

   Where:

   How:

   For what period of time can you commit to this practice? A week? A month? Start small; you can always re-up later.

6. How will you be supported in this commitment? Who will listen to you? Who can you check in with? What kind of structure do you need or want in order to fulfill this commitment?

# The Steps of Change

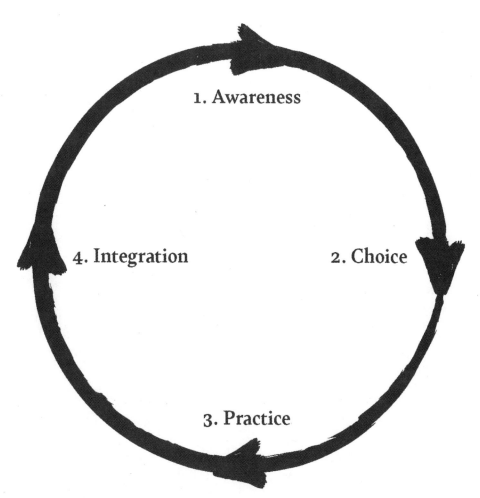

1. Awareness

2. Choice

3. Practice

4. Integration

First, you become aware of what is.

Second, you find you have choice.

Third, you choose what to practice. (Pro tip: Anything can be a practice!)

Last, what you practice integrates into who you are.

# Mapping Difficulties with Change

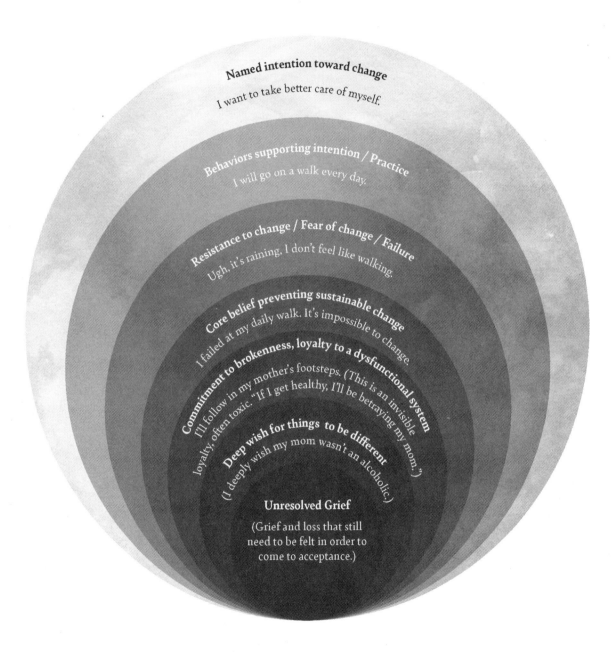

Named intention toward change

I want to take better care of myself.

Behaviors supporting intention / Practice

I will go on a walk every day.

Resistance to change / Fear of change / Failure

Ugh, it's raining, I don't feel like walking.

Core belief preventing sustainable change

I failed at my daily walk. It's impossible to change.

Commitment to brokenness, loyalty to a dysfunctional system

I'll follow in my mother's footsteps. (This is an invisible loyalty, often toxic: "If I get healthy, I'll be betraying my mom.")

Deep wish for things to be different

(I deeply wish my mom wasn't an alcoholic.)

Unresolved Grief

(Grief and loss that still need to be felt in order to come to acceptance.)

# Tips for Creating Sustainable Personal Change

- Awaken from denial.

- Place attention on an area in life that you wish were different.

- Honestly acknowledge the impact (costs and benefits) of your current practices.

- Seek external support for change, with some part of you believing change is possible.

- Set intentions from within, rather than allowing intentions to be imposed upon you from without or by another. Don't base your actions on "shoulds" or shame but instead on your deep desire for your own wellness.

- Decide how you will know when you have fulfilled the intention (i.e., your conditions for satisfaction).

- Find a good-enough reason for change so you can make decisions in the moment that support your intention (i.e., your "for the sake of what").

- Anticipate that resistance will probably happen at some point.

- Develop fierce self-compassion for the resistant self.

- Bring awareness and choice to habituated behaviors.

- Assess the difference between long-term and short-term self-care.

- Honor the value and gifts of resistance (usually protection from change).

- Uncover change-limiting beliefs that are probably subconscious (such as hidden loyalties to a system or person).

- Articulate specific and measurable commitments, and develop practices.

- Practice intentional behaviors over time.

- Track progress and resistance to progress.

- Tweak practices.

- When you realize that you're off your practices, tell someone ASAP.

- Honestly discern why you're off your practice. Is it no longer the right practice?

- Acknowledge honestly when you practice other things that are not in alignment with your commitment.

- Regularly assess where you are in relation to your intention.

- Celebrate the small moments of success, and string them together like twinkle lights.

- Understand that sustained personal change is not a linear process, but instead cyclical and spiraled, with layers of understanding that unfold over time.

- ¤ Practice the core belief that change is possible.

- ¤ Develop community that validates the self you are practicing instead of relationships that drag you back to where you were.

- ¤ To sustain change, seek purposeful support through periods of life transition (transitions wreak havoc on practices and routines!).

## What Is Freedom?

You are invited to dream into what freedom means to you.

# Workbook 8
## *Transformation*

Experiment with inviting in the erotic using each of the Tools for Arousal listed below. These can be done alone or with your partner—your choice. Maybe try both?

- ¤ Breath
- ¤ Movement
- ¤ Vocalization
- ¤ Sensation
- ¤ Senses

## Breath

### 1. Belly Breath

Breathe fully into the belly, as if the belly had nostrils. The shoulders are not moving upward for the most part, just a gentle rise and fall. The belly is soft and expansive, and you can feel and see it move as the breath enters and leaves.

### 2. Genitals Breath

Similar to the Belly Breath, now pay attention to your genitals as you breathe. Is there constriction or muscle tightness? What's happening in your asshole? The breath is full and relaxed, with all of the work on the inhale. During the exhale, the breath just falls softly out of the body.

### 3. Ecstasy Breath

Consciously breathe into the genitals during erotic encounters with yourself or others, almost like drinking in something delightful. Encourage erotic sensation to be present in the genitals through inviting it in, and deepen the pleasure once it is felt by staying with it. This breath is good to practice while lying down.

Once the breath is moving easily to the genitals, try breathing in through your heart and out through your genitals for two to three minutes.

Then try breathing in through your genitals and out through your heart.

# Movement

Try this right now: put on some music you love that has a sexy, sensuous rhythm, something you might like to have sex to. Wherever you are, start moving your pelvis. You can try lots of different kinds of movements: small circles, rotations, thrusting . . . it doesn't need to be anything in particular. Whatever feels good.

Once you've got a nice movement to the music going, try layering in being aware of the sensations in your pelvic region, including your genitals. If you replicate movements that you enjoy making during sex, you may find some erotic charge while doing this. Layer on top of this a breath that replicates breathing you might do when aroused: a fuller breath, relaxed chin and jaw, mouth partially open. Continue this practice for the entirety of the song.

Notice what happens when you invite the erotic into this moment, which is not in any context. How much arousal can you access when you turn your attention to it? How do you feel at the end of the song?

# Vocalization

Find a private time and place to experiment with vocalization. Invite in your erotic self, and see what noises want to be made.

It might be helpful to put on some music or to be near a river, an ocean, or a shower— anything that is already making noise—in order to give yourself permission.

What does your erotic self sound like?

# Internal Sensation

Perform this body scan procedure to identify your internal sensations:

1. Find a quiet time and turn your attention to the inward landscape of your body. You can try placing your attention at the top of your head and then slowly moving it down through every part of your body.

2. Allow yourself to just notice what is happening there on the level of sensation.

3. Take time to notice what happens in various parts of your body. As you pay attention—without trying to fix or change anything—what happens? Does the sensation stay the same, or does it change?

   Over time, practicing noticing internal sensations gives you access to greater embodiment.

4. Now invite in Eros. What happens if you consciously open to your hands feeling erotic? Your lips? Your back?

## PARTIAL LIST OF SENSATIONS

| | | | |
|---|---|---|---|
| Airy | Electric | Inflated | Restricted |
| Bloated | Empty | Itchy | Shaky |
| Blocked | Energized | Jagged | Sharp |
| Breathless | Expanded | Jittery | Smooth |
| Brittle | Expansive | Jumpy | Spacey |
| Bubbly | Faint | Knotted | Spacious |
| Buzzy | Flaccid | Light | Spinning |
| Calm | Floating | Luminous | Still |
| Clammy | Flowing | Moist | Streaming |
| Cold | Fluid | Nervous | Stringy |
| Cool | Flushed | Numb | Strong |
| Congested | Fluttery | Paralyzed | Suffocating |
| Constricted | Fragile | Pounding | Tense |
| Damp | Frozen | Prickly | Thin |
| Dark | Full | Puffy | Throbbing |
| Deflated | Fuzzy | Pulsing | Tight |
| Disconnected | Heavy | Queasy | Tingly |
| Dry | Heated | Quivery | Trembly |
| Dull | Hollow | Radiating | Tremulous |
| Dizzy | Hot | Ragged | Twitchy |
| Dense | Icy | Raw | Warm |

# Senses

Find a set of things that deliberately delight each of your senses, such as essential oils, flowers, food items, sounds, or textures.

Set aside at least thirty minutes.

Get into your body by using any of the aforementioned embodiment practices, or any other way. Give your erotic self time to experience each of the treats you have gathered for yourself. Allow yourself a long, sensual playtime that stimulates each of your senses.

Invite in the erotic without any pressure; nothing has to happen. You don't need to masturbate, have an orgasm, nothing! You are just playing with your senses and allowing arousal to be easy.

**What does a commitment to body positivity actually mean in practice? Here are some ideas:**

- ¤ For every minute you spend criticizing, spend two minutes saying loving, supportive things.
- ¤ Interrupt negative thoughts.
- ¤ Do mindset work around how you *want* to be with your body. How do you want to be treating yourself?
- ¤ Buy clothes that fit well and comfortably.
- ¤ Move in ways that feel good and affirming.
- ¤ Commit to noticing negative thoughts and interrupting them.
- ¤ Notice when you are comparing your body with other bodies. THOUGHT STOP. Send a mental good wish to the person you were comparing bodies with.
- ¤ Stop participating in body chat, fat chat, or any self-deprecating conversations with others.
- ¤ Tell others it's not okay to make comments about your body, and you won't listen.
- ¤ Develop a kind voice to talk with yourself.
- ¤ Make agreements with yourself about mirror time.
- ¤ Be conscious about how you choose to use a scale, and stick to your agreements.
- ¤ Work with a therapist to investigate your relationship with food.
- ¤ Notice when body shame comes up, and send some love to yourself.
- ¤ Be kind about body acceptance as a *process*. Some days are better than others. Don't beat yourself up if you misstep.
- ¤ Know that body acceptance doesn't start when you "lose that last bit of weight" or "after I have that procedure." Body acceptance is a daily practice. You have a body every day.

Add your own:

- ¤ _____.
- ¤ _____.
- ¤ _____.

Now pick one or two of these to try on for the next month, and see how it goes.

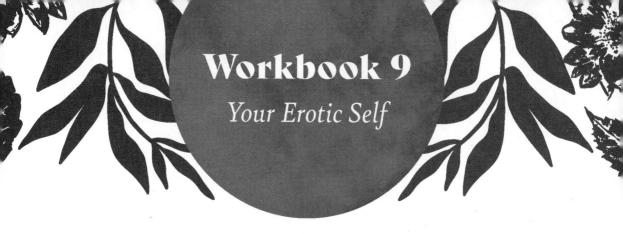

# Workbook 9
## *Your Erotic Self*

## Erotic Role Models

List at least three humans who you think rock their sexuality and really embody their erotic nature.

They can be living or dead, people you know or people you don't know, famous or otherwise. Perhaps there is a character in a movie who represents this for you.

Now consider what gives you this impression. How do they walk or move? What facial expressions do they use? Gestures? How do they dress? What about them conveys this confidence you long for?

*Out of these noticings, what can you turn into practices?*

## What Is Your Internal Sexual Self-Experience?

Make a list of at least twenty-five words to describe how you feel when your sexuality is most alive (just list words; no need to write in sentences).

## My Top 15 Life Turn-Ons

List at least fifteen things that turn you on. It can be a sexual turn-on, a sensual turn-on, or an aliveness turn-on. Whatever!

## The Triangle of Your Sexuality

Fill in the triangle with words that represent your experience as a sexual being. Notice the particular intersecting points. For example, how does the "other" experience of your sexuality touch your "inner" experience? And what's your experience of that intersection?

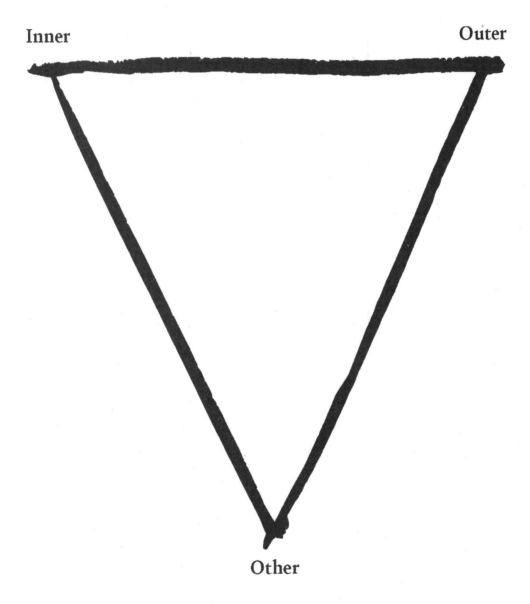

Inner

Outer

Other

# Erotic Vision Board

Find images that represent who you would like to see yourself be in your sexuality. These can be human or other-than-human.

Make a vision board of your emergent erotic self.

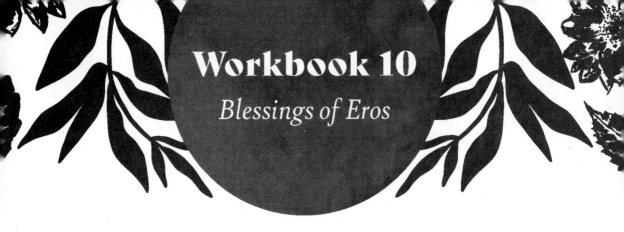

# Workbook 10
### *Blessings of Eros*

## What Are My Erotic Talents?

Give some thought to the special gifts of Eros that you possess, just by being you. We'll work together to uncover the erotic blessings from your ancestors. Here, list things about your sexuality that you admire, are proud of, or can give some cred to yourself for.

I'm good at …

My sexy superpower is …

I've been blessed with …

You can use these to get you started, or just go for it.

## Committing to Self-Pleasure Practice

What will I practice this month?
Some options include:

- ¤ Anointing
- ¤ Self-touch
- ¤ Erotic movement
- ¤ Erotic breath
- ¤ What else?

When will I practice? For how long?
Set the bar low: "I will do this one time, for three minutes," or something similar. You can always build on positive, successful experiences.

How will I be kind to myself if resistance comes up? To whom will I reach out for support?

## Some Thought Work

I hope you like making lists! Because this month, you are invited to make three separate lists for yourself. They relate to your sexuality and to the blessings that you are welcoming in your wider life.

The lists proceed in a particular order, and it might work best to follow the order given, although you are also welcome to trust your knowing.

### List 1

*If I knew what I wanted, what would it be?*

## List 2

Make a list dreaming wilder and wider dreams for your intimate self, your sexuality, your pleasure.

The new moon is a potent time to work this spell.

Start by writing this phrase: "Wouldn't it be nice if …" And continue with at least twenty-five things.

Post this list where you can see it.

The magic comes from the dreaming and the opening to receive.

This is a great technology that allows you to dream big and creative without needing to be overly concerned with outcome.

Create your list below.

*Wouldn't it be nice if …*

## List 3

Below is a list of major areas of life. Below each area, write down the blessings you're calling in for yourself in that area.

Self

Purpose

Spirit

Health

Pleasure

Prosperity


Work


Family


Partnership


Community

## My Contract for Sensual Aliveness

I, _____, invite and freely welcome these blessings, and I declare that I am available to receive this goodness in my life.


Signature and date: _____

(your name)

# Workbook 11

## Pleasure Moon

What is *your* definition of pleasure?

Other questions about pleasure you may wish to explore:

What feels pleasurable to you at this moment in your life?

How do you know pleasure when you feel it?

How do you regulate the amount of pleasure you experience?

For you, what is the relationship between pleasure and control?

For you, what is the relationship between pleasure and self-worth?

How does pleasure fit into your embodied existence?

What permission can you give yourself to experience more ethical hedonism in your life?

What other questions do you have about pleasure?

# Types of Pleasure

Try to write down at least one pleasure you experience for each of the pie slices:

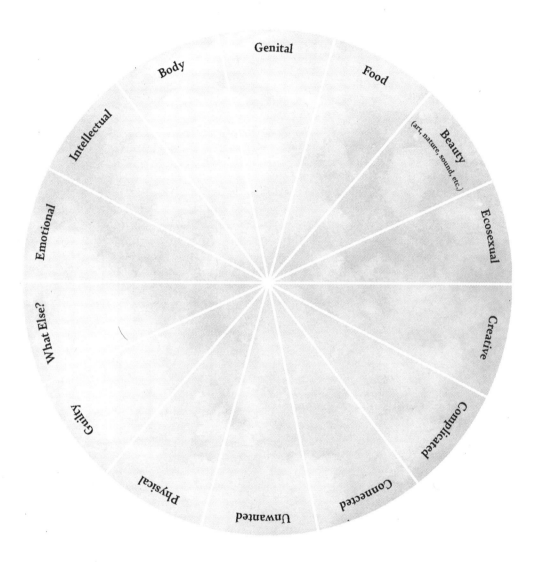

# **Workbook 12**
## *Ancestor Moon*

Who are your elders?

How do you engage with them?

How could you lean more on their wisdom?

How can you bring more of this work into your communities as a future elder?

# Genital Mapping

Lie down when you have a chunk of uninterrupted time, at least an hour. Allow yourself to downregulate by calming your breath and bringing your awareness into your body. You may wish to engage in some full-body self-touch as a way to wake up your body. When you feel ready, allow your hand to simply hold your genitals with tenderness. This practice is not about creating pleasure or arousal; it's simply about being with what is.

Breathe into your genitals, and notice what happens as you simply hold. Do this for some time, until you are not interested anymore. Be aware of the possibility that "not interested" could be a smoke screen for "can't hang out here."

One mapping practice involves imagining a clock face superimposed on your external genitals. With great presence, hold the place on your genitals that corresponds to 12:00, just breathing and noticing. Work your way around the clock an "hour" at a time, holding each point for three to five minutes if you can. Once you have completed this (or in another mapping session), do the same thing, but internally (if that's your anatomy).

Genital mapping can also be done with a partner, but again, this is not a practice of arousal or a lead-in to sex.

Make sure to have a way to make an audio recording of what comes up for you. You can take notes, but that's a lot of back and forth with paper and pen, so it's easier to just record your impressions and take notes afterward.

# Workbook 13
## Integration Moon

## Integrating Your Big Takeaways and Aha!s

Take some time to reflect on the concepts covered in *Tending the Bones*.
What have been your big learnings?
What has integrated into your erotic self?

| MONTH 1: CONTAINMENT MOON | |
|---|---|
| Intention | |
| Altar of healing | |
| Protection and discernment | |
| Boundaries: yarrow | |
| "No" work | |
| Community intimacy building | |

| MONTH 2: GROUNDING MOON | |
|---|---|
| Discernment: well and unwell; how to know who to work with | |
| Attachment | |
| Connection to land | |
| Eldership | |
| Choosing to heal with ancestors | |
| Working with ancestral guides: connection and discernment, establish relationship | |
| Prayer | |
| Offerings and devotion | |

| MONTH 3: BELONGING MOON | |
|---|---|
| Belonging | |
| Singing | |
| Spiritual hygiene practices | |
| Healing energies; trauma vortex | |
| Deepening with guides | |
| Containment of unwell energies | |

| MONTH 4: RESILIENCE MOON | |
|---|---|
| Somatic brilliance of trans-generational trauma | |
| Ancestral research | |
| Finding ground and finding center | |
| Somatic resourcing | |
| Positive resourcing: orienting, anchoring | |
| Shaking | |
| Practicing resilience: minutes and days | |
| Survival narratives | |

| MONTH 5: ACKNOWLEDGMENT MOON | |
|---|---|
| What is: power-over and rape culture | |
| Sites of shaping and perspective | |
| Acknowledging the impact: personal, lineage | |
| Acknowledging the full impact: looking at attachment wounds and relationships that are also affected | |
| Lineages of harm, lineages of healing | |
| Being clear in your responsibility: not more nor less | |
| Unpacking ancestral sexual burdens: How do I embody these? How do they affect me? | |

| MONTH 6: JUSTICE MOON | |
| --- | --- |
| Creating embodied justice: What is yours? | |
| Tending consent violations that you have experienced or committed | |
| Time-travel healing | |
| Degrees of healing | |
| Healing from consent accidents | |
| Rituals of repair | |
| Forgiveness: What is it? Is it for you? | |
| Self-forgiveness | |

| MONTH 7: FREEDOM MOON | |
| --- | --- |
| Shame | |
| Practice paradigm | |
| Placement of attention | |
| Choosing presence | |

| MONTH 8: TRANSFORMATION MOON | |
|---|---|
| Having a body: radical body acceptance | |
| Becoming three-dimensional | |
| Breathing | |
| Getting embodied | |
| Feeling and sensation | |
| Play and improvisation as antidote | |
| Visioning the pleasure body | |
| Where do you want to put your body/love? | |

| MONTH 9: SOVEREIGN MOON | |
|---|---|
| Who do I admire? Role models | |
| Vision board of your emergent erotic self | |
| Mindset work | |
| Inner, outer, other | |
| Agency | |

| MONTH 10: BLESSING MOON | |
|---|---|
| Unpacking ancestral sexual blessings | |
| Embracing your erotic gifts | |
| Self-love pleasure practices | |
| Oils and anointing | |
| Longing and desire as pathways to connection | |

| MONTH 11: PLEASURE MOON | |
|---|---|
| Ecstasy and ecstatic practices and ritual | |
| Sensual aliveness | |
| Ecosexuality | |
| RItualized pleasure | |
| Play | |

| MONTH 12: ANCESTOR MOON | |
|---|---|
| Ancestors of sexual liberation | |
| Ancestors and the erotic | |
| Elders | |
| Relationality | |
| Practicing belonging and attachment | |
| Sharing your sexual self | |
| Offering erotic energy and orgasms | |

| MONTH 13: INTEGRATION MOON | |
|---|---|
| Your pleasure bundle | |
| Love as protection | |
| Blessing descendants | |
| Writing your liberation story | |
| Integration and commitment | |

## Writing Your Liberation Story

If you were to tell a descendant the story of how you freed your sexuality, your erotic self, what story would you tell?

Write that story here, making up the bits you need to, so you reach the conclusion you want. (*Pro tip:* Write the conclusion first, and then fill in the details of how you got there.)

Conclusion you want to reach:

Even if this doesn't turn out to be exactly your path, it still means that a path exists.

## Your Pleasure Bundle

What did you receive in the pleasure bundle you received from your ancestors?

What else would have been helpful to receive?

Make a list of the things you want to include. These are the items you will gather to create an actual pleasure bundle.

# Resources

## Resources That Accompany This Book

Free, downloadable resources to support your practice, available at the author's website: www.pavinimoray.com/ttb-bonus.html

- ¤ Drumming
- ¤ Grounding meditation
- ¤ All thirteen rituals recorded
- ¤ All worksheets as downloadable PDFs

## Other Resources

### Podcasts

- ¤ *Bespoken Bones* podcast with Pavini Moray: bespokenbones.libsyn.com
- ¤ *Jewish Ancestral Healing* podcast with Taya Shere: www.jewishancestralhealing.com /season-1

### Books

- ¤ *Ancestral Medicine: Rituals for Personal and Family Healing* by Daniel Foor
- ¤ *Healing Sex: A Mind-Body Approach to Healing Sexual Trauma* by Staci Haines
- ¤ *Urban Tantra* and *Ecstasy Is Necessary* by Barbara Carrellas

### Video

High-quality video somatic sex education by Joseph Kramer:

- ¤ eroticmassage.com
- ¤ orgasmicyoga.com

## Practitioners

- ¤ Trained and certified Ancestral Lineage Healing Practitioners: ancestralmedicine.org /practitioner-directory
- ¤ Somatic Experiencing: traumahealing.org
- ¤ generative somatics: generativesomatics.org

## Genealogy

- ¤ Wisconsin Historical Society: www.wisconsinhistory.org/Records/Article/CS15307

# References

Aanavi, M. (2012). *The Trusting Heart: Addiction, Recovery, and Intergenerational Trauma*. Asheville, NC: Chiron Publications.

Abrahams, N., Devries, K., Watts, C., Pallitto, C., Petzold, M., Shamu, S., & García-Moreno, C. (2014). "Worldwide Prevalence of Non-partner Sexual Violence: A Systematic Review." *Lancet*, 383(9929), 1648–1654. doi:10.1016/S0140-6736(13)62243-6.

Acarturk, C., Konuk, E., Cetinkaya, M., Senay, I., Sijbrandij, M., Cuijpers, P., & Aker, T. (2015). "EMDR for Syrian Refugees with Posttraumatic Stress Disorder Symptoms: Results of a Pilot Randomized Controlled Trial." *European Journal of Psychotraumatology*, 6(1), [27414]. doi:10.3402/ejpt.v6.27414.

Addison, J. T. (1925). *Chinese Ancestor Worship: A Study of Its Meaning and Relations with Christianity*. Cambridge, MA: Church Literature Committee of the Chung Hua Sheng Kung Hui.

Aijmer, G. (1968). "A Structural Approach to Chinese Ancestor Worship." *Bijdragen tot de Taal-, Land- en Volkenkunde [Journal of the Humanities and Social Sciences of Southeast Asia and Oceania]*, 124(1), 91–98.

Ainsworth, M. D. S. (1969). "Object Relations, Dependency, and Attachment: A Theoretical Review of the Infant-Mother Relationship." *Child Development*, 40(4), 969–1025. doi:10.2307/1127008.

American Psychiatric Association. (2013). *Diagnostic and Statistical Manual of Mental Disorders* (5th ed.). Arlington, VA: American Psychiatric Publishing.

Andreasen, N. C. (2010). "Posttraumatic Stress Disorder: A History and a Critique." *Annals of the New York Academy of Sciences*, 1208, 67–71. doi:10.1111/j.1749-6632.2010.05699.x.

Asamoa-Tutu, S. R. (2013). "Walking Two Worlds: Healing from Trauma in the American Indian Community." Master of Social Work Clinical Research Papers, St. Catherine University and the University of St. Thomas, St. Paul, MN. https://sophia.stkate.edu/msw_papers/146/.

Atkinson, J. (2002). *Educaring: A Trauma Informed Approach to Healing Generational Trauma for Aboriginal Australians*. Goolmangar, NSW, Australia: We Al-li Pty. Ltd.

Avieli, N. (2007). "Feasting with the Living and the Dead: Food and Eating in Ancestor Worship Rituals in Hội An." In *Modernity and Re-enchantment: Religion in Post-revolutionary Vietnam*, edited by P. Taylor, 121–160. Singapore: ISEAS–Yusof Ishak Institute.

Banmen, J. (1986). "Virginia Satir's Family Therapy Model." *Individual Psychology: Journal of Adlerian Theory, Research & Practice*, 42(4), 480–492.

Barratt, B. B. (2005). *Sexual Health and Erotic Freedom*. Philadelphia, PA: Xlibris Corporation.

Barratt, B. B. (2013). *Emergence of Somatic Psychology and Bodymind Therapy*. London: Palgrave Macmillan.

Bass, E., & Davis, L. (1988). *The Courage to Heal: A Guide for Women Survivors of Child Sexual Abuse*. Bloomington, IN: Collins Living.

Basson, R. (2001). "Human Sex-Response Cycles." *Journal of Sex & Marital Therapy*, 27(1), 33–43. doi:10.1080/00926230152035831.

Baum, R. (2013). "Transgenerational Trauma and Repetition in the Body: The Groove of the Wound." *Body, Movement and Dance in Psychotherapy*, 8(1), 34–42. doi:10.1080/17432979.2013.748976.

Berceli, D. (2005). *Trauma Releasing Exercises (TRE): A Revolutionary New Method for Stress/Trauma Recovery*. Charleston, SC: BookSurge Publishing.

Berg, A. (2003). "Ancestor Reverence and Mental Health in South Africa." *Transcultural Psychiatry*, 40(2), 194–207. doi:10.1177/1363461503402004.

Berger, K. (2015). "Ingenious: Rachel Yehuda." *Nautilus*, December 31. http://nautil.us/issue/31/stress/ingenious-rachel-yehuda.

Berger, S. S. (2014). "Whose Trauma Is It Anyway? Furthering Our Understanding of Its Intergenerational Transmission." *Journal of Infant, Child, and Adolescent Psychotherapy*, 13(3), 169–181. doi:10.1080/15289168.2014.937975.

Bergmann, M., & Jucovy, M. E. (1982). *Generations of the Holocaust*. New York, NY: Columbia University Press.

Black, M., Basile, K., Breiding, M. J., Smith, S. G., Walters, M. L., Chen, J., et al. (2014). "Prevalence and Characteristics of Sexual Violence, Stalking, and Intimate Partner Violence Victimization: National Intimate Partner and Sexual Violence Survey, United States, 2011." *Morbidity and Mortality Weekly Report*, 63(SS08), 1–18.

Black, M. C., Basile, K. C., Breiding, M. J., Smith, S. G., Walters, M. L., Merrick, M. T., et al. (2010). *National Intimate Partner and Sexual Violence Survey (NISVS): 2010 Summary Report*. Atlanta, GA: CDC.

Bogopa, D. (2010). "Health and Ancestors: The Case of South Africa and Beyond." *Indo-Pacific Journal of Phenomenology*, 10(1), 1–7. doi:10.2989/IPJP.2010.10.1.8.1080.

Bojuwoye, O. (2013). "Integrating Principles underlying Ancestral Spirits Belief in Counseling and Psychotherapy." *Ife PsychologIA*, 21(1), 74–90.

Bojuwoye, O., & Edwards, S. (2011). "Integrating Ancestral Consciousness into Conventional Counseling." *Journal of Psychology in Africa*, 21(3), 375–381. doi:10.1080/14330237.2011.10820471.

Boring, F. M. (2012). *Connecting to Our Ancestral Past: Healing through Family Constellations, Ceremony, and Ritual*. Berkeley, CA: North Atlantic Books.

Bowers, M. E., & Yehuda, R. (2016). "Intergenerational Transmission of Stress in Humans." *Neuropsychopharmacology*, 41(4), 232–244. doi:10.1038/npp.2015.247.

Bowlby, J. (2005). *A Secure Base: Clinical Applications of Attachment Theory*. New York, NY: Routledge.

Bradshaw, J. (1988). *Healing the Shame That Binds You*. Deerfield Beach, FL: Health Communications.

Braga, L. L., Mello, M. F., & Fiks, J. P. (2012). "Transgenerational Transmission of Trauma and Resilience: A Qualitative Study with Brazilian Offspring of Holocaust Survivors." *BMC Psychiatry*, 12(1), 134. doi:10.1186/1471-244X-12-134.

Brandes, S. H. (2007). *Skulls to the Living, Bread to the Dead: The Day of the Dead in Mexico and Beyond*. Hoboken, NJ: Wiley-Blackwell.

Brom, D., Stokar, Y., Lawi, C., Nuriel-Porat, V., Ziv, Y., Lerner, K., et al. (2017). "Somatic Experiencing for Posttraumatic Stress Disorder: A Randomized Controlled Outcome Study." *Journal of Traumatic Stress*, 30(3), 304–312. doi:10.1002/jts.22189.

Browne, A., & Finkelhor, D. (1986). "Impact of Child Sexual Abuse: A Review of the Research." *Psychological Bulletin*, 99(9), 66–77. doi:10.1037/0033-2909.99.1.66.

Buhrmann, M. V. (1989). "Religion and Healing: The African Experience." In *AfroChristian Religion and Healing in Southern Africa*, edited by G. C. Oosthuizen, S. D. Edwards, W. H. Wessels, & I. Hexam, 25–34. Lewiston, NY: Edwin Mellin.

Carretta, C. M., & Burgess, A. W. (2013). "Symptom Responses to a Continuum of Sexual Trauma." *Violence and Victims*, 28(2), 248–258. doi:10.1891/0886-6708.VV-D-12-00011.

CDC. "Sexual Violence: Definitions." Centers for Disease Control and Prevention. https://www.cdc.gov/violenceprevention/sexualviolence/fastfact.html.

CDC. "Sexual Violence: Facts at a Glance 2012." Centers for Disease Control and Prevention. https://www.cdc.gov/violenceprevention/sexualviolence/prevention.html.

Chen, L. P., Murad, M. H., Paras, M. L., Colbenson, K. M., Sattler, A. L., Goranson, E. N., et al. (2010). "Sexual Abuse and Lifetime Diagnosis of Psychiatric Disorders: Systematic Review and Meta-analysis." *Mayo Clinic Proceedings*, 85(7), 618–629. doi:10.4065/mcp.2009.0583.

Chiakwa, V. N. (1999). "African Traditional Healing vis-à-vis Western Healing." In *Cross-Cultural Dialogue on Psychotherapy in Africa*, edited by S. N. Madu, P. K. Baguma, & A. Pritz, 193–208. Sovenga, South Africa: UNIN Press.

Clezy, B. (2017). "A Brief History of Transgenerational Trauma (Part III)." *Balkan Diskurs*, June 13. https://balkandiskurs.com/en/2017/06/13/a-brief-history-of-transgenerational-trauma-part-iii/.

Cohen, D. B. (2009). "Guilt, Responsibility, and Forgiveness: Lessons from Lifers in Prison." In *Forgiveness and Reconciliation*, edited by A. Kalayjian & R. F. Paloutzian, 137–151. New York, NY: Springer. doi:10.1007/978-1-4419-0181-1_9.

Cohen, D. B. (2009). "Systemic Family Constellations and Their Use with Prisoners Serving Long-Term Sentences for Murder or Rape." Ph.D. diss., Saybrook University, San Francisco. https://pqdtopen .proquest.com/pubnum/3344884.html.

Condon, J. R., & Cane, P. M. (2011). *CAPACITAR: Healing Trauma, Empowering Wellness*. Santa Cruz, CA: Capacitar International.

Coulter, C., Persson, M., & Utas, M(, 2008). *Young Female Fighters in African Wars: Conflict and Its Consequences*. Uppsala, Sweden: Nordic Africa Institute.

Coveney, J., & Bunton, R. (2003). "In Pursuit of the Study of Pleasure: Implications for Health Research and Practice." *Health*, 7(2), 161–179. doi:10.1177/1363459303007002873.

Crocq, M. A., & Crocq, L. (2000). "From Shell Shock and War Neurosis to Posttraumatic Stress Disorder: A History of Psychotraumatology." *Dialogues in Clinical Neuroscience*, 2(1), 47–55.

Daglieri, T., & Andelloux, M. (2013). "Sexuality and Sexual Pleasure after Sexual Assault." *Journal of Sexual Medicine*, 10(10), 2611–2612. doi:10.1111/jsm.12317.

Danieli, Y., ed. (1998). *International Handbook of Multigenerational Legacies of Trauma*. New York, NY: Plenum Press.

Danieli, Y. (2007). "Assessing Trauma across Cultures from a Multigenerational Perspective." In *Cross-Cultural Assessment of Psychological Trauma and PTSD*, edited by J. P. Wilson & C. S. Tang, 65–89. New York, NY: Springer.

Davidson, A. C., & Mellor, D. J. (2001). "The Adjustment of Children of Australian Vietnam Veterans: Is There Evidence for the Transgenerational Transmission of the Effects of War-Related Trauma?" *Australian & New Zealand Journal of Psychiatry*, 35(3), 345–351. doi:10.1046/j.1440-1614.2001.00897.x.

Davies, P., & Matthews, C. N. (2015). *This Ancient Heart: Landscape, Ancestor, Self*. Alresford, UK: John Hunt Publishing.

Davison, S. L., Bell, R. J., LaChina, M., Holden, S. L., & Davis, S. R. (2009). "The Relationship between Self-Reported Sexual Satisfaction and General Well-Being in Women." *Journal of Sexual Medicine*, 6(10), 2690–2697. doi:10.1111/j.1743-6109.2009.01406.x.

Edwards, S., Makunga, N., Thwala, J., & Mbele, B. (2009). "The Role of the Ancestors in Healing." *Indilinga: African Journal of Indigenous Knowledge Systems*, 8(1), 1–11.

Edwards, S. D. (2011). "A Psychology of Indigenous Healing in Southern Africa." *Journal of Psychology in Africa*, 21(3), 335–347. doi:10.1080/14330237.2011.10820466.

Ehrensaft, M. K., Cohen, P., Brown, J., Smailes, E., Chen, H., & Johnson, J. G. (2003). "Intergenerational Transmission of Partner Violence: A 20-year Prospective Study." *Journal of Consulting and Clinical Psychology*, 71(4), 741–753. doi:10.1037/0022-006X.71.4.741.

Emerson, D., & Hopper, E. K. (2011). *Overcoming Trauma through Yoga: Reclaiming Your Body*. Berkeley, CA: North Atlantic Books.

Evans-Pritchard, E. (1940). *African Political Systems*. Oxford, UK: Oxford University Press.

Fasholé-Luke, E. W. (1978). *Christianity in Independent Africa*. London: R. Collings.

Fatunmbi, A. F. (2005). "Ancestor Reverence: Building an Ancestor Shrine." *Africa Speaks*, July 3. http://www.africaspeaks.com/reasoning/index.php?topic=2775.0;wap2.

Firth, R. (1936). *We, the Tikopia: A Sociological Study of Kinship in Primitive Polynesia*. Oxford, UK: American Book.

Fogleman, E., & Savran, B. (1999). "Therapeutic Groups for Children of Holocaust Survivors." *International Journal of Group Psychotherapy*, 29(2), 211–235. doi:10.1080/00207284.1979.11491986.

Foor, D. (2017). *Ancestral Medicine: Rituals for Personal and Family Healing*. Rochester, VT: Bear & Company.

Frazier, K. N., West-Olatunji, C. A., St. Juste, S., & Goodman, R. D. (2009). "Transgenerational Trauma and Child Sexual Abuse: Reconceptualizing Cases involving Young Survivors of CSA." *Journal of Mental Health Counseling*, 31(1), 22–33. doi:10.17744/mehc.31.1.u72580m253524811.

Freedy, J. R., & Hobfull, S. E., eds. (1995). *Traumatic Stress*. Boston, MA: Springer.

Friedman, M. J. (2017). "History of PTSD in Veterans: Civil War to DSM-5 – PTSD." National Center for PTSD, May 31. https://www.ptsd.va.gov/public/ptsd-overview/basics/history-of-ptsd-vets.asp.

Gaillard, T. (2012). *Shamanism, Ancestors and Transgenerational Integration: Traditional Wisdom and Contemporary Practices*. Geneva: Écodition Éditions.

Gampel, Y. (1992). "Thoughts about the Transmission of Conscious and Unconscious Knowledge to the Generation Born after the Shoah." *Journal of Social Work and Policy in Israel*, 5–6, 43–50.

Gardner, F. (1999). "Transgenerational Processes and the Trauma of Sexual Abuse." *European Journal of Psychotherapy & Counseling*, 2(3), 297–308. doi:10.1080/13642539908400814.

Goodwin, J., McCarthy, T., & DiVasto, P. (1981). "Prior Incest in Mothers of Abused Children." *Child Abuse and Neglect*, 5(2), 87–95. doi:10.1016/0145-2134(81)90025-9.

Grimassi, R. (2016). *Communing with Ancestors: Your Spirit Guides, Bloodline Allies, and the Cycle of Reincarnation*. Newburyport, MA: Weiser Books.

Guarino, K., Soares, P., Konnath, K., Clervil, R., & Bassuk, E. (2009). *Trauma-Informed Organizational Toolkit*. Rockville, MD: Center for Mental Health Services.

Gumede, M. (1990). *Traditional Healers: A Medical Practitioner's Perspective*. Braamfontein, Johannesburg, South Africa: Skotaville.

Gutiérrez, R. n. A., Scalora, S., Beezley, W. H., & Salvo, D. (1997). *Home Altars of Mexico*. Albuquerque, NM: University of New Mexico Press.

Haagen, J. F. G., Smid, G. E., Knipscheer, J. W., & Kleber, R. J. (2015). "The Efficacy of Recommended Treatments for Veterans with PTSD: A Metaregression Analysis." *Clinical Psychology Review*, 40, 184–194. doi:10.1016/J.CPR.2015.06.008.

Haines, S. (2007). *Healing Sex: A Mind-Body Approach to Healing Sexual Trauma*. San Francisco, CA: Cleis.

Hamilton, A. (2018). "Extraordinary Life: He Gave a Voice to Holocaust Survivors." *Hartford Courant*, August 26. http://www.courant.com/obituaries/hc-extraordinary-life-dori-laub-08226-story.html.

Harner, M. (1999). "Science, Spirits, and Core Shamanism." *Shamanism*, 12(1), 1–2.

Harris, M., & Fallot, R. D. (2001). "Envisioning a Trauma-Informed Service System: A Vital Paradigm Shift." *New Directions for Mental Health Services*, 89, 3–22. doi:10.1002/yd.23320018903.

Hawkins, K., Cornwall, A., & Lewin, T. (2011). *Sexuality and Empowerment: An Intimate Connection*. Brighton, UK: Pathways of Women's Empowerment.

Hellinger, B. (2003). *Peace Begins in the Soul: Family Constellations in the Service of Reconciliation*. Heidelberg, Germany: Carl-Auer-System-Verl.

Higgins, J. A., Mullinax, M., Trussell, J., Davidson, J. K., & Moore, N. B. (2011). "Sexual Satisfaction and Sexual Health among University Students in the United States." *American Journal of Public Health*, 101(9), 1643–1654. doi:10.2105/AJPH.2011.300154.

Hochschild, A. (2011). *To End All Wars: A Story of Loyalty and Rebellion, 1914–1918*. Boston, MA: Houghton Mifflin Harcourt.

Holt, L. (2004). "The 'Voices' of Children: De-Centring Empowering Research Relations." *Children's Geographies*, 2(1), 13–27.

Honwana, A. (1999). "The Collective Body: Challenging Western Concepts of Trauma and Healing." *Track Two: Constructive Approaches to Community and Political Conflict*, 8(1). https://api.semantic scholar.org/CorpusID:74696905.

Jablonka, E., & Raz, G. (2009). "Transgenerational Epigenetic Inheritance: Prevalence, Mechanisms, and Implications for the Study of Heredity and Evolution." *Quarterly Review of Biology*, 84(2), 131–176. doi:10.1086/598822.

Jakobsen, M. D. (1999). *Shamanism: Traditional and Contemporary Approaches to the Mastery of Spirits and Healing*. Brooklyn, NY: Berghahn Books.

Jelinek, E. M. (2015). "Epigenetics: The Transgenerational Transmission of Ancestral Trauma, Experiences, and Behaviors—As Seen in Systemic Family Constellations." PhD diss., California Institute of Integral Studies, San Francisco, CA. https://pqdtopen.proquest.com/pubnum/3726301.html.

Kalischuk, R. G., Solowoniuk, J., & Nixon, G. (2008). "Introducing a Transpersonal, Spiritual, Healing Framework for the Aftermath of Trauma." *International Journal of Healing and Caring*, 8(3). https://irp-cdn.multiscreensite.com/891f98f6/files/uploaded/Kalischuk-8-3.pdf.

Kaltman, S., Krupnick, J., Stockton, P., Hooper, L., & Green, B. L. (2005). "Psychological Impact of Types of Sexual Trauma among College Women." *Journal of Traumatic Stress*, 18(5), 547–555. doi:10.1002/jts.20063.

Kellermann, N. (2001). "Transmission of Holocaust Trauma – An Integrative View." *Psychiatry: Interpersonal and Biological Processes*, 63(3), 256–267. doi:10.1521/psyc.64.3.256.18464.

Kellermann, N. P. (2013). "Epigenetic Transmission of Holocaust Trauma: Can Nightmares Be Inherited?" *Israel Journal of Psychiatry and Related Sciences*, 50(1), 33–39.

Kellermann, P. F., & Hudgins, K. (Eds.). (2000). *Psychodrama with Trauma Survivors: Acting Out Your Pain*. London: Jessica Kingsley Publishers.

Kestenberg, J. S. (1980). "Psychoanalyses of Children of Survivors from the Holocaust: Case Presentations and Assessment." *Journal of the American Psychoanalytic Association*, 28(4), 775–804. doi:10.1177/000306518002800402.

Kestenberg, J. S. (1993). "What a Psychoanalyst Learned from the Holocaust and Genocide." *International Journal of Psycho-analysis*, 74(6), 1117–1129.

Kim, Y. (2012). "Historical Perspective of PTSD and Future Revision in DSM-5." *Seishin Shinkeigaku Zasshi*, 114(9), 1031–1036.

Krystal, H., & Danieli, Y. (1994). "Holocaust Survivor Studies in the Context of PTSD." *National Center for Post-Traumatic Stress Disorder PTSD Research Quarterly*, 5(4), 1–5.

Kuek, J. C. (2012). "Culture and Trauma: An Ethnographic Study of Transpersonal Approaches to Trauma Recovery from a Sudanese Perspective." PhD diss., Sofia University, Palo Alto, CA. https://scinapse.io/papers/2318114099.

Lang, A. J., Rodgers, C. S., Laffaye, C., Satz, L. E., Dresselhaus, T. R., & Stein, M. B. (2003). "Sexual Trauma, Posttraumatic Stress Disorder, and Health Behavior." *Behavioral Medicine*, 28(4), 150–158. doi:10.1080/08964280309596053.

Larsen, S. E., Hopkins, S., & Harris, I. (2024). "Addressing Religious or Spiritual Dimensions of Trauma and PTSD." PTSD: National Center for PTSD. https://www.ptsd.va.gov/professional/treat/txessentials/spirituality_trauma.asp.

Laumann, E. O., Paik, A., Glasser, D. B., Kang, J. H., Wang, T., Levinson, B., & Gingell, C. (2006). "A Cross-National Study of Subjective Sexual Well-Being among Older Women and Men: Findings from the Global Study of Sexual Attitudes and Behaviors." *Archives of Sexual Behavior*, 35(2), 143–159. doi:10.1007/s10508-005-9005-3.

Lawrance, K., & Byers, E. S. (1995). "Sexual Satisfaction in Long-Term Heterosexual Relationships: The Interpersonal Exchange Model of Sexual Satisfaction." *Personal Relationships*, 2(4), 267–285. doi:10.1111/j.1475-6811.1995.tb00092.x.

Lebowitz, L., Harvey, M. R., & Herman, J. L. (1993). "A Stage-by-Dimension Model of Recovery from Sexual Trauma." *Journal of Interpersonal Violence*, 8(3), 378–391. doi:10.1177/088626093008003006.

Lehmann, A. C., & Myers, J. E. (1985). *Magic, Witchcraft, and Religion: An Anthropological Study of the Supernatural*. California City, CA: Mayfield.

Levine, P. A., & Frederick, A. (1997). *Waking the Tiger: Healing Trauma*. Berkeley, CA: North Atlantic Books.

Liebling-Kalifani, H., Mwaka, V., Ojiambo-Ochieng, R., Were-Oguttu, J., & Kinyanda, E. (2011). "Women War Survivors of the 1989-2003 Conflict in Liberia: The Impact of Sexual and Gender-Based Violence." *Journal of International Women's Studies*, 12(1), 1–21.

Lindau, S., Schumm, L., Laumann, E., Levinson, W., Waite, L., & O'Muircheartaigh, C. (2007). "A Study of Sexuality and Health among Older Adults in the United States." *New England Journal of Medicine*, 357(8), 762–774.

Loya, R. M. (2014). "Rape as an Economic Crime: The Impact of Sexual Violence on Survivors' Employment and Economic Well-Being." *Journal of Interpersonal Violence*, 30(16), 2793–2813. doi:10.1177/0886260514554291.

Lunday, M. (2010). *Running Head: Addressing the Spiritual Impact of Trauma in Therapy*. Destin, FL: Lunday Counseling Center.

Magliocco, S. (2004). *Witching Culture: Folklore and Neo-paganism in America*. Philadelphia, PA: University of Pennsylvania Press.

Maltz, W. (1991). *The Sexual Healing Journey: A Guide for Survivors of Sexual Abuse*. New York, NY: William Morrow.

Martinson, A. A., Sigmon, S. T., Craner, J., Rothstein, E., & McGillicuddy, M. (2013). "Processing of Intimacy-Related Stimuli in Survivors of Sexual Trauma: The Role of PTSD." *Journal of Interpersonal Violence*, 28(9), 1886–1908. doi:10.1177/0886260512469104.

Masters, W. H., & Johnson, V. E. (2010). *Human Sexual Response*. Bronx, NY: Ishi Press International.

McCabe, G. (2008). "Mind, Body, Emotions and Spirit: Reaching to the Ancestors for Healing." *Counseling Psychology Quarterly*, 21(2), 143–152. doi:10.1080/09515070802066847.

McCarthy, B., & Farr, E. (2011). "The Impact of Sexual Trauma on Sexual Desire and Function." *Advances in Psychosomatic Medicine*, 31, 105–120. doi:10.1159/000328919.

McClelland, S. I. (2010). "Intimate Justice: A Critical Analysis of Sexual Satisfaction." *Social and Personality Psychology Compass*, 4(9), 663–680. doi:10.1111/j.1751-9004.2010.00293.x.

McGowan, P. O., Sasaki, A., D'Alessio, A. C., Dymov, S., Labonté, B., Szyf, M., et al. (2009). "Epigenetic Regulation of the Glucocorticoid Receptor in Human Brain Associates with Childhood Abuse." *Nature Neuroscience*, 12(3), 342–348. doi:10.1038/nn.2270.

McNally, D. (2014). *Transgenerational Trauma and Dealing with the Past in Northern Ireland*. Belfast: WAVE Trauma Centre.

Menzies, P. (2008). "Developing an Aboriginal Healing Model for Intergenerational Trauma." *International Journal of Health Promotion and Education*, 46(1), 41–48. doi:10.1080/14635240.2008.10708128.

Metzger-Brown, E. (1998). "The Transmission of Trauma through Caretaking Patterns of Behavior in Holocaust Families: Re-enactments in a Facilitated Long-Term Second-Generation Group." *Smith College Studies in Social Work*, 68(3), 267–285. doi:10.1080/00377319809517531.

Morgan, R., & Reid, G. (2003). "'I've Got Two Men and One Woman': Ancestors, Sexuality and Identity among Same-Sex Identified Women Traditional Healers in South Africa." *Culture, Health and Sexuality*, 5(5), 375–391. doi:10.1080/1369105011000064146.

Morrison, Z., Quadara, A., & Boyd, C. (2007). *Ripple Effects of Sexual Assault*. Melbourne: Australian Institute of Family Studies.

Motta, R. W., Joseph, J. M., Rose, R. D., Suozzi, J. M., & Leiderman, L. J. (1997). "Secondary Trauma: Assessing Intergenerational Transmission of War Experiences with a Modified Stroop Procedure." *Journal of Clinical Psychology*, 53(8), 895–903.

Mouledoux, A., Legrand, G., & Brackett, A. (2013). "The DSM-5's New PTSD Diagnostic Criteria." *MBLB News*, June 14. https://mblb.com/admiralty-maritime/the-dsm-5s-new-ptsd-diagnostic -criteria.

Mullen, P. E., Martin, J. L., Anderson, J. C., Romans, S. E., & Herbison, G. P. (1996). "The Long-Term Impact of the Physical, Emotional, and Sexual Abuse of Children: A Community Study." *Child Abuse and Neglect*, 20(1), 7–21. doi:10.1016/0145-2134(95)00112-3.

Munthali, A. C. (2006). "Health Problems That Require No Medication: The Case of Ancestor-Related Illnesses among the Tumbuka of Northern Malawi." *Nordic Journal of African Studies*, 15(3), 367–379.

National Sexual Violence Resource Center. (2010). "The Impact of Sexual Violence: Fact Sheet." https:// www.nsvrc.org/sites/default/files/2012-03/Publications_NSVRC_Factsheet_Impact-of-sexual -violence_0.pdf.

Nipps, L. (2018). "How Do Constellations Help?" Convivium Constellations. http://www.convivium constellations.com/how-do-constellations-help.

Oldstone-Moore, J. (2003). *Taoism: Origins, Beliefs, Practices, Holy Texts, Sacred Places*. Oxford: Oxford University Press.

Olssen, M. C. (2013). "Mental Health Practitioners' Views on Why Somatic Experiencing Works for Treating Trauma." Master's thesis, St. Catherine University and the University of St. Thomas, St. Paul, MN. http://sophia.stkate.edu/msw_papers/244.

Oshun, I. O. (2011). *A Festival of Bones: Celebrating the Ancestors*. Oakland, CA: Orikire.

Parad, H. J., & Spark, G. (1973). *Invisible Loyalties: Reciprocity in Intergenerational Family Therapy*. Philadelphia, PA: Lippincott Williams and Wilkins / Harper & Row.

Parker, C., Doctor, R. M., & Selvan, R. (2008). "Somatic Therapy Treatment Effects with Tsunami Survivors." *Traumatology*, 14(3), 103–109.

Pascoal, P. M., Narciso, I. d. S. B., & Pereira, N. M. (2014). "What Is Sexual Satisfaction? Thematic Analysis of Lay People's Definitions." *Journal of Sex Research*, 51(1), 22–30. doi:10.1080/00224499 .2013.815149.

Pearsa, K. C., & Capaldi, D. M. (2001). "Intergenerational Transmission of Abuse: A Two-Generational Prospective Study of an At-Risk Sample." *Child Abuse and Neglect*, 25(11), 1439–1461.

Piaget, J. (1930). *The Child's Conception of the World*. New York, NY: Harcourt, Brace and World.

Picard, A. (2017). "Sexual Violence: The Silent Health Epidemic." *Globe and Mail*, April 13. https://www .theglobeandmail.com/opinion/sexual-violence-the-silent-health-epidemic/article33915008.

Planned Parenthood. (2007). "The Health Benefits of Sexual Expression." https://www.plannedparenthood .org/files/3413/9611/7801/Benefits_Sex_07_07.pdf.

Pratt, C. (2007). *An Encyclopedia of Shamanism, Volume One: A-M*. New York, NY: Rosen Publishing Group.

Prechtel, M. (2015). *The Smell of Rain on Dust: Grief and Praise*. Berkeley, CA: North Atlantic Books.

Price, C. (2005). "Body-Oriented Therapy in Recovery from Child Sexual Abuse: An Efficacy Study." *Alternative Therapies in Health and Medicine*, 11(5), 46–57.

Rakoff, V. M. (1966). "Long Term Effects of the Concentration Camp Experience." *Viewpoints: Labor Zionist Movement of Canada*, 1, 17–22.

Ralph, N., Hamaguchi, K., & Cox, M. (2006). "Transgenerational Trauma, Suicide and Healing from Sexual Abuse in the Kimberley Region, Australia." *Pimatisiwin: A Journal of Aboriginal & Indigenous Community Health*, 4(2), 116–136.

Rape, Abuse, & Incest National Network. (n.d.). "About Sexual Assault." https://www.rainn.org/about -sexual-assault (accessed April 3, 2024).

Realmuto, G. M. (1994). "Shattered Assumptions: Towards a New Psychology of Trauma." *Journal of the American Academy of Child & Adolescent Psychiatry*, 33(4), 597–598. doi:10.1097/00004583 -199405000-00028.

Romm, C. (2018). "A Sexuality Researcher Explains a Big Unanswered Question in Sex Studies." MSN, July 26. https://www.msn.com/en-us/lifestyle/whats-hot/a-sexuality-researcher-explains-a-big-unanswered-question-in-sex-studies/ar-BBL6og7.

Rosen, R. C., & Bachmann, G. A. (2008). "Sexual Well-Being, Happiness, and Satisfaction, in Women: The Case for a New Conceptual Paradigm." *Journal of Sex and Marital Therapy*, 34(4), 291–297. doi:10.1080/00926230802096234.

Royce, A. P. (2014). *Becoming an Ancestor: The Isthmus Zapotec Way of Death*. Albany, NY: State University of New York Press.

Rymut, J. (2016). "How to Prepare for Meditation: 9 Ways to Ground Yourself." About Meditation, March 24. https://aboutmeditation.com/how-to-prepare-for-meditation.

Saigh, P. A., Green, B. L., & Korol, M. (1996). "The History and Prevalence of Posttraumatic Stress Disorder with Special Reference to Children and Adolescents." *Journal of School Psychology*, 34(2), 107–131. doi:10.1016/0022-4405(96)00002-7.

Salberg, J. (2015a). "Introduction: On the Evolution of Witnessing and Trauma Transmission." *Contemporary Psychoanalysis*, 51(2), 185–194. doi:10.1080/00107530.2015.1036724.

Salberg, J. (2015b). "The Texture of Traumatic Attachment: Presence and Ghostly Absence in Transgenerational Transmission." *Psychoanalytic Quarterly*, 84(1), 21–46. doi:10.1002/j.2167-4086.2015.00002.x.

Sánchez-Fuentes, M. d. M., Santos-Iglesias, P., & Sierra, J. C. (2014). "A Systematic Review of Sexual Satisfaction." *International Journal of Clinical and Health Psychology*, 14(1), 67–75. doi:10.1016/S1697-2600(14)70038-9.

Sarivaara, E., Maatta, K., & Uusiautti, S. (2013). "Who Is Indigenous? Definitions of Indigeneity." *European Scientific Journal*, 1, 369–378. doi:10.19044/esj.2013.v9n10p%25p.

Schützenberger, A. A. (1998). *The Ancestor Syndrome: Transgenerational Psychotherapy and the Hidden Links in the Family Tree*. London: Routledge.

Schützenberger, A. A., & Devroede, G. (2005). *Suffering in Silence: The Legacy of Unresolved Sexual Abuse*. Metairie, LA: Gestalt Institute Press.

Shapiro, F. (1996). "Eye Movement Desensitization and Reprocessing (EMDR): Evaluation of Controlled PTSD Research." *Journal of Behavior Therapy and Experimental Psychiatry*, 27(3), 209–218. doi:10.1016/S0005-7916(96)00029-8.

Shapiro, J. (2018). "The Sexual Assault Epidemic No One Talks About." NPR, January 8. www.npr.org/2018/01/08/570224090/the-sexual-assault-epidemic-no-one-talks-about.

Sigal, J. J., & Weinfeld, M. (1989). *Trauma and Rebirth: Intergenerational Effects of the Holocaust*. Santa Barbara, CA: Praeger.

Širokogorov, S. M. (1999). *Psychomental Complex of the Tungus*. Berlin: Schletzer.

Smith, A., & LaDuke, W. (2005). *Conquest: Sexual Violence and American Indian Genocide*. Durham, NC: Duke University Press.

Solkoff, N. (1992). "Children of Survivors of the Nazi Holocaust: A Critical Review of the Literature." *American Journal of Orthopsychiatry*, 62(3), 342–358. doi:10.1037/h0079348.

Sorsdahl, K., D. Stein, A. Grimsrud, A. Seedat, A. Flisher, D. Williams, and L. Myer. (2009). "Traditional Healers in the Treatment of Common Mental Disorders in South Africa." *Journal of Nervous and Mental Disease*, 197(6), 434–441. doi:10.1097/NMD.0b013e3181a61dbc.

Sprecher, S., and R. Cate. (2004). "Sexual Satisfaction and Sexual Expression as Predictors of Relationship Satisfaction and Stability." In *The Handbook of Sexuality in Close Relationships*, edited by J. H. Harvey, A. Wenzel, & S. Sprecher, 235–247. Mahwah, NJ: Lawrence Erlbaum Associates Publishers.

Srivastava, P., and Hopwood, N. (2009). "A Practical Iterative Framework for Qualitative Data Analysis." *International Journal of Qualitative Methods*, 8(1), 76–84. doi:10.1177/160940690900800107.

St. Just, A. (2009). *A Question of Balance: A Systemic Approach to Understanding and Resolving Trauma*. North Charleston, WV: BookSurge Publishing.

Starhawk, and Macha NightMare, M. (1997). *The Pagan Book of Living and Dying: Practical Rituals, Prayers, Blessings, and Meditations on Crossing Over*. San Francisco, CA: Harper Collins.

Steadman, L., Palmer, C., and Tilley, C. (1996). "The Universality of Ancestor Worship." *Ethnology*, 35(1), 63. doi:10.2307/3774025.

Steele, K. (1987). "Sitting with the Shattered Soul." *Pilgrimage: Journal of Personal Exploration and Psychotherapy*, 15(6), 19–25.

Stobie, C. (2011). "'He Uses My Body': Female Traditional Healers, Male Ancestors and Transgender in South Africa." *African Identities*, 9(2), 149–162. doi:10.1080/14725843.2011.556792.

Stolorow, R. D. (2003). "Trauma and Temporality." *Psychoanalytic Psychology*, 20(1), 158–161. doi:10.1037/0736-9735.20.1.158.

Strauss, A., and Corbin J. (1998). *Basics of Qualitative Research: Techniques and Procedures for Developing Grounded Theory*. Thousand Oaks, CA: Sage.

Strozzi-Heckler, R. (2014). *The Art of Somatic Coaching: Embodying Skillful Action, Wisdom, and Compassion*. Berkeley, CA: North Atlantic Books.

Swanson, G. (1964). *The Birth of the Gods: The Origin of Primitive Beliefs*. Ann Arbor, MI: University of Michigan Press.

Talbot, N. L., Houghtalen, R. P., Duberstein, P. R., Cox, C., Giles, D. E., and Wynne, L. C. (1999). "Effects of Group Treatment for Women with a History of Childhood Sexual Abuse." *Psychiatric Services*, 50(5), 686–692. doi:10.1176/ps.50.5.686.

Tatje, T., and Hsu, F. (1969). "Variations in Ancestor Worship Beliefs and Their Relation to Kinship." *Southwestern Journal of Anthropology*, 25(2), 153–172. doi:10.1086/soutjanth.25.2.3629199.

Teach Trauma. (n.d.). "Types of Trauma." http://www.teachtrauma.com/information-about-trauma/types-of-trauma (accessed April 4, 2024).

Thompson, R. F. (1995). "Face of the Gods: The Artists and Their Altars." *African Arts*, 28(1), 50–61. doi:10.2307/3337250.

Thwala, D., Pillay, J., Anthony, M., and Sargent, C. (2000). "The Influence of Urban/Rural Background, Gender, Age & Education on the Perception of and Response to Dreams among Zulu South Africans." *South African Journal of Psychology*, 30, 1–5. doi:10.1177/008124630003000401.

Tourame, G. (1975). "Moreno's Psychodrama." *L'Encephale*, 1(3), 249–253.

Utas, M. (2009). *Traditional Healing of Young Sexual Abuse Survivors: (g)local Prospects in the Aftermath of an African War*. Uppsala: Nordic Africa Institute.

Van der Kolk, B. (2017). "How Trauma Lodges in the Body." *On Being*, March 9. https://onbeing.org/programs/bessel-van-der-kolk-how-trauma-lodges-in-the-body-mar2017.

Van der Kolk, B. A. (2015). *The Body Keeps the Score: Brain, Mind, and Body in the Healing of Trauma*. New York, NY: Penguin Books.

Van Etten, M. L., and Taylor, S. (1998). "Comparative Efficacy of Treatments for Post-traumatic Stress Disorder: A Meta-Analysis." *Clinical Psychology & Psychotherapy*, 5(3), 126–144. doi:10.1002/(SICI)1099-0879(199809).

Ventegodt, S., Braga, K., Kjølhede Nielsen, T., and Merrick, J. (2009). "Clinical Holistic Medicine: Holistic Sexology and Female Quality of Life." *Journal of Alternative Medicine Research*, 1(3), 321–330.

Ventegodt, S., Kandel, I., Neikrug, S., and Merric, J. (2005). "Clinical Holistic Medicine: Holistic Treatment of Rape and Incest Trauma." *Scientific World Journal*, 5, 288–297. doi:10.1100/tsw.2005.38.

Volkas, A. (2009). "Healing the Wounds of History: Drama Therapy in Collective Trauma and Intercultural Conflict Resolution." In *Current Approaches in Drama Therapy*, edited by D. Johnson & R. Emunah, 145–171. Springfield, IL: Charles C. Thomas.

Wajnryb, R. (2001). *The Silence: How Tragedy Shapes Talk*. Crows Nest, NSW, Australia: Allen & Unwin.

Walker, M. (1999). "The Intergenerational Transmission of Trauma: The Effects of Abuse on the Survivor's Relationship with Their Children and on the Children Themselves." *European Journal of Psychotherapy & Counseling*, 2(3), 281–296. doi:10.1080/13642539908400813.

Weingarten, K. (2003). *Common Shock: Witnessing Violence Every Day—How We Are Harmed, How We Can Heal.* New York, NY: Dutton.

Weinhold, B. (2006). "Epigenetics: The Science of Change." *Environmental Health Perspectives*, 114(3), A160–A167.

Weinhold, J., Hunger, C., Bornhäuser, A., Link, L., Rochon, J., Wild, B., et al. (2013). "Family Constellation Seminars Improve Psychological Functioning in a General Population Sample: Results of a Randomized Controlled Trial." *Journal of Counseling Psychology*, 60(4), 601–609. doi:10.1037/a0033539.

Wekerle, C., Wall, A. M., Leung, E., and Trocmé, N. (2007). "Cumulative Stress and Substantiated Maltreatment: The Importance of Caregiver Vulnerability and Adult Partner Violence." *Child Abuse and Neglect*, 31(4), 427–443. doi:10.1016/j.chiabu.2007.03.001.

Wellbriety Training Institute. (2015). *Mending Broken Hearts: Healing from Unresolved Grief and Intergenerational Trauma.* Colorado Springs, CO: Coyhis Publishing.

Wolynn, M. (2017). *It Didn't Start with You: How Inherited Family Trauma Shapes Who We Are and How to End the Cycle.* London: Penguin Books.

Wu, C., and Morris, C. (2001). "Genes, Genetics, and Epigenetics: A Correspondence." *Science*, 293(5532), 1103–1105. doi:10.1126/science.293.5532.1103.

Wylie, M. S. (2004). "The Limits of Talk: Bessel van der Kolk Wants to Transform the Treatment of Trauma." *Psychotherapy Networker*, 28(1), 30–41.

Yehuda, R. (2002). "Post-traumatic Stress Disorder." *New England Journal of Medicine*, 346(2), 108–114. doi:10.1056/NEJMra012941.

Yehuda, R. (2013). "Epigenetic Markers in the GR and FKBP5 Genes in Children of Holocaust Survivors." *Neuropsychopharmacology*, 38, S54–S55. doi:10.1038/npp.2013.278.

Yehuda, R. (2015). "How Trauma and Resilience Cross Generations." *On Being*, July 30. https://onbeing.org/programs/rachel-yehuda-how-trauma-and-resilience-cross-generations.

Yehuda, R., Daskalakis, N. P., Bierer, L. M., Bader, H. N., Klengel, T., Holsboer, F., et al. (2016). "Holocaust Exposure Induced Intergenerational Effects on FKBP5 Methylation." *Biological Psychiatry*, 80(5), 372–380. doi:10.1016/j.biopsych.2015.08.005.

Yellow Horse Brave Heart, M. (1998). "The Return to the Sacred Path: Healing the Historical Trauma and Historical Unresolved Grief Response among the Lakota through a Psychoeducational Group Intervention." *Smith College Studies in Social Work*, 68(3), 287–305. doi:10.1080/00377319809517532.

Yellow Horse Brave Heart, M., and L. M. DeBruyn. (1998). "The American Indian Holocaust: Healing Historical Unresolved Grief." *American Indian and Alaska Native Mental Health Research*, 8(2), 56–78.

Yount, K. M. (2014). "Worldwide Prevalence of Non-Partner Sexual Violence." *Lancet*, 383(9929), 1614–1616. doi:10.1016/S0140-6736(13)62333-8.

Zerubavel, E. (2013). *Ancestors and Relatives: Genealogy, Identity, and Community.* Oxford, UK: Oxford University Press.

# About the Author

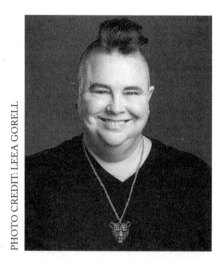

PAVINI MORAY is an author with over thirty years of experience as an educator, activist, somatic coach, and serial entrepreneur. They support humans and organizations to develop thriving relationships. They hold an MEd in Montessori curriculum design and a PhD in somatic psychology. Pavini is a queer, trans, nonbinary human walking the glitter path of dancing bones, ridiculous delight, and old magick. They are available to provide somatic coaching and training. Learn more at www.pavinimoray.com.

# About
# North Atlantic Books

North Atlantic Books (NAB) is an independent, nonprofit publisher committed to a bold exploration of the relationships between mind, body, spirit, and nature. Founded in 1974, NAB aims to nurture a holistic view of the arts, sciences, humanities, and healing. To make a donation or to learn more about our books, authors, events, and newsletter, please visit www.northatlanticbooks.com.